C000010266

Chris Cairns

Hamish McDouall

Chris Cairns

Hodder Moa Beckett

FRONT COVER PHOTO
Simon Baker
BACK COVER PHOTO
Photosport

National Library of New Zealand Cataloguing-in-Publication Data

Cairns, Chris, 1970-
Chris Cairns / Chris Cairns, Hamish McDouall
ISBN 1-86958-910-6
1. Cairns, Chris, 1970- 2. Cricket players — New Zealand — Biography
I. McDouall, Hamish, 1968- II. Title
796.358092—dc 21

ISBN 1-86958-910-6

© 2002 — Design and format Hodder Moa Beckett Publishers Limited
Published in 2002 by Hodder Moa Beckett Publishers Limited
[a member of the Hodder Headline Group]
4 Whetu Place, Mairangi Bay, Auckland

Designed by Tradewinds, Auckland
Produced by BookNZ, Auckland
Film by Microdot, Auckland
Printed by PrintLink, Wellington

This book is dedicated to every person who has ever crossed my path and contributed to who I am today. And to Thomas, for humbling me.

About the Writer

HAMISH McDOUALL was born and bred in Wanganui. Two of his great passions, cricket and writing, developed there. He wrote creatively for the first time when he was eight years old on his grandmother's typewriter, and played his first game of cricket a year later on Victoria Park (caught behind for one).

At the University of Otago he studied English, completing a Masters degree. When he was twenty he won 'Sale of the Century', and become the youngest winner of 'Mastermind' a year later. In 1993 his first book *The Who's Who of New Zealand Cricket* was published. In 1996 he went overseas and lived and worked in London, Sweden and Russia for the next four years. While there he had articles published in *The Observer*, the *Evening Standard* (London), *When Saturday Comes* and numerous New Zealand papers.

Hamish has been lucky to have witnessed, first hand, several significant moments in Chris Cairns' cricketing career in Zimbabwe and the West Indies. He has watched Chris play cricket at Lancaster Park and Lord's and many places in between.

This year Hamish has been living in Dunedin, and while writing this book has been studying to complete a law degree.

Contents

Acknowledgements 8

Foreword 9

1 Oaks and acorns 11

2 Six and out 22

3 Fern fronds 33

4 Tickets, passport, whites 47

5 The big break 62

6 Of mice and men 74

7 MCG or bust 83

8 The county drudge 89

9 Sour times 93

10 The shire 100

11 Louise 103

12 His Achilles heel 106

13 The summer of our discontent .115

14 Scorching 121

15 Grand tour 129

16 First century and second cup 138

17 Paradise razed 150

18 Change for the better 161

19 A new dawn fades 165

20 Out there and back again 179

21 Without whom 195

22 Renaissance 198

23 The quest 202

24 BTB 212

25 Big hits green grass 221

26 All's fair (or, love in a hot climate) 236

27 Joyful and triumphant 244

Epilogue 260

Statistics 263

Acknowledgements

I owe several people special thanks in helping make this book possible. Carin van den Berg for challenging me on what I really thought and for giving me the space to complete the task. My mum for all the newspaper clippings she so lovingly collected. Warren Adler and Kevin Chapman of Hodder Moa Beckett for their full support. Leanne McGoldrick for her professional and tireless work on the book's production. Hamish McDouall, who along with being a cricket junkie, is one heck of a writer. And to everyone who gave up their time to speak to Hamish and give him insight into my life.

Chris Cairns
August 2002

Thanks to the following for their help and inspiration in writing this book — Gerald and Shirley McDouall, Bruce and Diana Taylor, Adam Watson, Ken Bertenshaw, Matthew Parry and Vanessa Manhire, Felix Geiringer, Andrew McDouall, Rachael and Michael Hay, Nicole Roberton, Glenn Campbell, Philip and Tracy Brown, Rod Nye, the partners at Horsley Christie, the staff of the Otago Law Faculty, the Master and residents of Knox College, John Milnes, Aunt Fay and most especially Juliet Taylor for her unerring support. Warmest thanks also to Chris Cairns, Leanne McGoldrick, Warren Adler, Kevin Chapman for their patience and faith. Thanks also to Francis Payne for his statistical input. Hamish's part in this work is dedicated to his father.

Hamish McDouall
August 2002

Foreword

I remember meeting Chris as a lad through being a friend of the family. It's always good to see a lad come on. I know his father is very proud of him and quite rightly. He's a terrific cricketer.

I played against Chris quite a few times when he was with Notts. I was always impressed with his ability. He had a big act to follow because his father was somewhat of a legend in New Zealand. But he's coped with it and gone on from there. Lance and Chris share a great friendship now. There's so much genuine affection and good humour between them. I've been told I'm the only person to dismiss both a father and a son in test cricket — quite a double for me!

Chris is a terrific cricketer, a true all-rounder. He's a good bowler. He tends to bowl within himself, saving himself for the extra-effort balls. He uses his head. He's learned over the years to get the ball in the right place more often than not. He's learned control — that spell he started off against England last summer when he got two wickets in the first over had everything.

His batting has really come on. He's such a clean striker of the ball. I saw the hundred he got in Brisbane in the one-dayers. That was magnificent. He showed composure, he showed style when he went onto the attack. He turned the whole innings around. It was a very mature innings. A lot of guys would have given it away, thinking 'It's all over, red rover!' but not him. He showed so much determination.

He's a good performer. He fills two positions for Stephen Fleming — a genuine bowler and a genuine batsman. And a good fielder! I think he has more to offer with his leadership potential too.

It's such a shame that he has had such bad luck with injuries. He'd be a big loss to any side but to a side like New Zealand it really is a big blow — you have to replace two players.

It's also a shame he wasn't playing in the era of the all-rounders, in the '80s — against Imran Khan, Kapil Dev, Richard Hadlee and me. He would have enjoyed playing then. His batting is similar to mine in some respects — he hits the ball straight down the ground, which is where I used to try and score. He does that very well. When he hits the ball it stays hit.

Chris has so much ability and he works so hard at his cricket. But he's also good company. He is a great friend.

Ian Botham
August 2002

1

Oaks and acorns

Cricket ran in Sue Roberts' blood. Her grandfather had played. Her father, a stores officer in the Air Force, had played for Combined Services. Her brother Barry played for Marlborough. The sound of cricket, either commentary on radio or bat on ball, was so familiar it was soothing. It was a perfectly natural thing for the pretty, vivacious teenager to head down to Horton Park, Blenheim, to watch a match on a Saturday afternoon in the late '60s. She would see some friends, lie in the sun, watch her brother and relax. And she would keep a casual, discreet eye on the boy she had seen playing the week before, a boy with a clumsily effective way of swinging both ball and bat. He was tall, handsome and his hair was curly and bleached blond by the Marlborough sun. He was 20 years old. His name was Lance.

Lance Cairns was from Picton. He and his mother, Daisy, and four brothers lived in a modest house near Nelson Square, Picton's bonsai cricket ground. His father had deserted the family when Lance was an infant and times were hard financially. In his final year at primary school Lance had been bright enough to be dux, but this was the early '60s, the time of school milk, six o'clock closing and Dr Spock. Children of solo mothers were not the type to be awarded the top academic prize. A pupil who was better connected won the prize instead.

It was an innocent time when kids had to make their own fun. Lance would play in the bush or fish but, with a cricket ground at the end of the street, it was ball-sports that he took to. He would run after the ball, a willing retriever for adults who might let the kid bowl for five minutes at some stage near the end of practice.

When Lance transferred to Marlborough Boys College he struggled. There was no intermediate school in Picton and the step from primary to secondary education was too great. He lost interest in schoolwork. Instead he discovered the sports field and was soon playing for Marlborough age-group teams. Success came first in hockey, where he was propelled into the full Marlborough side aged just 14, a boy playing among men. But he was becoming obsessed with cricket. Even though Gary Bartlett was the local hero with his hurricane bowling, Lance's icon was Dick Motz, the paceman from Christchurch who went on to take 100 test wickets. But it was Motz's hitting that Lance marvelled at the most, the big swings towards, to and over the boundary.

Sue had followed the transient existence of children of the Services. She had been born in Palmerston North, when her father had been stationed at Ohakea. He moved to Woodbourne, then Nelson and Sue spent her growing years there. She went to Nayland College, but school wasn't for her. She was the prettiest of the five Roberts girls, and she wanted to earn money and have fun. There was no persuading her to stay at school after she passed the voluntary leaving age. When her parents moved back to Blenheim, she followed and took a job in a chemist's shop.

Lance played for the Picton Cricket Club at first but when that folded he went down the road to the little community of Spring Creek, 8 km north of Blenheim.

It was to give him a nickname ('Springers'), a test career and a wife.

As soon as he turned 15, Lance left school and began working in the freezing works at Picton's Shakespeare Bay. He was a typical Kiwi teenager, working hard, partying hard, and on Saturdays, in summer, playing cricket hard.

When Barry Roberts asked Sue to babysit one night she made a deal with her brother. She would look after the two children as long as her brother introduced her to his team-mate Lance. Barry honoured his end of the bargain and one summer night at the clubhouse they met. The set-up worked and the two started dating. When Sue brought Lance home to meet her parents he was wearing bare feet. He was a country boy!

The romance was nearly a year old when Sue discovered she was going to have a baby. The pair got engaged and at Easter 1970, at the Church of the Nativity in Blenheim, Lance and Sue married.

Most of New Zealand has passed through Picton. From the ferry people drive south, maybe stopping for some fish and chips or petrol before motoring along State Highway 1, around the cricket oval where Lance played as a lad, then up and out of the valley towards Blenheim.

Most people spend five minutes passing through Picton. Chris Cairns spent five years doing that. He arrived in the maternity ward of Picton hospital early on 13 June 1970. He had exhausted his mother (which was another thing he was to spend more than five years doing) after a 24-hour labour. He was finally induced just after midnight. Lance was overjoyed — not only did he have a son, but also he got home in time to watch the US Open golf on television. Three grandparents and Sue's large family gathered around to see the new entrant who, like many babies and most cricket balls, was red and smooth. He was called Christopher Lance.

Sue's sister Lynette Allport was missing, however. Nine days earlier she had given birth to a son, Wayne, in Blenheim. These newborns were destined to become best friends.

The new parents rented a series of houses in Picton before finally moving into a tiny little cottage sandwiched between Highway 1 and the Main Trunk Line. This was the first home that Chris would remember — two rooms and a kitchen, not three metres from the country's main thoroughfares. When trains out back weren't shaking the house the traffic was shaking it out the front. The two males of the house were to build reputations from this house. Lance was to become known throughout the nation as a test cricketer. Christopher was to become known throughout Picton as a testing child.

Lance's cricketing prospects improved in 1970–71 when Central Districts sent an under-23 team to compete for the Rothmans Cup. Previously Lance had had to travel over Cook Strait for Wellington age-group trials and the lads from the provinces encountered parochial selectors and patronising treatment. Lance had to content himself with playing for Marlborough. But now he was in a tournament playing on the national stage against his peers — players like Warren Lees, Jeremy Coney, Geoff Howarth and a fast but inconsistent bowler whose father had captained New Zealand, a bloke by the name of Hadlee.

New Zealand selectors were there to assess the potential of these tyros. This was Lance's first cricket trip away from Sue and Christopher, the start of a lifestyle that was to strain, and eventually break apart, the marriage.

CAIRNS FAMILY

The Cairns family. Lance and Sue (holding baby Louise) and a mischievous young fellow named Christopher, front and centre.

When Lance was away Sue had her hands full with Christopher. As a toddler he went a thousand miles an hour in every direction. He never kept still, or quiet, and Sue would have to be vigilant or else he would be off. He would dash into the nearby dairy, grab a lolly, eat it and dash out before the shopkeeper could say 'sugar fix'.

He was a demanding child, wanting to be the centre of everything. If a photograph was being taken he wanted to be in the frame. If food was being eaten he wanted it. If toys were being played with he wanted them in his hands. He also had the size to back up these demands with force — he was a big baby. He dwarfed his older cousin Wayne and most other kids of his age. He was also more independent than most of them. When it all got too much for Sue she would put Christopher on the bus to Blenheim, sitting him in the seat behind the driver, to be picked up by grandparents or one of his aunts. He would then tear around their house for the rest of the day. Thankfully a human torpedo needs to rest and the one blessing was that Christopher was a big sleeper. Once he was in his cot he was down for the night.

In 1971–72, in Dunedin, Central won the Rothmans Cup outright and Lance was one of the star performers. He was selected for the New Zealand under-23 team for a short internal tour that culminated in a first-class match against Otago at Carisbrook. Lance had only been to one test ground before that (he had gone to Lancaster Park to see Gary Sobers play in 1969). The first thing that struck him was the size of the

13

boundaries. They seemed so close. Invitingly close. The next summer Lance broke into the Central Districts Plunket Shield side and had a full, if unspectacular, season. The highlight was a victory over the touring Pakistanis at Wanganui. Lance regularly took wickets and usually batted at 9. His approach to batting seemed too random to justify a place higher in the order.

Cricket was part of Chris' life from the earliest moments. As a toddler he would wander around Horton Park trailing an oversized bat. His first exposure couldn't have been at a better place — a tree-ringed oval with an almost rural atmosphere. It was grass-roots cricket. There is little wonder Chris grew to love the game. He soaked up the relaxed summer atmosphere and mimicked the adults.

The greatest sporting moments of Lance's life didn't occur at the MCG or Headingley but at Lansdowne Park, Blenheim. After Marlborough won the Ranfurly Shield, beating Canterbury 13–6 in July 1973 at Lancaster Park, they then held the 'log o' wood' for six challenges at Lansdowne Park before losing to South Canterbury the following season. At Christmas the Roberts whanau gathered at the home of Chris' Aunty Gail, in Blenheim. Next door lived the president of the Marlborough RFU, Jim Fraser, who just happened to have the Ranfurly Shield in his lounge. It was soon shown around the gathering. While the adults returned to their Christmas cheer, Wayne Allport and Christopher examined the shield. It seemed the perfect size and shape to the two boys, who proceeded to use the premier trophy in New Zealand sport as cricket wickets.

Wayne and Christopher didn't need props, however, and would play imaginary cricket with full commentary and actions from a very young age. Test matches lasting

Having wanted the central position behind the famous log o' wood back in 1973, Chris lets his cousins, Wayne (left) and Donna Allport (centre) know he is not happy.

hours would be played in the pair's minds. When they got a bat or a ball all the better, but lack of the appropriate equipment didn't stop them 'playing' cricket. Once, having got hold of a ball, Christopher sent it through a window. Sue got ready to spank the errant child but Daisy stopped her, saying, 'Lance used to do that all the time when he was that age.' The message was clear. Smashed windows were collateral damage.

Lance was eager to introduce his son to the national game, and built probably the worst set of goal-posts ever erected. It was obvious why Lance was a freezing worker rather than a chippy. It was also obvious why Chris never became an All Black. Seven or eight pieces of wood were nailed loosely together to make the mere suggestion of a capital H. Lance also hated mowing lawns, but Chris and Wayne would still tear through this backyard jungle and dot a ball down underneath the rickety construction.

The Herds, who lived opposite the Roberts in Gascoigne Street, saw a lot of Chris. He loved playing on their big front lawn, and the Herd kids, Tonia and Warren, would often be lassoed into a game of cricket. They became proxy babysitters. Mrs Herd was a golfer and one day Chris took a driver and was attempting to hit a ball in the backyard. The four-year-old was swinging wildly so Mrs Herd gave the little chap a putter — she was worried about windows. As she watched from the kitchen she saw a golf ball disappear over the neighbour's fence. Chris had cleared his first boundary — with a putter.

The Cairns family were never well off. Pleasures were simple and cheap, and sometimes death-defying. One Christmas Lance bought a second-hand bike, Sue painted it and they presented it to Chris. The excited kid leaped onto the bike and cycled down the drive towards the highway. Unfortunately the bicycle lacked one thing — brakes — and Chris, unable to stop, collided with the house.

Brakes were a problem for the family generally — one evening Sue, Chris and his aunt were driving home when the brakes on the old Ford Prefect failed. Sue couldn't stop and proceeded to drive around and around the block trying to work out how to stop. On each circuit, as they passed their home, Chris would lean out the window and shout 'Dad!' until Lance heard the high-pitched yells and came out to save them.

A sister for Christopher, Rachel Louise, was born on 13 November 1973. While Sue was in hospital Lance ran the household in his inimitable way. He cooked roasts and gave Christopher exactly half the amount of meat and potatoes he himself was having. After all, Chris was half his height. Again little wonder that Chris towered over the other Picton pre-schoolers. But Sue was soon left to cope on her own with a newborn and a toddler.

In November 1973 Lance was invited to a New Zealand trial at Hagley Park. The national selectors, in their amateur way, had decided a closely contested net session would be the best way to find replacements for Richard Collinge and Bruce Taylor, who were both crocked. The selectors were seeking someone who could swing the ball and who could face the short-pitched bowling that was likely in Australia. It was a terrible set-up, a trial by ordeal, but at the end of it Lance Cairns, 23 years old, with only a handful of first-class matches behind him, was selected for the Australian tour. He was to be selected for every overseas tour from then on until he retired. It was a shock to everybody, not least to the man himself.

The family went south to stay with the Allports at Wigram Air Force base, where

Brotherly love. Chris cradles his newborn sister Louise in 1973.

Christopher and Wayne could play in the huge new gymnasium. Chris was, in fact, the first to put a hole in the wall of the gym.

There was a second more important reason to go — Lance was playing for New Zealand for the first time, in a warm-up match against Canterbury. Sue and Lynette took Wayne, Christopher and Louise to watch. It was the first big game Chris had seen and there was his dad playing in the same uncomplicated manner as he always had. The two boys acted up, as always, and to Lynette and Sue's embarrassment they were asked to leave the Number One Stand.

The family all saw Lance off at Christchurch Airport. He was wearing a tie for the first time — the Allports' neighbour had taught him how to tie one that afternoon. Even with a black blazer and a silver fern on his chest, Lance Cairns was still unmistakably a country boy.

His workmates took up a collection so Sue could cope financially while the family's provider was touring. It was the early '70s and New Zealand could claim only one professional cricketer — Glenn Turner. The rest were amateurs. The money that was given to players on tour barely covered the necessities, let alone providing any income for families at home. Sue occasionally sub-let the house in Picton and moved back with her parents to cut costs. Chris would then scoff scores of Nana Roberts' legendary mince pies and annoy his grandfather by running off with the copy of *Best Bets* as he sat in front of the racing programme.

In January 1974 Lance walked out onto the Adelaide Oval to become the first Picton-born test cricketer. Chris was immensely proud of him. When Lance returned home from Australia a few days later Christopher went to the garage and, leaning on the Ford Prefect, he dressed up in his father's gear — whites, pads, gloves and all. He had seen big cricket and he liked what he saw. His name was Christopher Cairns, he was almost four and he wanted, more than anything else in the world, to play cricket for New Zealand.

The lifestyle of an international cricketer meant that Lance was rarely home. He would work long hours at the freezing works when he wasn't away with cricket and Chris would see him twice a day — when Sue and he push-started the Prefect in the morning, and sometimes at night when he wasn't working overtime. In weekends it was cricket in summer and golf in winter. Then in December 1974 Lance was off again, this time to play the English at Christchurch. Lance scored 39, including a mighty six.

In June 1975 Chris went to school for the first time and his neighbourhood breathed a sigh of relief. His first teacher at Picton School was a Mrs Bunt. She wrote Christopher's first school report, stating that Chris often 'listens well', 'gets along with other pupils' and 'shows concentration'. But it also related that he seldom 'works quietly', 'waits turn patiently' or 'accepts criticism cheerfully'. Mrs Bunt wrote: 'When Christopher learns to settle quietly to work and not

Hoping one day to emulate the cricket deeds of his father, Chris tries out Lance's gear. CAIRNS FAMILY

organise everyone around him his work will show better progress. His habit of trying to be first in all situations poses problems for him with other children.' That first school report reads like a blueprint for an aggressive opening bowler.

But the Cairns' time in Picton was soon over. The 1975–76 season was a great one for Lance. He batted brilliantly, scoring 538 runs at 41.38, but the figures didn't tell of the vicious fours and capricious sixes. The speeds of the innings were remarkable. And this from a specialist bowler. The *New Zealand Cricket Almanack* declared him their 'Batsman of the Year'. That kind of form attracted the attention of the manager of the Ravensdown fertiliser works in Dunedin, Paul Sawers, who was also president of the North East Valley Cricket Club. He offered Lance a job with provision to tour with the New Zealand side. Lance would play for NEV and Otago. He would replace Glenn Turner, New Zealand's star batsman, who had left the province for Northern Districts. To be paid to play cricket was too good an opportunity to pass up. The Cairns family migrated south.

The first thing Christopher noticed arriving in Dunedin was the cold. This, after all, is the city with the southernmost test ground in the world. Penguins live on nearby beaches and the southerly wind travels unhindered directly from Antarctica. It was a world apart from the dry heat of Marlborough. One day arriving home from Maori Hill School Chris was so cold that he did the most obvious thing he could think of. He started lighting paper in the middle of the living room, trying to start a fire so he could fend off the cold.

Sue was shocked when she discovered the little pyromaniac and a pile of ashes. Chris knew what was coming, changed into his pyjamas and went to bed mid-afternoon, hoping his father would have mercy on a sleeping child. When his father got home one specific part of Christopher's body got a lot warmer. It was one of the only times that Lance had cause to discipline him physically.

Lance also experienced an unfamiliar climate. In November 1976 he went away to India and Pakistan on the most physically taxing tour of all. There is a whiff of good fortune about Lance's early career. He was often selected only for the last test of the season and would do enough to get on the end-of-season tour. This was how he had got on the plane to the World Cup in 1975 and again on the three-month, six-test epic through the sub-continent. Lance had his first extended run in the national side. He scored his first half-century (v Pakistan at Karachi) and his first five-wicket bag (v India at Madras).

Sue would listen to the wireless to keep up with her husband's exploits, but she never knew that Chris would be lying in bed with a scratchy transistor radio under his pillow pretending to be asleep but listening to ethereal reports from far-off ovals.

Sue made friends among the other cricket wives. She became close to Bernie Bracewell, Chris Petherick, Heather Boock, Judy Lees and Sukhi Turner, Glenn's wife, who had newly arrived from India, and who was struggling with the loneliness and difficulties of immigrating to Dunedin. Sukhi and Sue in particular provided support for each other. For Chris it became a perfectly ordinary thing to be around famous cricketers like Warren Lees and Glenn Turner.

The family moved out towards St Kilda beach. Chris and Louise went to Musselburgh School. Chris was a good pupil at the tiny south Dunedin school. His school reports tell of an ability at mathematics and a broad vocabulary. They also reveal the gift he was carrying. Early on the teacher ticks the 'always' box next to the words 'Enjoys active games'. Another teacher writes, 'Excels at all games', while a third comments with two simple words: 'A natural'. He was a natural at athletics, winning the school sprint competitions. He loved soccer, too, but he had king leather and linseed oil in his genes. Cricket was his game.

Lance had never pushed Chris in any particular direction. A proud parent, certainly, as his eldest belted his first-ever six from a pitch on the Oval into the traffic on lower Princes Street, but not someone who felt the need to hothouse his son, to make this boy in his own image. But there were similarities. Christopher swung the bat very fast for his size, and when he hit, the ball stayed hit. Christopher had also developed a similar chest-on style and was bowling huge in-swingers.

In 1978 while he was touring England with a disappointing New Zealand team, Lance was spotted by a group of men from a village in the north-east of England. They noted that his hitting had a certain blacksmith quality about it. They saw that his bowling action looked untouched by the rigours of coaching. He looked like any ordinary burly villager playing cricket — except that he was playing test cricket. He was the perfect combination of ordinariness and talent. The Whitburn Cricket Club contacted him.

League cricket is to the English what club rugby is to New Zealanders. It is the foundation of the national game. Throughout the counties of Cheshire, Lancashire, Worcestershire and Yorkshire, hard-fought leagues are played on picturesque ovals: elm trees, deck-chairs, mock-Tudor pavilions and nearby village pubs. The quality of

OTAGO DAILY TIMES

Chris has been under the media spotlight virtually his whole life. Here he strikes a pose with Lance for a photograph which appeared in the Otago Daily Times.

the cricket is high — the leagues are full of overseas professionals and talented locals who can't find the time to play county cricket. Learie Constantine, Ray Lindwall, John Richard Reid and Brian Lara played league cricket. The great Sydney Barnes preferred playing in the Staffordshire league between tests, rather than for Warwickshire. It is every cricketer's dream to play in England and Lance couldn't refuse a season in the Durham League. He would probably be in England again the next year anyway, competing for the second World Cup. But this time he'd bring his family.

The journey in April 1979 wasn't straightforward, however. Driving to Christchurch in terrible weather the family, with all their luggage, had to negotiate several floods, where rivers had burst their banks and spilled over the main highway. Chris still remembers water coming up through the floor of the car as Lance motored on through the deluge.

The Cairns family discovered a harsh reality when they finally arrived in England. They found a terraced house straight out of *Coronation Street* or *Billy Elliot*, in a grim suburb of Sunderland near the local football ground. The weather was often wintry, even at the height of summer, with winds howling off the North Sea. It made Dunedin seem tropical. The streets were intimidating for the young Cairns. The kids in the neighbourhood were the products of a hard northern lifestyle. They were tough and spoke in the impenetrable Wearside accent. And they were poor. The economic downturn of the '70s had hit that part of Britain particularly severely. Crime was rife — and the small backyard had glass embedded in the walls to stop intruders.

It wasn't just the streets that had an aggressive atmosphere. As a treat, Lance took Christopher to a football match — a Division 2 encounter at nearby Roker Park. Sunderland was playing Newcastle United in the ferocious north-east derby — the Geordies versus the Mackems. Soccer in England had reached its lowest ebb — hooligans were regularly fighting at every match, sharpened coins would be tossed at opposing fans, it was a world of Stanley knives and skinheads. Occasionally people would be killed. Amid all this, Lance took Chris through a sea of red and white stripes to his first really big sports event. But there was a problem, adults and children had to enter the stadium by separate entrances. Chris got inside and turned to look for Lance. He wasn't there. Surrounded by thousands of people on Roker's terraces, Chris felt completely alone and did what any other nine-year-old would do. He burst into tears.

The next sporting event he attended with his father was a lot happier. The World Cup began in June and Sue and the kids drove down the A1 to Nottingham. This was Chris' first visit to the ground that was to become his second home a decade later. Chris had a surprise waiting for him. For several years he had asked his dad if he could go into the dressing room to look around. As his birthday present Lance took Christopher into the New Zealand dressing room. There were familiar faces — Mr Turner, Mr Lees, Mr McKechnie — and there were stars like Mr Hadlee, Mr Burgess and Mr Howarth. Then Lance took his son into the opponents' dressing room — the West Indies. They were the gods in Christopher's world — Mr Holding, Mr Greenidge, Mr Lloyd, Mr Garner and the greatest — Mr Richards. Chris was overwhelmed. Standing next to 'Big Bird', the 2 m-plus Joel Garner, Chris only came up to his navel.

New Zealand lost that match but proceeded to the last four anyway. The semi-final was played at Old Trafford. England were their opponents and there was a sell-out crowd. Christopher was again in awe. He imagined himself walking out onto the tessellated turf to play a match of that importance. But in spite of a late charge by Lance and Warren Lees, New Zealand fell short of the England total by just nine runs, after Chris Old and Geoffrey Boycott bowled tightly. Not for the last time New Zealand had been a whisker away from appearing on cricket's greatest stage.

In September the family returned to Dunedin but not before Lance arranged to

Lunching with a legend. Chris and Louise with Karen Hadlee (left), Lance (centre) and
Sir Richard Hadlee (right). This photo was taken at the Hadlees' 'local' in Nottingham in 1979.

return to the north-east the next year — he signed a two-year contract with a new team, Bishop Auckland, to play in the south Durham/north Yorkshire league.

Back in New Zealand, cricket's honeymoon began. New Zealand beat the world champion Windies in the last over of a one-day match at Lancaster Park. Then the test series began in Dunedin. Christopher was delirious — his heroes were in town. He wasn't there on the Friday when his father took to the spinner Derek Parry and hit three sixes into, onto and over the Burns Street stand, but the next morning he was there watching Colin Croft, Joel Garner and the smoothest of all bowlers — Michael Holding.

At lunch Chris, like a hundred other small kids, went out onto the Carisbrook oval. He had a mission. He walked to the point near the sight-screen where Holding, 'Whispering Death' as he was known, began his run-up. There Chris could see the indentations in the turf extending 40 yards, all the way to the popping crease, that Holding's feet had made on his way to releasing the ball at near 100 mph. It was magical to see the great man's footprints. They seemed to go on forever. Chris began to run, throwing his nine-year-old legs in order to reach the next step. His stride was huge but as he ran he got into a rhythm, like Holding, a rhythm as smooth as single malt, and as he approached the wickets, he could see himself as a fast bowler running in to bowl in a test.

2

Six and out

One morning in January 1980, on the front page of the *Otago Daily Times*, a little article appeared concerning the upcoming primary schools cricket tournament to be held at Dunedin's Logan Park. The article focused on the sons of famous fathers competing, including the offspring of All Black Fergie McCormick and test cricketer Brian Hastings. Alongside the article was a photo of two young children staring at the lens with a combination of childhood shyness and excitement. There was Paul Campbell (son of cricketer Keith) and, with his blond curls exploding from beneath an Otago cap, Chris Cairns.

Sue Cairns took scissors and carefully cut out the article and glued it onto the first page of a scrapbook. From then on she would carefully scan the sports pages whenever there was a possibility of Chris being mentioned and cut and paste any appropriate article. As the years went by it developed into a remarkable record of the feats of a prodigy. The pages filled and Chris got bigger, more assured in front of the camera. His jaw squared, his hair darkened. The boy grew into an adolescent, then a man, and the deeds recorded in this treasury of column inches remained extraordinary.

In that first photograph Chris was just nine years old. He is the same size as his team-mate Paul Campbell (who later played first-class cricket for Otago), who was 11. Chris was always playing cricket with boys older than him. And men. The next page in the scrapbook tells that aged 11 he played President's Grade against cricketers 20 and 30 years his senior, and took 4-28 one week, and 4-24 the next. At a schoolboy tournament he took 5-19. Against Kaikorai Valley High School he took 6-8. For Otago, against his birthplace, Marlborough, he top scored with 29, having taken 5-14 off 16 overs. At the South Island Primary Schools tournament that year, played at Greenmeadows in Nelson, he scored 53 and 36 and took 3-16 and 2-10. Phrases like 'sparkling innings' and 'bowled with fire' rose out of the blocks of newsprint. But it wasn't only cricket reports that Sue found. He also acted in Musselburgh School's pantomime. Almost inevitably he had captured the most important role — he was Prince Charming. At the Dunedin Primary Schools Athletics tournament, Chris won both the 75 m and the 800 m. Later that year he turned 12.

Chris was at Tahuna Normal Intermediate for his Form 1 year but instead of playing with a soft ball for his school team he had been playing for the Dunedin club (3-6 and 40 runs versus Taieri, according to one clipping) and was selected as captain of the Otago Primary Schools team for the 1983 tournament in Oamaru. The team included Aaron Gale, who was later to play alongside Chris in the national side, and Dayle Shackel, the future Black Caps physio. A half-century in a warm-up tournament was followed by incredible figures, recorded by Sue in this archive of precocity. Against Marlborough he scored 53 and took 4-52. In the next match he took 6-16 and 5-11 (South Canterbury all out for 13 in the second innings). Against North Canterbury he scored 67 and had bowling figures of 3-28. They reached the final but lost to a strong Canterbury side that

CAIRNS FAMILY

Chris (seated with cup) was captain of Otago Primary Schools in 1982–83. The team finished runner-up to a Chris Harris-inspired Canterbury team. Dayle Shackel, the current Black Caps physio, is seated at the far right.

included a lad with a bunch of floppy blond hair called Chris Harris.

Chris Cairns had now played in four primary schools tournaments in a row. But his spectacular season hadn't quite finished. On 5 February 1983, against St Edmunds Blue, Chris scored 119, his first century, an innings full of straight hits and smart running between the wickets. A week later he scored 99 not out. All these innings, all the reports, all the smallest mentions of 'C.Cairns' in the fine print, lovingly recorded by a mother in a scrapbook with Goofy, Donald Duck and Pluto on the cover.

In that first clipping Chris was quoted — 'Dad has taught me all I know about cricket.' But at that time two important people came into Chris' life. John Bracewell was a young, competitive off-spinner. John and his partner, Bernie, would sometimes babysit Christopher. The kid was entertained very easily — John tied a cricket ball to the washing line — and Chris would go outside and practise hitting the ball with a straight bat. He would do that for hour after hour, until the long southern evenings melted away. Next morning, after a breakfast of leftover curried sausages, Chris would be out in the yard again.

As his talent became more evident he was noticed by one of the greatest batting coaches to bless the New Zealand game — Khalid 'Billy' Ibadulla. Billy Ibadulla had played four tests for Pakistan in the mid-60s before he emigrated to New Zealand and began teaching the youngsters of Dunedin the tao of batting. Glenn Turner was perhaps his most successful pupil, but he coached Ken Rutherford, Brendon McCullum — and even greats like David Gower and Alvin Kallicharran had sought his advice. While his knowledge of technique and the mechanics of batting was detailed, Ibadulla's greatest ability was to read a young person's game, read the personality behind the strokes.

In Turner he had discovered a dour accumulator without the timing and strength to hit the ball off the pitch, but with all the defensive technique and determination in the world. Ibadulla introduced attacking strokes to this blank canvas and Turner hit a century of centuries. With Rutherford, the reckless aggressor, he taught shot selection.

With Chris Cairns, the tyro with the big swing, he taught the value of patience and defensive discipline. Chris attributes Ibadulla with the foundation of the batting technique he uses to this day. He also taught Chris the ethos of cricket. The elite group of children who Ibadulla gathered were ruled strictly but wisely. They wore whites and addressed him as 'Mister Ibadulla'. He was the Yoda of New Zealand cricket. It is ironic, bearing in mind subsequent events, that one pupil did not absorb the main tenet of the Ibadulla philosophy — to tailor the coaching according to the temperament of the player — when he, Glenn Turner, later took up coaching.

If Ibadulla acted as Chris' mentor, the sculptor of his batting technique, then Lance and Sue had at least provided the raw materials. Chris had been exposed to cricket since year zero. He had grown up swinging a bat in backyards and on sidelines since he was old enough to lift one. Billy Ibadulla fed the fire, but the fire was hereditary.

By the time Billy met Chris he had a vast amount of cricket behind him and cricket played to a high standard. Ever since playing in that first primary schools tournament he had been on a steep learning curve. In England, in 1980, while Lance was playing for Bishop Auckland, Chris would occasionally fill in for the under-18s with boys seven years older and half a foot taller than him. It was the first time Chris had ever worn long trousers to play cricket.

That second season in England was a magic time for the family. Lance was working on a farm when he wasn't playing cricket, and drove a rusting car whose door had to be held shut as it was driven along the motorways. When Lance was playing cricket he was being spectacular — his figures almost match what Chris was doing during the New Zealand summer. The Bishops won the league, and Lance took 261 wickets at 9.55 (best bowling 9 for 12). One time they bowled the opposition out for six. Six all out. Against Middlesbrough he took 8-82 then hit 106 not out. He was selected for Durham, and the Minor Counties composite team.

For Chris and Louise it was all wonderful. Their father was a hero in Bishop Auckland. At the clubhouse the kids were treated wonderfully — they were given pints of duckhams — blackcurrant and lemonade. They'd look wide-eyed at the dark ale, the sepia pictures on the wall. They fed fruit machines with 20p coins. They listened to stories told in a strange accent. Louise eventually picked up the brogue. School was fun, even if the Kiwi kids struggled with the English syllabus. Christopher played soccer and again produced minor miracles in athletics. Those memories stuck readily in the head of Cairns junior. He grew to love England, and loved the romance that cricket possesses there and loved the fact that he was the son of a cricketing Zeus.

The family continued following the summer, returning to New Zealand when the days got shorter in Britain. At the end of a busy domestic season New Zealand played a series against India. The last match was in Auckland — a lame draw. Christopher and Louise waited for their champion to come home after his long absence. They waited several days but Lance didn't arrive. Sue contacted several of the other New Zealand players to ask his whereabouts but was confronted by a mist of denial and dissembling.

Lance — with Sue, Chris and Louise — about to leave on another tour.

Disappointingly, even people who Sue considered close friends reacted with a 'what goes on tour stays on tour' mentality. Her husband was AWOL and the New Zealand cricket team displayed a similar lack of conviction in facing Sue as they had displayed in the last test facing Ravi Shastri.

Sue was a woman of action and flew to Auckland the next day to find Lance. Several days later her sister Gail gathered Christopher and his little sister onto a plane and the three joined Sue in Auckland. Sue had discovered that Lance had begun a romance with a woman and she was determined to make him meet his responsibilities, to explain his actions to her and the kids.

One night in Auckland the children were playing on the floor of a motel unit when there was a knock on the door. Lance came in, hugged them both then calmly told the two children that he loved them very much and that he was not leaving the family because of them. They would see him in the holidays. For Christopher that was sufficient. However traumatic the previous days had been, from then on the break-up of the family was never an issue, never an excuse for his own behaviour. He would always love his father. In those days, when divorce was not yet in vogue, it was a refreshingly adult view from a 10-year-old. For little Louise it must have been much harder. She was so much younger and craved her father's presence.

The lifestyle of the touring cricketer, the financial pinch, the long absences from home — all these things were mixed into the separation of Sue and Lance. Seventeen years later the same pressures would affect Chris' life. Perhaps the painful edge was knocked off the split by the fact that when New Zealand, or Lance's new province of Northern Districts, were playing in the south Chris would be there to watch his dad and soak up the atmosphere. He sometimes gave Richard Hadlee throw-downs, or played games against the younger members of the test team — Ian Smith and

Martin Snedden — in the bowels of the stands at Carisbrook or Lancaster Park. Young Martin Crowe was amazed at this sponge — this boy who would listen to all advice with the eagerness of a Jack Russell terrier. He saw, in his determination and love of the game, something of himself, something of the marriage of latent talent and inevitability. But Chris was never allowed to forget that this was a rare privilege — Lance demanded that he was always polite and even the youngest member of the side, not even 20 years old, was addressed as Mr Crowe.

Chris' 99 not out in 1983 wasn't the most spectacular innings that weekend by someone with the surname Cairns. Lance was in Australia with the New Zealand side competing for the World Series Cup. He had been used as a pinch-hitter, floating in the order to create havoc and panic, particularly amongst the English spinners Geoff Miller, Vic Marks and Eddie Hemmings. He scored 36 off 26 balls in the first match against England, and then in a record-breaking match at the Adelaide Oval he scored 49 off 24 balls to help the Kiwis get 298 to beat Bob Willis' side. Lance had been using the specially designed Newbury bat — the Excalibur, a bat with no shoulders and the weight redistributed, as much a Kiwi icon as L&P and black singlets.

The Kiwis reached the final on the backs of those victories. This was the holy grail of New Zealand cricket — the World Series Cup final. Two years earlier Lance had watched from the enclosure as Trevor Chappell had rolled a grubber along the pitch to prevent Brian McKechnie from hitting a six to tie the match. New Zealand had been incensed — the team, the populace, Prime Minister Muldoon. The word 'underarm' entered trans-Tasman folklore. Now, in early February 1983, that same folklore was to get a hero.

The first final was lost because of a rain readjustment. The second final was, for the most part, a disaster, as the Aussies posted a record score of 302. New Zealand batted terribly. Turner, Howarth, Wright, Coney, Jeff Crowe and John Morrison were in the hut by the time Lance strode to the wicket. In New Zealand it was tea-time, families throughout the country were watching. Cricket is all about timing, as is becoming a folk hero, and Lance Cairns got his timing spot on. He had no intention of pushing the ball about lamely. It was bang not whimper. He hit Ken Macleay for two sixes, then launched into Dennis Lillee, hitting the great bowler for another brace of sixes. The second six off Lillee went well over the longest boundary on one of the biggest grounds in international cricket. And it was one-handed. And unintentional. Two more sixes off Rodney Hogg and Lance Cairns had hit the fastest one-day 50 of all time.

Chris watched, like the rest of New Zealand, stunned and joyous. Lance was out eventually and New Zealand lost, but it had been a marvellous display — not just of hitting power but of bravado, of élan, of Kiwi guts. The history of New Zealand cricket had been about glorious defeats — the Sutcliffe–Blair partnership at Ellis Park, the 'underarm' final, the Trent Bridge fight-back in 1973. Lance had simply added to this tradition and in such a way that he became a cult hero on both sides of the Tasman Sea. Daisy Cairns even became a minor celebrity — being interviewed about what she had fed her growing son.

Even though he was principally a bowler, even though six months later he took 10-144 in a test at Headingley (and was awarded Man of the Match) in New Zealand's historic maiden victory on English soil, he is still remembered for a carefree innings in a doomed match. That day in Melbourne, in barely an hour, Lance had become an icon.

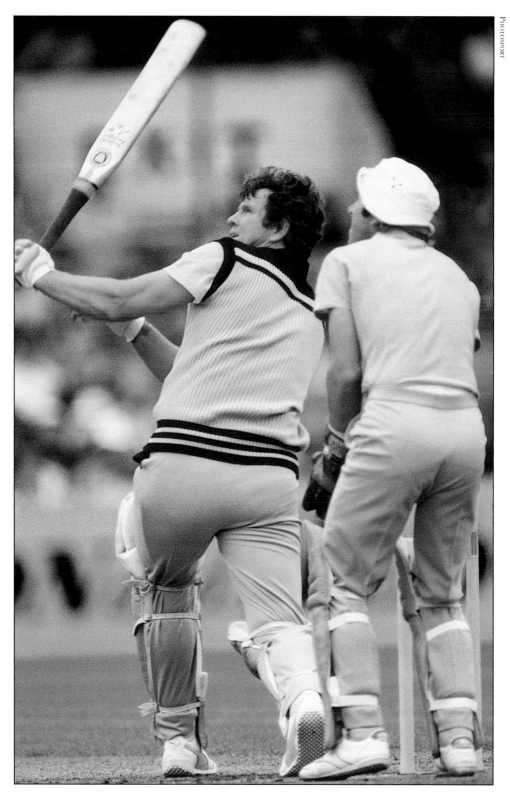

Lance and Chris still often debate who is the biggest hitter. Here Lance displays his signature shot — the one-handed six. (Although Chris would never admit it to his father, he thinks Lance would 'hit bigger'.)

When the pyjama game arrived a week later in New Zealand, with England playing three one-day matches, the Cairns frenzy continued. The Eden Park crowd was one of the most vocal, excitable crowds ever to gather for a cricket match in New Zealand. Geoff Howarth helped the party along by sending Lance out at first drop, and as the first six disappeared into the ecstatic crowd someone unfurled a banner — 'Lance Cairns for Pope'. One of the commentators said that Lance could even beat Robert Muldoon for the safe Tamaki electorate.

That mini-tour changed Lance Cairns' life. Money started to roll in from sponsorships and endorsements. The days of penury of the mid-70s were long gone. It also changed the immediate future of Chris Cairns. The surname was the same, the talent fairly evident and Newbury Bats began supplying Chris with gear through their agent, John Guy, the former test cricketer.

At that stage Chris was bowling fast. His pace worried most of his contemporaries and the balls would swing into the body of right-handed batsmen. That year (1983) in a friendly against South Canterbury, several mothers were so concerned that their sons were being exposed to unnecessary danger that they asked the umpire to stop Chris from bowling.

When Chris later hit one of the boys on the arm, fracturing it, he was promptly banned from the bowling crease. A couple of years earlier he had hit another opponent on the toe. As the kid hopped around in pain Chris grabbed the ball and ran him out. Again parents were in high dudgeon.

As a treat Christopher and Nana Roberts went on a trip to visit the Allports, who had recently moved to Singapore. Graeme was in charge of physical education at the New Zealand Services base there and had a brand-new gym. Again Chris was the first to put a hole in the panelling. A couple of men noticed Chris and Wayne playing cricket and asked to join in — but soon after seeing the first couple from Chris they beat a tactical retreat. It was left to Wayne Allport to play with Chris — and they reverted to a familiar pattern: Chris would bat for ages, then when he was finally out, Wayne would keep Chris out for only a handful of balls.

That Singapore trip was a rare treat as the family of three did not have a large income. Sue worked hard to cover the costs of rearing two children, one of whom could make the contents of a fridge evaporate with every pass. The gear sponsorship was a huge bonus. Nana Roberts, living in Timaru, was also a great support for Sue coping with divorce, and came down to Dunedin regularly to help out.

Sue and the kids moved up to Christchurch for the new school year in 1983. Initially they lived with Karen and Richard Hadlee in Bishopdale, then rented the home when the Hadlees left for another season in Nottingham. Karen knew all about being a cricket widow and the two wives of New Zealand's new ball attack shared an understanding.

Chris spent his Form 2 year at Casebrook Intermediate. He continued to work well at school and his report was sprinkled with As and Bs for effort and 2s (language, science, art) and 3s (maths, woodwork, music) for ability but even his teacher, Mr Wardrop, recognised that for Chris the classroom time was the 'bit in between' his sport. Complimenting Chris' 'mature' attitude the teacher used a cricket metaphor to describe the future — 'Your high school innings is about to commence, you have an excellent strip to bat on, and your form likewise is excellent.'

Five days after Mr Wardrop wrote those words on 21 December 1983, Chris scored his second century, against Marlborough. He was captain of the Canterbury primary schools team and batted for 91 minutes and scored 117 runs. After Christmas the team went to Westport for Chris' fifth primary schools tournament — a record. He had never won with Otago, coming close in the last two years, but he was now captain of defending champions Canterbury and instead of being younger than the rest he was now the oldest and biggest. Against North Otago Chris hit 76 off 71 balls (four sixes, seven fours) then took 3-18. He got 6-20 against Eastern Southland and then a bravura effort against South Canterbury, 5-23. Canterbury won the tournament, and he was named captain of the tournament team. As he received the United Building Society's cup he towered over administrator Don Hazlett. He was only 13 years old.

That summer England arrived to play three tests. In Wellington young Martin Crowe and veteran Jeremy Coney scored maiden centuries, and Lance hit his highest test score (64, 10 fours, one six), but Chris was not so interested in the Kiwis' performance. He admired Hadlee's bowling and studied Crowe's technique. But he was watching someone else, a rather rotund player who threw himself around the field, who leaped into the crease with his bottle-bleached curls bouncing on his shoulders, who batted like he had a plane to catch. Ian Botham had a great match at the Basin — he scored 100 and took five wickets not for the first or last time in a test. But it wasn't just the quality of the performance that attracted Chris. 'Beefy' was a performer with a big personality that filled the expanse of a cricket oval. He was expressive, passionate and charismatic. When he took a wicket his back arched in triumph and his arms jabbed at the air above him. When he hit hard and straight he beamed with satisfaction.

It's been suggested that the popularity of W.G. Grace — in particular the doctor's compelling skill and roguish demeanour — began the concept of spectator sport. Ian Botham was the inheritor of that tradition, like Sobers, like Miller, like Trumper, the most watchable, entertaining cricketer of his generation (with apologies to his good friend Viv). Chris had seen Botham, recognised the same extrovert traits in his own game, and wanted to be like him.

In February Chris walked along the drive of Christchurch Boys High School, wearing its dark-blue uniform. To the left was the ivy-covered main block, to the right was the broad green plain of the cricket field, the 'sacred acre'. It could have been difficult for him — sons of famous fathers have often had tough times at school — but Chris' size, talent and temperament made such abuse seem hollow. Chris arrived at secondary school not only as the son of Lance Cairns but, potentially, his successor.

On his second day at school Chris was selected in the CBHS First XI, the first time a third-former had been called into the team. The team was talented — Lee Germon, 15, was wicketkeeper, while seventh-former Blair Hartland had already been selected for provincial youth teams. As the young'un of the side, Chris bowled first change and batted down the order and occasionally regretted not playing in his age group.

There was a familiar face at school in the third form — Wayne Allport. Chris' cousin and best friend had returned from Singapore. For someone who seemed to shift schools every second year it was a point of stability. Chris was popular among his peers, not just for his sporting prowess and reflected fame, but also for his wit. While he was never a smart aleck he occasionally had his classmates in fits. Mr Holmes, for example, the French teacher, had a strange accent. He didn't have a typical New Zealand twang, nor did he have a real French accent. Chris asked him whether he had

On the way to Auckland for the inter-school match between Christchurch Boys High and Auckland Grammar. Chris was still wearing a fourth-form uniform back then and had to borrow this senior uniform for the trip.

been conceived in France, New Zealand or on the flight in-between. For his cheekiness he was caned but earned the long-term respect of his class comrades.

He wasn't often on detention lists however, and was quite popular with his teachers, who all remembered his interest and enthusiasm. He was in the top bracket of the class in English and maths, was exceptional at social studies, and in spite of a studied *ennui* that probably had something to do with old-fashioned Kiwi machismo, he was very good at French, coming second in the class.

Soccer was his winter code. He played for the top junior team at school and was selected in Canterbury age-group sides. He also began playing rugby, at first casually at lunch-times, but later, in Form 4, he took up New Zealand's national game more seriously, mainly because his friends Craig Rogers and Toby Ellis played it. They were his cycling companions, boys Chris had met at the school's entrance exam. Together the three journeyed every morning in convoy, negotiating the 8 km from Papanui, and became lifelong friends.

In the summer of 1984–85 Chris, just 14, was selected to play for the South Island under-17 cricket side for a match against the North Island at Horton Park. The team included future first-class player Mark Lane and nascent All Black Simon Culhane. A young Hamilton lad, Shane Thomson, took the bowling honours for the opposition.

Chris took two wickets and his pace again hurried and harried batsmen. It was a good work-out for the young teenager against players of quality and experience. Chris Cairns was on the rise.

Lance's cricket career, however, seemed to be winding down. In 1984 Lance went with Jeremy Coney's team to Pakistan. The pitches took spin and, to accommodate Evan Gray, Lance was left on the sidelines, the first time he'd been dropped from the side for five years. On the tour of the West Indies, Lance again found himself carrying the drinks on two occasions as the selectors chose more pace (young Derek Stirling) or left-arm variation (Garry Troup). He perhaps shouldn't have been surprised. In a hoary attack (Hadlee 34, Chatfield 35, Cairns 36), he was the hoariest. The selectors had already begun trawling for successors to the aged trio. Mark Carrington, Sean Tracy, Gary Robertson and Richard Webb had all been given a whiff of international cricket.

Lance had also had a bit of a shake-up. He didn't wear a helmet unless the pitch seemed really lively or the bowlers were likely to send deliveries headwise. He had, after all, been brought up on the bounciest wickets in the country and not had too much difficulty. But on a cool Dunedin afternoon Lance, helmetless, received a bouncer from Pakistani fast bowler Wasim Akram, a southpaw. Maybe it was the extra pace of the young bowler, or the odd angle, or the sheer fact that Lance's reactions had slowed, but he lost sight of the delivery and it struck him above his ear. Blurred vision and concussion followed — and Lance went to hospital for X-rays to see if his cranium had been fractured.

Cricket began to dominate Chris' study to the extent that every one of his teachers mentioned the adverse effect his sporting commitments were having on his schoolwork in the Term 1 report of 1985. He would work hard to catch up, but the sheer number of days absent took their toll. A balance had to be negotiated. In winter the marks picked up — football lasted only 80 minutes as opposed to several days — but his fourth form was a mediocre year. In summer, time simply evaporated.

Lance had been going progressively deaf over a period of several years. This was probably a legacy of years at the Shakespeare Bay works in the days when earmuffs were luxuries. Maybe the blow on the head from Akram also hastened the hearing loss, but for a cricket player it was a worrying disability. All sports might be primarily visual, but cricket has an important audio quality to it — to hear the calls of other players, no-balls from the umpire and, most important, the fine sound of a ball grazing a bat. Lance knew that this was a big problem for his cricket.

There was soon another problem. At the end of the tour of the West Indies, Geoff Howarth, struggling with form and fitness, was dropped. The new captain, Jeremy Coney, brought in Glenn Turner as 'cricket manager' to help replace the leadership experience that was missing from the side. It was a good idea, as Coney was green in the captaincy role — and Turner had captained New Zealand and Worcestershire. The problem for Lance Cairns was that Turner thought the most effective bowling was that which went away from the bat.

Lance was selected for the tour to Australia but was left out of the team for the first test at the Gabba. It was a strange decision — the pitch seemed like it would suit seamers, Australia had five left-handers in their batting line-up and the first day dawned humid. It was a bitterly disappointing moment, made all the more disappointing as Hadlee exploited the ideal conditions to take 9-52, which Chris

CAIRNS FAMILY

Chris' first national honours came in this 1985–86 NZ under-18 team which undertook a short tour of the South Island. As well as containing several future first-class cricketers, this team also produced All Black Jon Preston (far right, back row), a useful left-handed opening batsman. Chris is pictured third from left in the middle row.

considers as the most complete display of seam bowling he has witnessed.

Lance realised that his time as a test cricketer was approaching its end. He couldn't shake the idea that Turner had brought a 'new broom' mentality to the side and that he was following Howarth into cricketing oblivion. He played the third test in Perth, another victory over Allan Border's Australians, and the Kiwis completed a maiden series win in Oz. But Lance hadn't taken a wicket in the series, nor scored a run. On his return to New Zealand he announced his retirement from first-class cricket. He had taken 130 test wickets, hit 39 sixes in one-day internationals and his only first-class century was the fastest ever scored in New Zealand (52 minutes, 45 balls — against Wellington at Lower Hutt in 1980). For Lance it was all over. One month later after the national under-18 tournament in Palmerston North, Chris was selected for New Zealand, for the under-18 side. For Chris it had just begun.

3

Fern fronds

With his retirement from cricket, Lance's priorities swung 180 degrees. Having coached Christopher long-distance, Lance began to put all his energies into helping the boy reach his potential. Chris and Louise spent several weeks with their father in Te Puke before Christmas 1985. It was the first time since the separation that the kids had spent more than a couple of days with their dad. It was an important time — Chris, nearing adulthood, began developing a mature relationship with his father, while for Lance bonding with his children helped him cope with a tragedy. His first child with new wife Angela, a son Hayden, had died of cot death several months earlier. Chris never met his infant half-brother but his father's sadness was obvious. Cricket provided a salve.

Lance felt his 'teach yourself' batting technique was not a good thing to pass on to the next generation and he'd chastise his son for playing shots across the line. Chris' fast in-swingers became even more pronounced with the expert help. He also developed some vicious leg-cutters.

With his open-chested action, the 15-year-old was bowling quickly enough to have Lance ban the bouncer from net sessions as both discipline to bowl the fuller ball and precaution against a repeat of the Carisbrook incident. Lance was a little intimidated by his son's speed and high action. It could be claustrophobic in the nets. Chris was fast, with the expectation that as he grew bigger and broader, as the cocoon of adolescence was cast off, he would become even faster.

After Christmas, Chris played the under-18 tournament, while Lance, still enjoying the one-day competitions, played for Northern Districts in the Shell Cup. Canterbury won the under-18 tourney easily and Chris was only one of several well-performed players, albeit easily the youngest competing. Seven Canterbury players were selected, after the event, in the national side, including Lee Germon, Mark Hastings and Jon Preston, an opening bat who would one day be an All Black halfback. The strength of the Canterbury side is evident when you consider that the rest of the victorious team included two players, Chris Harris and Andrew Caddick, who would one day play international cricket.

When Chris was young Nana Roberts had knitted him a cricket jersey. Chris wanted three black stripes around the collar — the New Zealand insignia. In 1985, Chris earned the real McCoy — a New Zealand jumper. It was a huge buzz pulling it over his head for the first time. He was so proud of it he wore it everywhere.

The under-18 side had a small three-match tour around the South Island and Chris started to produce headlines. He was two years younger than most of the rest of the side. Yet again he was being extended beyond his age and he rewarded the selectors' faith. Against Nelson, during an innings of 34, he sent one ball over the Trafalgar Park grandstand into a motel swimming pool. Against Ashburton he took five wickets. But his match-winning performance was against South Canterbury at Geraldine. Having taken 3-23 in the second innings, Chris, batting at number 8, strode to the crease with

Keeper Lee Germon leads the NZ under-18 team onto the pitch at Geraldine. Chris, third from left, shared the new ball with Shane Thomson, at Germon's right.

31 needed off five overs. He struck two sixes and in the last over cover drove for four to win the match. The youngsters had won by one wicket with three balls to spare. Chris had scored 28 not out. The headline in the *Press* read 'Cairns clout lives on'.

That headline may have been surprising but a feature article in the *Australian* was extraordinary. Writing about the remarkable New Zealand team of the mid-80s journalist Terry Brindle warned that Richard Hadlee, the vanguard of Kiwi cricket, would be retiring soon and that the NZCC were searching for potential replacements. 'The New Zealand Cricket Council has enlisted the aid of Dennis Lillee to run the rule over likely candidates. There are none, or at least none capable of remotely approaching Hadlee's class in the foreseeable future . . . Kiwis who know are already talking about a flop cycle when the team will be spearheaded by medium-pacers.'

The writer then mentioned some of the emerging young pacemen — Brian Barrett, Gary Robertson, Fred Beyeler and Willie Watson. And one other. 'Longer-term optimism already centres on a strapping 15-year-old called Chris Cairns. He is son of Lance, bats impressively and looks as though he could be really quick. It is an engaging thought, if an ominous one for New Zealand, that the next eminent generation of Kiwi cricketers could be led by a man called Cairns.' Chris Cairns was just 15 and already pundits across the Tasman were watching him.

On the under-18 tour, Chris had acquired the nickname 'Son of' because every newspaper article mentioned his father. His heritage was unshakable and all-pervasive. Yet he never once regarded it as a burden — never used his genes and the expectation that arose from them as an excuse for under-performing or misbehaving. In fact, far from being a source of pressure, Chris used the attention. He knew that because of his name certain people — selectors, coaches, scouts — might look at him just that little bit longer than if his name was Brown, Johnson or Tyler. And he was, in the end, a different player from his father — a faster bowler and a more technically correct batsman. Like Chris Harris, Richard Reid or Dayle Hadlee, Chris could play his own game without having to 'be like Dad'.

Chris had emerged from the shadow cast by his father but there was another shadow to crawl from under. A tall, mustachioed silhouette with big feet — Richard Hadlee's. The fact that there was speculation about Chris' future in committee rooms and media cabals tells not only of his obvious ability, but also the lack of evident depth in fast-bowling circles.

Any promising fast bowler who emerged from the time Hadlee had turned 30 was eyed as a potential replacement. By 1986 the search was desperate. Hadlee and Chatfield were not quite over the hill, but they were certainly working their way up it. Even young Martin Snedden was showing signs of wear and tear. So the New Zealand selectors reacted as they always have — they selected players who had the word 'promising' attached to their job description. Brian Barrett, Derek Stirling and Willie Watson found themselves journeying to England. One of them, surely, would be the replacement for Hadlee.

The plan was fatally flawed, of course. The idea of 'replacing' the greatest New Zealand bowler was as unlikely as trying to develop a very big chicken to replace the moa. The three bowlers wilted under the pressure. Stirling and Barrett never played for New Zealand again. Willie Watson contented himself with being a solid line and length bowler — a kind of diluted Chatfield. There were others in the next tier — including Danny Morrison. Morrison was short but powerful. He was faster than Watson, more accurate than Stirling and had greater endurance than Barrett. And he had one less kidney than the lot of them. His action owed more to D.K. Lillee than R.J. Hadlee but there was something to work on. In the age-group results names like Thomson, Millmow, Pringle, Caddick and Su'a appeared regularly, but there was hope, and any number of crossed fingers, that the young fellow Cairns might make it further.

At the start of 1986, his fifth-form year, with the spectre of the nationwide School Certificate exam at the end of the year Chris set himself high standards for both cricket and schoolwork. Hard work, diligence and application would see him through — he aimed for excellence. One teacher, Paul Crowe, remembered Chris' singular focus, a focus that would occasionally lead to self-absorption. Chris as an infant, a child and an adolescent had always listened politely to the advice and ideas of others, then promptly ignored them — a true cricket captain in the making. On the strength of such determination Chris breezed through School C with one A and four Bs.

It was a great record for someone with such demanding extra-curricular activities. That included his first season in the CBHS Second XV. Operating at either first five-eighth or fullback, he showed pace and vision and one hell of a long punt. Defence, however, was not his strong point. Nevertheless he was good enough to be noticed first by the Canterbury selectors, then the South Island selectors and finally the national selectors. In just his second season of rugby union he was picked for the New Zealand under-17 squad as cover for fullback Andre Bell, the future Maori All Black. Others in the squad included future Canterbury hooker Matt Sexton, and Rene Naufahu, who found fame playing Sam the ambulance driver in the soap opera 'Shortland Street'.

That wasn't Chris' only sporting success of the winter. Indoor cricket was in its

One of Chris' most prized photos. The 1987 NZ under-17 rugby team which played Australia at Athletic Park. Even though he was a reserve, Chris (back row, second from right) treasured the fact he got to wear the black jersey.

honeymoon period and warehouses throughout the land were being bedecked with nets and metal stumps. Chris loved the indoor game. It had a familiar 'working-class' atmosphere like league or softball and a social aspect he hadn't experienced before. His team-mates were hard-working and hard-drinking. The game itself was constant action. He could jog in and bowl fast and short. He would also get top reward for straight hits. And, most important, the pressure of aiming at the highest level was off. This was simply good fun and could only benefit his outdoor cricket. He played for Canterbury in the national tournament and helped the team reach the semi-finals. Then he was selected for the South Island team. It was his first year playing competitively.

All these activities required cash and Sue worked hard to provide for both her kids. Louise had a unique dress sense, and Chris demanded the best equipment. He wanted to upgrade from Bata Bullets to adidas. To supplement Sue's modest income and pay the difference, Chris took a job stocking shelves at the local supermarket. The check-out girls were the top of the tree and the shelvers dreamed of taking one of these goddesses out. Chris became the envy of the Woolworth's boys when he achieved this feat.

Financial pressures were also eased when Chris won a Le Coq Sportif Scholarship. He was the youngest of the five recipients, which also included Lee Germon. Lee and Chris had spent a lot of time together over the preceding three years. Lee had captained Chris in the First XI, Canterbury under-18s, South Island under-17s and New Zealand under-18s. Their destinies seemed to be linked. It seemed very likely that Germon would captain Cairns for the province, and maybe even for the national side.

Even in the first major controversy of Chris' career, Germon played a role. Two clubs, Lancaster Park and Woolston Working Men's Club, tried to woo Chris into playing senior cricket but were told by Canterbury Cricket that the 16-year-old was too young. Lee Germon, 18 months older, but still at school, was granted permission to play seniors for Sydenham and the other ambitious clubs complained of double standards.

The Canterbury Cricket Association was particularly protective of their protégé. Chris was slated to play alongside his father for a Marlborough invitation XI in a benefit match at Horton Park. Several first-class names would be playing and there was the novelty of having a father and son taking the new ball. But Wayne Wilson, coach of the Canterbury under-20s, demanded he appear in a minor fixture. Lance was disgusted and Chris disappointed but he grudgingly realised that there were priorities and commitments, even the less glamorous ones.

But in fact he was fighting kismet. Wayne had ordered Chris to play because he wanted Sue Cairns to come to the match so he could court her. He continued to arrange team barbecues and gatherings. The two started dating a year later and in 1992, Wayne and Sue married. Chris was happy that his mum had found such a top bloke, who absolutely adored her. Chris' nemesis aged 16 became his stepfather by the time he was 21.

Lance had other concerns about his son. During Chris' annual stays in Te Puke, after hours in the nets, Lance had got his son swinging the ball in a long way from the off and at a very fast pace. Wayne Allport could confirm the speed. He had taken Lee Germon's place behind the stumps for the CBHS First XI. Keeping wicket to Chris the ball gave his hands a pounding, and he often stood nearly halfway to the boundary on many grounds, such was the carry.

Chris' action was a little unorthodox. He ran in conventionally but would open up in his delivery stride. It was this last movement, the open-chested style, that resulted in so much swing. It was an action that had developed naturally, without coaching, and Lance was a great believer in letting players retain their 'natural' style.

However, this was the mid-80s and bowling theory had a new model. Richard Hadlee's fluid side-on action was considered the standard. He had, after all, just taken his 300th test wicket. Kids all over the country were mimicking Hadlee, and those who didn't were encouraged to change. New Zealand Cricket brought Dennis Lillee over to work with the most promising young quicks. He was the greatest of all Australian fast bowlers, the epitome of aggression, and NZC was tapping into his knowledge. Lillee encouraged Chris to get ever more side-on in his delivery stride, working to get his feet positioned correctly, working to get every centimetre of pace out of Chris' young body. The template had to be followed — after all, nobody had any better ideas and Lillee and Hadlee were essays on the power of the side-on action.

Chris listened and soaked up the knowledge imparted. After a workshop over several days Chris had closed his action. He was still bowling very quickly, was learning to seam the ball both ways and was now bowling on a line just outside off stump. He never bowled his open-chested style again. He also never consistently swung the ball again — for the rest of his career.

In retrospect Chris does not think that there was a good return on the investment New Zealand Cricket made with the Lillee clinics. While Chris kicked on and used the refinement in his technique to great effect, he can list 30-odd cricketers who he was involved with but who fell by the wayside. There was no follow-up. Once the boys got

Dennis Lillee shows New Zealand's young talent the fast bowling ropes.

back to their clubs and provinces other coaches influenced them, suggested other things and the Lillee wisdom was diluted.

In December 1986, Chris went with the Canterbury under-20 team to the national tournament in Lower Hutt. It was to be the most difficult and least enjoyable moment of his cricket career to that point. Fresh from the stress of School Certificate he was now playing alongside men. Several players had played first-class cricket while Brian Barrett, in the Northern Districts side, had even played for New Zealand. Mark Douglas, just over a year older than Chris, had a full beard. Germon was there, but so were Darrin Murray and Blair Hartland, batsmen both destined to open for their country and both almost four years older than Chris.

For the first and last time in cricket, Chris felt totally out of his league. The bowling was fast and the atmosphere testosterone-filled. He had a poor tournament. Canterbury struggled and Chris managed only one major contribution — 42 against Auckland. His form was disappointing and he wondered whether he was playing too much cricket, and simply whether he was good enough.

It was the same old story, Chris thrown into a situation beyond his years. Like his first primary schools tournament, like the Bishop Auckland under-18s, like his first week at high school, he was left to flounder in the deep end.

When he did get to play against his contemporaries he enjoyed himself. At the annual under-18 tournament, Canterbury won for the second year running, winning every match. Chris stood out as a bowler, taking 4-9 against Wellington and 4-39 against CD and extracting bounce and movement from the truest pitches.

Cairns and Germon and Chris Harris were all selected for the national under-18 side (as was Shane Thomson and the hirsute Mark Douglas) to play their Australian under-19 counterparts. The first international was played at Oamaru. Shane Thomson picked up four wickets and Australia made 236. New Zealand were always behind the run rate until Greg Collinge joined Chris at the crease. In just eight minutes the Collinge–Cairns partnership racked up 55 runs for the eighth wicket. Chris was out for 18, with 10 still needed, while Collinge scored a phenomenal 61 from only 46 deliveries to win the match. It was the only defeat the Australians suffered on their whole tour.

The Australians, led by future test player Stuart Law, won the second match, in Dunedin, easily. That night an incident was to occur which, to this day, Lee Germon would not be proud of — an incident, says Chris, which would sour the relationship between the two players for ever.

At school Chris was constantly playing catch-up. The report for the first term of his sixth-form year, 1987, tells of 21 half-days missed. In spite of this he passed all his subjects, with particularly solid marks in English, biology and physical education. He was clearly a good pupil, slightly above average but without the time and commitment to get the highest marks. He had other areas of achievement and both he and his teachers were aware of it.

This was his first year in the First XV. He had been moved to first five-eighth, where his ball-handling and punting would be most effective. CBHS had an average year but in July Chris flew to Wellington to join the New Zealand under-17 squad for a one-off test against Australia under-17, a team that featured two gun centres, Tim Horan and Jason Little. Chris was reserve fullback on the day and although he didn't get on the field in the 16–3 loss, he had pulled on a black jersey with a silver fern on the breast. Most New Zealand boys, even those predestined to play cricket, still dream of one day wearing a black rugby strip and facing Australia. For Chris, at the cavernous Athletic Park, this dream came true.

Brian Hutchison (captain, left) and Chris about to do battle for the Canterbury under-15 rugby team. Chris loves his rugby, and while he would never exchange his Black Cap for an All Black jersey, he is an avid All Black supporter.

For all this success Chris was realistic about the future. Whatever the mystical attraction of playing for the All Blacks, he knew that to become a double All Black like Curly Page or Brian McKechnie was a dream too far. Footie was simply fun. Maybe in a parallel reality he could have committed himself to rugby and gone further. But rugby was always going to have an unfair fight with naked cricketing ambition. Already, aged just 16, he stated his aims to friends and cricket colleagues. He wanted to become the best all-rounder in the world.

While rugby fell by the wayside, indoor cricket provided an appropriate balance between his chosen sport and a casual pastime. His indoor team, Russley, which included future test cricketers Mark Priest and Michael ('Millie') Owens, won the South Island championship. Again Chris was selected for Canterbury and the South Island. He couldn't go to Australia with the national side because of finance. It was, after all, the outdoor game he loved and he had to concentrate his energies and money there.

During that tournament Chris acquired the nickname 'Forgetful'. He managed to lose an incredible amount of his possessions. The list included:

- one shoe (size 12)
- one jersey
- two T-shirts
- one watch
- the championship trophy lid
- a 'man of the match' cup
- his way home

Something that was unforgettable was Chris' selection in August 1987 in the full Canterbury squad to prepare for the forthcoming provincial season. It included several talented youngsters — Hartland, Priest, Stu Roberts — some older first-class heads like Rod Latham and Chris Flanagan and even a test player, Paul McEwan. Among this distinguished company was Chris, a schoolboy, just 17. However, he had to withdraw from the squad — he would again be spending the summer in the Bay of Plenty with his father. He was also in demand for club cricket. He was invited to make his senior debut for the Lancaster Park club at the Burwood Oval. Eager to make an impression, Chris steamed in and bowled ferociously. One of his deliveries skidded through and smashed painfully into the keeper's hand, breaking a bone.

Soon after, the match was rained out. It had been an all-round disaster. No result and the keeper, Graeme Kench, out for the best part of the season. Worse still for Lancaster Park, Chris remained committed to the CBHS First XI for Saturday cricket. He did agree to play some one-day matches for the club, until he went back to Te Puke, a few weeks later.

Chris loved playing in Te Puke. He worked on a kiwifruit orchard and had a casual job as groundskeeper at the local oval. He could bowl for hours in the nets. Chris remembers a 12-year-old kid keeping to his bowling. The boy dropped a lot of the balls but worked very hard. The kid's name was Robbie Hart and 15 years later he played for New Zealand.

The regular sunshine hard-baked the cricket strip. The Bay of Plenty weather provided great bowling conditions for the young speedster — with bounce and carry.

He could bowl at his very fastest — bowling for nicks to the keeper and slip cordon and with a bouncer in ready reserve for the more stubborn batsmen. He had never been able to bowl short regularly on Canterbury's slow, low pitches. There was also advice and motivation to be gleaned from Lance, from former test cricketer the late Andy Roberts, and from Glamorgan professional John Derrick.

Chris' debut for Te Puke, alongside his father, Roberts and Derrick, was so spectacular that the entire first innings scoreboard can be happily reproduced.

ALBION-OLD BOYS

Friis		b. Cairns C.	0
Kibblewhite	c. Parsons	b. Cairns L.	18
King	lbw	b. Cairns L.	15
Williamson		b. Cairns C.	4
A. Blake		b. Cairns L.	0
Wilson	c. Kensington	b. Cairns C.	0
Elton		b. Cairns L.	0
Jacques		b. Cairns L.	1
Neal	c. Leigh	b. Cairns C.	0
T. Blake	c. Roberts	b. Cairns C.	0
Emmett	not out		0
extras			10
Total			**48**

Fall of wickets: 0, 42, 43, 43, 46, 47, 48, 48, 48, 48.

Bowling	O	M	R	W
Cairns C.	8	5	10	5
Derrick	10	2	39	0
Cairns L.	9.4	5	6	5

The father and son demolition team took all ten wickets, the last nine for six runs. (Not everybody got the story right though. Lance was shopping when a man asked him if he was the Cairns fella who had taken all the wickets. He replied that he was and the bloke said, 'Gee, you and your dad must have bowled well!') The older players in the unfortunate Albion side conceded it was the fastest bowling ever seen in the local competition, while the Te Puke wicketkeeper, former ND keeper Jeff Leigh, who had kept to Richard Collinge among others, considered that only the young expressman, Alan Jordan, had been quicker.

All of the older, experienced men saw the incredible potential of this boy. And when he had finished with the ball he picked up a bat and scored 63 beautifully timed runs. With John Derrick, Chris put on 115 runs. It was described by an effusive local reporter as a 'gem' of an innings.

His bowling was great, his batting even better. A senior player from the opposition summarised what most people thought — that Chris was a better prospect than some of the players who had just been selected in the Northern Districts team. Speculation started to mount in the press. Would Chris get into the Shell Cup side? The selectors would have to confer with the Shell Cup captain. His name was Lance Cairns.

As symmetrical and sentimental as it would have been to have Cairns *père* and Cairns *fils* in the same side in a competitive match, Shell Cup cricket, particularly the way it was played by Lance, was no place for symmetry or sentiment. In the end Chris wasn't selected. Northern Districts had several good new-ball specialists — Karl Treiber, Brian Barrett and Lance himself could fill that position — and several good medium-pacers. In the end there was simply no vacancy. Perhaps Lance also wondered how nepotistic it would look. And maybe he looked at it from the other, paternal, angle and saw a young man who had always been advanced to a level well above his calendar age. Perhaps Lance saw the Shell Cup as too much, too soon. When Chris had been pushed into the under-20s the year before he had hated the experience. Indeed because of that he had made himself unavailable (for either Canterbury or Northern Districts) for the very same tournament that December. Maybe this season Chris would be better off just playing with his peers and achieving his short-term ambition — the 1988 Youth World Cup.

At the national under-18 tournament in Dunedin Chris starred — this time in the maroon cap of Northern Districts. ND had finished bottom, pointless, the season before but it was all different this year. Chris scored 45, 59, 41 and a match-winning 72 not out against his old province. He didn't feel too bad about defeating Canterbury — most of his old team-mates had graduated to the under-20s, anyway — and he took 3-51 when the Cantabrians batted. He also took 4-28, 3-37 and 4-29 in other matches to finish as leading wicket-taker. Northern, and appropriately Canterbury, were joint champions. And Chris had been captain. When the New Zealand under-19 team to play India was selected they had a familiar look to them. Germon was captain, Caddick, Douglas and Thomson were all there, and Aaron Gale and Chris Pringle had made the step up. Mark Hastings, son of former New Zealand batsman Brian, was also selected. Chris was appointed vice-captain. After a tour by India the squad would travel to Australia to play the Youth World Cup. Chris had set, then met his goal.

In January 1988 a small bespectacled 19-year-old, with a headband holding his anarchic hair, took a record 16 wickets on his test debut. His mixture of googlies, top-spinners and leg-breaks confounded the great West Indies batting line-up. His name was Narendra Hirwani and a month later he was bowling to Chris Cairns.

The record-breaker was part of the Indian under-19 squad preparing for the Youth World Cup. It included other players that Chris would eventually play in test cricket — Nayan Mongia and Venkatapathy Raju, but Hirwani was the star. In the first innings of the first match — a four-day game at Seddon Park — Chris was beaten by the subtlety of Hirwani's flight — stumped for 45, the top score.

In the second innings, Hirwani's wrong'un trapped Chris in front for 20. It was the first time Chris had come up against international quality leg-spin, and he had lost the contest. He was to find leg-spin difficult for the next decade. The problem was not attacking the spinners — he loved to dominate and he estimated that no boundary would be long enough if he connected properly. The major problem was to defend leg-breaks. But while the New Zealanders were having problems with the Indian spinners, the Indians were having bigger problems with the New Zealand pace attack. Chris took 3-36 in the first innings, while Shane Thomson finished with 6-21. The pair took seven wickets in 34 minutes (including a drinks break) on the second morning. Martin Kimber and Hamish Kember then spun New Zealand to victory in the second innings.

Following through for Northern Districts under-18s against Otago at University Oval in Dunedin.
Playing in his own age group for the first time, Chris captained ND to a joint share of the national title
in the 1987–88 season.

It was a great win but Germon rolled his ankle and was out of the following one-day match. Chris was appointed captain of a New Zealand team for the first time — but the under-19s batted poorly and India won.

After these matches Chris travelled to Wanganui to play in Lance's benefit match, under lights. It was a family occasion — 6000 turned up to the tiny ground to watch a New Zealand XI, all players with test experience, play Lance Cairns' XI — a team including Jeremy Coney and Tony Blain, Chris Broad and John Emburey from the touring English team, Shane Thomson and Barry Cooper and the two Cairnses.

This was Lance's last hurrah. He had decided it was time to hang up his flannels for good. Not that there had been a noticeable drop in form — Lance had even been asked to join the New Zealand team for the World Series Cup a couple of months earlier. But Lance felt that his time was up. The benefit match was a disappointment — after 25 overs it rained and the game was abandoned. Lance didn't get the chance to size up the small Cook's Gardens boundaries.

But it wasn't a complete disappointment — one player had time to shine. Chris took the wickets of Trevor Franklin (a second-ball yorker), John Wright, Mark Greatbatch and Martin Crowe — four international batsmen with 99 tests and over 5000 test runs between them. Chris finished with 4 for 21. And his figures could have been better. A catch was dropped at slip off Wright. The culprit was his dad.

A week later the under-19 squad arrived in Adelaide on their big quest. Cricket had taken Chris over a national border for the first time. The tournament was played on picturesque gum-ringed ovals across the South Australian countryside, at places like Berri and Wentworth. The eight teams included players, here and there, who would dominate the game in the 1990s. Pakistan looked likely prospects with talented youngsters Basit Ali, Mushtaq Ahmed and a large clumsy fellow called Inzamam-ul-Haq. England had Cambridge student Michael Atherton captaining a side which included Nasser Hussain and Mark Ramprakash. Sri Lanka boasted Sanath Jayasuriya. But for every player who advanced to greater heights, there was a player like West Indian Samuel Skeete, a person who oozed confidence and talent, an all-rounder who looked as if he would bestride cricket for the next decade. Skeete was a swaggering superstar at the age of 19 — and a cricketing nobody a few years later.

New Zealand began well — beating Sri Lanka, but then lost to the West Indies. It was the first time Chris encountered the Caribbean attitude of breezy self-confidence. These players were the apprentices to Richards, Greenidge, Garner and Walsh. One, short of stature, batting at first drop, whistled as he batted and played delicate shots from the start of his innings. He scored a good-looking 20 and when the Kiwis later looked in the score-book they read the name Lara.

New Zealand recorded only one more victory — over an ICC composite side — and finished second to last. It was a disastrous tournament. The batting had been poor — only three Kiwi batsmen hit half-centuries in seven games. Chris scored just 88 runs at 12.57 with a high score of 34. Twice he fell to leg-spinners (Hirwani, again, and little Mushtaq Ahmed).

Chris' bowling was a different story altogether. His 15 wickets in the tournament (at 16.40) was the fourth-highest total overall. Among his peers from throughout the world, Chris, at least with ball in hand, looked the match of anyone.

The tournament was won by Australia. Strangely only two of that team went on to play test cricket — Stuart Law played just one test, while Alan Mullally went on to play 19 tests — for England. Mullally wasn't the only youngster to change allegiance. Andy Caddick, the Hadlee clone from Christchurch, was disappointed to have played only one match at the Cup. A short time later he left New Zealand to try his luck in the mother country. Chris remembered an aloof, focused character, someone who didn't mix well within the team environment. Caddick went to England and played first for Somerset and then for England. Andy Caddick provides one of the great 'what ifs' of New Zealand cricket.

Back in Christchurch, Chris returned to school for his seventh-form year. He was deputy head prefect. But in spite of the benefits of being a senior student, he felt unhappy from the first day. He had missed the first month of term, was behind on schoolwork, and missed the glamour of touring and cricket. Once he'd tasted his exciting future it was hard to go back to the mundane present. There were things to look forward to — a rugby tour to Australia with the First XV and the school dance, but that month school proved tiresome and frustrating. Then Chris received a phone call from Richard Hadlee which was to change his life.

The year before Hadlee had finished his 10-year stint at Nottinghamshire. It had been a glittering county career including the first double of 1000 runs and 100 wickets since Fred Titmus in 1973. He was consistently in the top bracket of the bowling

Chris (seated, third from left) as vice-captain of the under-19 Youth World Cup team. This side contained future Black Caps Shane Thomson, Chris Pringle, Mark Douglas and also New Zealand's biggest loss to the game in recent seasons, Andy Caddick (seated, second from right), who went on to represent England.

averages and hit several memorable centuries. Both he and his close comrade Clive Rice had retired from the County Championship and Notts were looking to unearth some more talent to foster.

Hadlee had seen Chris perform, indeed had watched the boy grow up and recognised the same desire for success that was such a part of his own game. He made a recommendation to the Notts committee, who eagerly agreed to employ Chris on their staff. All that was needed was Chris' acceptance of the offer.

The phone call detailing the offer came in the mid-evening just after Chris had got home from school. He was busy wolfing down dinner. The Notts deal was combined with a scholarship from Air New Zealand together with New Zealand Cricket. Chris was stunned. It was not just the crystallisation of a nebulous dream to play in England, this was even greater, even fuller. This was one of the most famous cricket teams — a team that had produced Harold Larwood, the Gunns, Arthur Shrewsbury.

When he told his mother she panicked inside. It was a wonderful offer, and she believed fully in her son's talent, but this was 1988. No employer could guarantee a job for life any longer. The economic buzz-words were restructuring, efficiency and Black Tuesday. Surely he should see out his seventh form and then follow the plan he'd sketched out several years before — play league cricket in England for a year and then maybe go to university.

She told Chris her concerns and encouraged him to speak to someone at school about his dilemma. The next morning, over breakfast, Chris turned to his mother and

Sue, Chris and Louise. A dedicated follower of fashion, Chris displays the characteristic 1980s bouffant hairstyle.

simply told her that he was thinking of buying new rugby boots. Sue's heart leaped. It was a subtle code. He was going to stay.

Life-changing decisions always seem to have a large element of luck attached to them and Chris' was no different. When he went to school that day he had pretty much decided that maybe it was too soon, that he was too young, that his mother was right. He went to see the deputy headmaster, Lyall Frenchwright, because Ian Leggat, the principal, was away. When he had finished explaining the offer to Mr Frenchwright, the teacher, a big sports fan, gave his opinion — he said that if it was plumbing or carpentry he would advise the student to accept the offer of an 'apprenticeship'. Cricket was just like other trades. Chris' mind was made up. He accepted the offer and in less than a month he was in Nottingham.

Maybe the whole narrative of his career would have been different had he spoken to Ian Leggat that day rather than Lyall Frenchwright. A few weeks later Sue asked Mr Leggat what he would have advised. He said, 'I wouldn't have made it so easy for him to leave.'

4

Tickets, passport, whites

Many young New Zealanders experience the big OE, but few are as young as Chris was when he took his in 1988, and few have such a dream job. Instead of working in a bar, driving trucks or shuffling papers in an office, Chris was playing cricket for Nottinghamshire. However, a lot of other aspects of his first year at Nottingham would be very familiar to those Antipodeans who have lived in Britain for any length of time. He lived in a 1920s bungalow with purple carpet, 'The Purple Palace', in the suburbs of Nottingham, opposite an off-licence.

The house had four residents from different corners of the British Empire. Chris shared a room with a South African all-rounder, Dave Callaghan (seven years later Callaghan hit an amazing 169 not out against New Zealand in a one-day international). He was 22 and as inept as Chris around the house. The dishes piled high and they didn't change their bed sheets for the entire summer. Also in the house was the big West Indian Franklyn Stephenson and an Englishman, Duncan Martindale, a born-again Christian and professional cricketer. It was squalid but happy, and the quartet of strangers socialised often.

Stephenson was Nottinghamshire's overseas professional, brought in to replace Hadlee and he must rank as one of the best players never to have played test cricket in the modern era, along with Clive Rice and Vincent van der Bijl. He had been

The house lawn mower at the 'Purple Palace' in Nottingham left a lot to be desired.

banned from international cricket for playing on one of the West Indian rebel tours to the apartheid state of South Africa. The irony of a black player being banned because of sporting contacts with a racist white nation was lost somewhat on the authorities.

Stephenson was a captain's dream, willing to bowl at any time on any pitch. He was capable of running through sides with his speed, but if the pitch was true he was equally capable of limiting totals with accurate, strangulating bowling. Batting was always an adventure with Franklyn. He swung the bat in a very liberated, and occasionally effective way. In short he was the perfect professional, a match-winner.

Callaghan was one of the best timers of the ball Chris has ever seen. His chances for South Africa were limited, perhaps, because he was not a God-fearing man like Cronje, Rhodes or Wessels. He was a hedonist who enjoyed the barbecues and reggae parties at the Purple Palace. Chris was amazed that Dave would run daily but never seemed to lose kilos. Dave's rationale was that with the amount of booze they were drinking he had to train constantly just to maintain his weight!

Chris began playing alongside Callaghan in the Second XI. This was usually on ovals in the backblocks of the major counties, at the same time the first teams were playing each other. The Second XI comprised young players on their way up, and older professionals on their way down, a potpourri of talent and ambition. Life was certainly not as glamorous as Chris had imagined. He seemed to spend an inordinate amount of time in cheap hotel rooms in strange towns. Besides the cricket there were mundane tasks like carrying drinks and cleaning gear as part of the staff. All the time he was soaking up the experience, the history of Trent Bridge, and the wisdom of Nottinghamshire's test players — Bruce French, Chris Broad, Tim Robinson and Derek 'Arkle' Randall. That old cricketing walrus Eddie Hemmings, in particular, took Chris under his wing.

In the weekends he turned out for Blidworth Colliery in the local pit league. There is a deep connection between cricket and coal — Harold Larwood, Wilfred Rhodes and Geoffrey Boycott were all from mining towns. Playing with the miners' team was great fun — none of his team-mates were stars but most of them had reams of experience, and they helped Chris with his acclimatisation to English wickets and conditions.

Blidworth began the season well on the back of great performances by the 17-year-old Kiwi, even though their home ground, with a horizon of towering pithead wheels and slag heaps, did not have a wicket conducive to fast bowling. One afternoon was particularly memorable — Blidworth was all out for just 94. Chris then took 6-28 and their opponents, Welbeck Colliery, were dismissed for 69 in reply.

Chris loved playing for Blidworth and enjoyed the company of his team-mates at the welfare social club — people like Mark Tiplady, a lusty middle-order hitter and nude off-spin bowler, who provided chauffeur and accommodation services for the teenager. Perhaps the small-town atmosphere reminded Chris of his time growing up in Bishop Auckland. Perhaps, even, it reminded him of the days way back in the past at Spring Creek. Like father like son, both Cairnses had some of their happiest cricket experiences playing for small teams in forgotten corners of England.

For the Second XI, however, Chris didn't think that he was playing particularly well in those first weeks. But halfway into a three-month contract, a minor miracle occurred. Franklyn Stephenson, attempting to play the hook against Gloucestershire,

CAIRNS FAMILY

Some of Chris' team-mates from Blidworth, his first club team in England, 1988. Mark Tiplady (far left) took Chris (far right) under his wing, but all club members did their best to ensure the young Kiwi felt part of the 'family'.

had his nose broken, and required surgery. At the same time former Wellington speedster Andy Pick was also injured. Notts, famed for its fast-bowling stable, was suddenly short a new-ball bowler. They looked only as far as their second team and saw a lightning-fast 17-year-old.

There was a flurry of messages between the New Zealand Cricket Council and Nottinghamshire, as Chris' 'overseas player' registration was sought and sorted out. Chris' contract was extended to the end of the season. Suddenly he was in the side to face Kent. Eleven days shy of his eighteenth birthday, the youngest New Zealander to make his county debut, Chris walked onto a ground to play first-class cricket.

Dartford is one of the least likely places for a great career to begin. It is a small Kentish town at the very margins of Greater London, and gives its name to the Dartford tunnel and bridge complex, which allows the M25 motorway to go both under and over the Thames estuary. It has few sights of any note. The cricket ground is a midden, surrounded on two sides by busy roads, and brick bungalows of 1930s council estates. Kent played at Dartford just once a year. In 1988 they were to play Nottingham there.

It should have been an unforgettable moment for Chris, but Nottinghamshire played so poorly that to forget the game completely was preferable. When Chris walked to the wicket, his first action in first-class cricket, the score was 54 for six. Notts had been destroyed. Soon afterwards they were all out for 64. It was the lowest total the county had managed for nigh on 80 years. The humiliation was tangible. Tim Robinson had eked out 31 runs. The next highest scorer was debutant Chris Cairns. He had managed seven not out. While this boy played straight, four wickets had fallen, in a matter of minutes, at the other end.

It was only just past lunch on the first day when Chris was thrown the ball to open

Franklyn Stephenson — friend, team-mate, flatmate — joins Chris on the 'dance floor' during a flat party in 1988.

the bowling with Kevin Cooper. After a nervous couple of overs, and an accidental beamer or two, he built up good pace. Soon, however, the mix of adrenalin coursing through his body and the exertion of bowling at top speed had exhausted the young Kiwi. The Kent openers, including England player Mark Benson, started building a partnership and hitting Chris around. A wicket fell at the other end and Chris was bowling to left-hander Simon Hinks. The barefaced 17-year-old was bowling with velocity and venom but scattered the ball around and Hinks, a journeyman with several seasons of cricket behind him, saw a short wide ball and cut it ferociously.

And aerially. Paul Pollard standing at point caught the ball. Strictly he had to take it as it had been struck so hard that it could have decapitated him. Chris had his first first-class wicket.

While Hinks may have started it all, Chris' third wicket had extra significance. Chris Cowdrey was, like his namesake Cairns, the son of a famous father. He was a player who never lived up to the enormous freight of expectation that came from being the child of Colin Cowdrey, one of the great stylists of English cricket. Chris Cowdrey had played several tests as a bits-and-pieces all-rounder in the mid-80s but had faded, it seemed, from the selectors' scope. He was now Kent's captain. Would Chris Cairns be the same? A player never set to repeat the feats of his father? When Cowdrey edged a Cairns ball to slip he became the first test cricketer Chris had dismissed in top-level cricket. Two months later Cowdrey was selected out of the blue as England's captain to play the Windies.

Chris finished with 4-70 on debut. He had proved a good, if raw, replacement for Stephenson, but he thought that he hadn't bowled that well. He had exhausted himself quickly. After six overs he was a physical wreck. He clearly had to learn how to bowl long spells and to conserve his energy.

In the second innings Chris scored 15 and Notts fared much better. Kent had a tricky 111 runs to win on a poor pitch. This was not the time to give a 17-year-old the responsibility both to get wickets and to keep the runs down. Cooper and Saxelby bowled throughout the innings and very nearly secured an unlikely victory. In the outfield Chris was angry. He wanted to help. A word came to him — contribute. As he watched other players play the game he vowed that never again would he not contribute.

Kent won by just two wickets. Chris was one of the positives for the defeated side. He had enjoyed the experience immensely and hadn't looked out of place. He was selected for the next match against Warwickshire at their headquarters. A famous ground. Edgbaston.

The *Sunday Times* two days later published a match report by Malcolm Winton. It began:

> Edgbaston yesterday saw the appearance of a future test fast bowler. He stands 6ft 2in, is broad in the beam, the way good fast bowlers are traditionally meant to be, and won't be 18 till next Sunday. Unfortunately he isn't English. His name is Christopher Lance Cairns . . .

His first day at the grand Birmingham ground had been very successful. He had taken three wickets including England internationals Andy Lloyd and Geoff Humpage. On a green wicket Chris bowled aggressively. Occasionally he strayed down leg, trying too hard, but only the experienced Humpage had looked comfortable facing his pace and movement. Running in from 30 yards with the enthusiasm of youth, he would follow through all the way inside the batsman's personal space. Chris bristled. The fact that these players were 10 and 20 years his senior didn't faze him. With every glare, with every ball that arrowed into the keeper's gloves 20 yards behind the stumps, with every stride Chris announced his arrival. He was here to stay.

The rest of the match was not quite as successful. Chris took one more wicket to finish with 4-89, but Notts batted poorly (Cairns bowled Merrick 7) and Warwickshire set a target of 206 to win. Notts managed to score just 44 of them.

Chris got his first duck. It seemed that this champion side was falling apart — it was their sixth loss from eight matches. It was the first time Chris had faced somebody of genuine pace — West Indian Tony Merrick. Merrick was big, sharp and a huge challenge for the rookie.

The emergence of Chris Cairns caused a buzz around the county circuit. Test veteran Chris Broad declared him the fastest 17-year-old he'd ever seen. Alvin Kallicharan, the Warwickshire coach, considered him the best quick bowler of his age on the planet. The great West Indian noted his devastating fast ball. Some English cricket writers compared him to the young West Indian quicks who were touring England at the time — players like Ian Bishop, Patrick Patterson and Curtly Ambrose. Test players. Chris' future seemed assured. Not even 18 and he was slated for international cricket. In fact his exposure to international cricket came a lot sooner than expected.

Franklyn Stephenson was back in the side for the next match and Chris dropped down to the reserves (10 days later he hit a century off 46 balls with 4 fours and 8 sixes against Sheffield University, the second 50 coming off just 15 balls). But there was an exception to the 'one overseas professional' rule. For tour matches counties could play as many foreigners as they liked. Notts was to play two matches against touring teams that season. The first was against the West Indies. All the residents of the 'Purple Palace' were selected to play.

The West Indian team of the '80s was one of the greatest of all sides. Gordon Greenidge and Desmond Haynes were a great opening pair, followed by the Leeward Islanders Viv Richards and Richie Richardson. Then there was the fury of Malcolm Marshall and Courtney Walsh. It was an array of wilful destruction that may not ever be assembled again. When the Windies arrived in Nottingham like a spring storm they led the five-match test series 3–0 with one to play. They were in the middle of the third 'blackwash' to be inflicted on England within four years.

It was incredible for Chris. It wasn't even a decade since he had watched the Windies at Carisbrook. Now he was on the same paddock as Gordon Greenidge. The great batsman started to scythe the opening bowlers around on his way to a century. Chris was first change. Other colts might have been overwhelmed, but not Chris. A quick yorker sent Jeffrey Dujon towards the pavilion. Then Carl Hooper edged to the keeper. Viv Richards, the 'Master Blaster', the irresistible force of cricket in the latter half of the 20th century, walked to the wicket, without a helmet. Viv Richards, Chris' paragon.

Chris spent a few overs bowling the ball directly into the middle of Richards' bat but he wasn't flustered. Fuelled by the invincibility of youth, Chris bowled a ball that rose from a length, just outside off stump. It moved ever so slightly away from the batsman, who had been surprised a little by its pace. The leather had been achingly close to kissing the willow. In the one-on-one joust that is the essence of cricket, Chris had scored points.

Then something strange happened. Normally when a batsman is beaten the slips will sigh, the keeper will exhort and the bowler will remind the batsman of his responsibilities, but this time there was nothing but an eerie silence. This type of thing didn't happen to Viv Richards. Chris didn't know the protocol and just stood mid-pitch, amazed. There was no clapping, no sledging. Then in an Antiguan accent as thick and rich as a chocolate gateau, the batsman shouted a simple compliment

Bowling for Notts against the West Indies at Trent Bridge, 1988. It was in this match Chris would come up against one of his idols, Viv Richards, the 'Master Blaster'.

to his 18-year-old opponent, 'Well bowled, maaan.'

Unsure what to do Chris just said 'Thanks!' and walked back to his mark.

Chris took two lower-order wickets to finish with 4-82, and the match degenerated into batting practice for the Caribbeans. Chris had an opportunity to bat late on the last day. He was nervous and enervated. It was his first innings at Trent Bridge. As Chris walked down the steps with Notts members clapping politely he put on his batting gloves. But there was something wrong — there was something rubbery stuck in his glove. He reached in and pulled out a condom that his team-mates, laughing away on the balcony above, had put there earlier. It gave a new spin to the term 'protective gear'.

Chris had always dreamed about facing really fast bowlers and had spent all week practising with a bowling machine facing short balls. However, when it came his turn to bat, the quicks were resting — Keith Arthurton and Carl Hooper were ambling through some overs of spin.

It had still been marvellous. In just his third first-class match he had played the greatest cricket side in the world. He had bowled in tandem with the marvel Franklyn Stephenson. And his father was in the crowd. A month later Notts played the touring Sri Lankan side and Chris took another three international scalps.

The season was winding down. Notts couldn't repeat the trophy haul of the year before but finished mid-table, thanks largely to the brilliance of Stephenson, who achieved the 'double' of 100 wickets and a thousand runs. Remembering what Billy Ibadulla had done for Glenn Turner when the latter had scored his 100th hundred, Chris took a drink (rum and coke) out to the crease for the Bajan when Franklyn scored his thousandth run of the season. Stephenson hadn't just replaced Hadlee, he had matched his achievement.

Another player that the English press were comparing to Hadlee was young Chris, who had taken 15 wickets at a little over 25 runs each. He had loved his first season — the socialising, the travelling, and the endless days of cricket. The cricket ground was his office. Sure bowling day-in day-out was hard on the body but professional cricket seemed to be what this body had been designed for. Before he headed back across the equator, Chris cemented his future — he signed up for another season with Notts as the county's second overseas player.

Chris may have expected a few months' rest in the three-month gap between the Northern and Southern Hemisphere seasons but soon after his return to New Zealand he was called in as a reinforcement on the Young New Zealand tour to Zimbabwe. The team included eight players (Vance, Rutherford, Greatbatch, Blain, Morrison, Watson, Franklin and Horne) who had already played test cricket. Chris was replacing his mate Shane Thomson, who had broken a finger. Having never played a single first-class match in New Zealand, Chris was selected as one of his country's representatives.

Zimbabwe were up-and-comers. They had performed creditably at the World Cup in 1987 and had already given the world the belligerent batting of Graeme Hick. The country was undergoing a huge sea change — from racist colony to African democracy. The autocratic president Robert Mugabe had dismantled most things colonial, but cricket had survived. The apocryphal story was that the Rhodesian Government, hoping to torture Mugabe psychologically, had piped cricket commentary into his prison cell while he was being held captive in the '60s. Incredibly, the future president had grown to love the game because of this and went to see the touring Kiwis when they played in Harare.

When Chris arrived in the country, he encountered a Zimbabwe team of competent, doughty fighters. The home team had already won the 'test' series 2–0. Chris played in the last three one-day games. His bowling, however, proved expensive and loose and it was only with the bat that Chris excelled. He scored 19 in his first match, and had a breakneck partnership of 72 (Chris' contribution 38) with young Gavin Larsen in the next. New Zealand narrowly lost the last two matches, and the series 3–2.

On his return home Chris played in a fifth-grade match (!) for Lancaster Park. Sydenham complained that he was playing below his grade. Just slightly. It was his only game for Lancaster Park that season though, as, despite an offer from the club of $10,000 to stay in Christchurch, he wanted to spend another summer accruing knowledge from his old man. Lance was now living in Whangarei and the pair made their Northland debut in the same match — a U-Bix Cup playoff. Chris hadn't even played club cricket in Northland when he was picked but proved up to the task with nine wickets in the match.

Chris flatted with Barry Cooper and spent the weeks working as a labourer on a dairy factory being constructed near Whangarei. But he was mainly in the Far North to learn and one Sunday morning he learned a lot. On the Saturday, Chris had performed particularly well for his club, Onerahi-Central, against Bay of Islands. He scored 68 in the first innings, then took 5-12. His dad took 4-8. At one stage Bay of Islands were 9 for 8, but rallied to reach 22 all out.

Afterwards with a few team-mates, Chris had a big night — a great evening of dancing, flirting and imbibing. The next morning he arrived at the ground feeling worse for wear. The captain saw that his new-ball bowler was looking haggard and careworn and threw the ball to him. On a blistering Northland summer's morning, Chris was forced to bowl over after over after over. He sweated alcohol from every pore, and craved water and rest. It was a lesson in restraint, a tutorial in moderation — cricket came first. The captain was Lance Cairns.

Chris led the Northern Districts under-20 team in the annual tournament in Auckland in December. The competition that had intimidated him so much two years previously became his domain. Competing against his peers was so much easier (and more fun) than striving against the world's best. With scores of 33, 47, 70, 71 not out and 136 against Central Districts, he was the nonpareil of his generation. He matched that with the ball — 14 wickets at an average a fraction less than 15. Northern Districts, with a team that included future New Zealand representatives Matthew Hart, Simon Doull (9-28 v CD), Kyle Wealleans and Mark Bailey, and coached by Richard 'The Rock' Collinge, won with acreage to spare. It was time for Chris to graduate.

He made his debut for Northern Districts in the limited-overs Shell Cup competition after Christmas. His returns were relatively modest, but in his second game, against Otago, he made an impact — 10-1-27-3 with the ball was followed by a six-ball innings for 15 including a huge six off paceman Vaughn Johnson.

In the New Year, the Shell Trophy began. The first match against Central Districts at McLean Park pitted the two best young captains in New Zealand against each other — Chris Kuggeleijn and Martin Crowe. Northern had the two great white hopes in Thomson and Cairns. There was Brendon Bracewell, all-rounder Grant Bradburn, and promising keeper Bryan Young. Finally, in Graeme Hick they had one of the most powerful batsmen in the world, a player who had scored 405 in an innings for Worcestershire and 'a thousand runs in May'. The Zimbabwean sensation could maul any attack.

Central batted and Chris took three wickets (including New Zealand rep Tony Blain) and the Northern middle order knocked off the deficit and built a lead. Chris scored a quick 21, including his first six in first-class cricket off off-spinner Paul Unwin. Then Crowe scored one of his peerless centuries, on a turning pitch. With Hick matching Crowe's century, the game swung towards Northern, and with one over to go they needed just 14 to win. A six, a wicket, a bye, a wicket and another wicket and Central had conjured an unlikely victory. Chris was disappointed, but this was cricket as he loved to play it — absurdly close, evenly matched and exciting. Crowe seemed to be a strategist with a touch of genius — a future test captain for sure. Chris imagined that he would enjoy playing under his leadership.

In his sixth-ever first-class match Chris finally took part in a victory as Northern's bowlers proved too good for Otago's batsmen. Chris twice knocked the top off the southern batting order. The next match he pushed his highest score to 32 (seven fours) against Wellington batting at number 10 (!) and took a further three top-order wickets.

After that, success with the ball evaporated. In six more matches Chris took just nine more wickets. Perhaps he wasn't the force majeure that everybody hoped he was. In truth it was a terrible year for a fast bowler to make his debut. It seemed like there was not a single pitch that offered seamers any help at all. Eden Park, Seddon Park and the Basin Reserve were simply batsmen's paradises. Bowling careers could be ruined on the shirt-fronts carefully ironed and starched by groundskeepers around the country. Records tumbled like the sweat off bowlers' brows. In the 1988–89 season an incredible five double-centuries and 40 centuries were recorded in 29 first-class matches. Luckily for Chris' season, one of those centuries was his.

Against Auckland at Seddon Park in Hamilton, Chris joined Graeme Hick with Northern 93-6 and wilting. Hick was being watchful and Chris suddenly found himself playing as if HE was the senior partner. He pushed Danny Morrison and friends for singles and hammered the loose ball when it came. Two wickets fell quickly and the veteran Brendon Bracewell joined Chris.

This was the kind of situation Chris adored — a team in crisis relying on his performance. He breezed past the 50 mark and began to take to the Auckland spinner Neutze. A couple of shots flew over the boundary. When Bracewell's aggressive innings ended, Chris was still four short of his century with Brian Barrett the last man in. Displaying a calm not usually seen in an 18-year-old, Chris pushed three singles then hit a boundary off Bill Fowler to score his maiden century. He became the fifth-youngest century-maker in the history of New Zealand cricket.

When he was out a few minutes later, he had scored 110 runs off 145 balls with nine fours and two sixes. It was a magic moment. The modest crowd at Seddon Park had seen something special, the final confirmation, if it was ever needed, that here was an all-rounder of international class, still in his teens. The future was as bright and wide as his smile.

Seddon Park was the scene of another highlight. Chris was selected, along with Bracewell, to play for a President's XI in the first official match of Pakistan's tour. The Pakistanis had one player who was on another level altogether. Imran Khan, the 'Lion of Lahore', was the greatest cricketer Pakistan had produced, a player who ranked equal to, or even above, the other great all-rounders of the '80s — Kapil Dev, Botham and Hadlee. Imran would have been selected either as a batsman or bowler in the Pakistan side, so adept was he at both disciplines. He had charisma and charm that was enviable. He was inspiring to the players he led, full of confidence towards his opposition and a sexual icon to women. In short, he was everything Chris wanted to be.

Pakistan batted first and Chris experienced the rugged brilliance of Javed Miandad for the first time (Javed averaged 150 this tour). Chris picked up the wicket of young Ijaz Ahmed, but didn't bowl particularly well. The New Zealanders had some good batting practice, and Chris came to the crease and looked solid. He faced Imran Khan — and Chris was determined not to go out, determined to get behind the ball. He did both things, but not in the way intended. Imran took the second new ball and bowled a beautiful bouncer. Although Chris tried to duck, the ball beat him for pace, swung in and hit him on the helmet. It was travelling so quickly that it slipped between the face grill and the visor and struck Chris flush on the forehead. For the second time in four years a Pakistani had levelled one of the Cairns family with a short-pitched ball. This delivery had some freight behind it — it was a welcome from one generation of world-beaters to another, an initiation into the all-rounders club. Having scored 25, Chris was forced to leave the field for stitches in a wound above his right eye. Chris felt like he'd gone a round with Mike Tyson.

The Hawke/U-Bix Cup is New Zealand's oldest cricket trophy. It was gifted in 1903 by the patrician cricketer Lord Hawke and became the symbol of supremacy beyond the urban centres. A challenge trophy, like the Ranfurly Shield, its idiosyncratic rules mean that the cup can be won on a first-innings victory. Often games are slow essays in run accumulation, with the accent on defence and concentration. The rivalry was fierce and the sledging notorious and this unique style has produced many fine New Zealand cricketers — including Bevan Congdon and Ken Wadsworth (Nelson), Jack Alabaster (Southland) and Harry Cave (Wanganui). The 1988–89 season saw the arrival of the Cairns family into the Hawke Cup history.

After the playoffs, Northland was confirmed as challenger and the team journeyed to New Plymouth in February to meet the holders, Taranaki. The Northland team were replete with seasoned first-class players — Murray Child, Karl Treiber, Bryan Young, Derbyshire pro Bernie Maher and Barry Cooper and, of course, the father and son pincer movement. Between the steep terraces of Pukekura Park, Chris bowled steepling deliveries on a flat wicket and finished with 5-94. His father took 2-56. The solid Northland top order built an innings slowly and surely and when the total pushed past Taranaki's 324 the game was as good as won. Neither Cairns was even required to bat and the Cup journeyed to the northernmost association for the first time in five years.

The domestic season was soon over — Northern finishing a close third to Auckland in spite of the Cairns-inspired victory at Seddon Park. Most first-class cricketers packed up their gear and stowed it away in forgotten cupboards and spent another winter doing the ordinary things in life, going back to jobs or family or study. Not Chris Cairns. Together with Chris Harris, Mark Richardson, Shane Thomson, Matthew Hart, Llorne Howell, Mark Douglas and, again, skipper Lee Germon, he journeyed to Australia with the under-20 team to play a three 'test' series against their trans-Tasman contemporaries.

The New Zealanders were outclassed. Chris scored 91 against a District XI but against the might of Young Australia he didn't have much success. The Aussies had several good stroke-makers including Michael Bevan, Michael Slater and Brendan Julian, and a stork of a bowler, Phil Alley (6' 8"), whose hand would come from above the sight-screen, and who ran through the Kiwis with regularity.

The Australians managed a clean sweep, though there were encouraging moments. In Germon's absence, Chris captained in one of the one-dayers. Defending just 141, Chris bowled 11-3-25-4 and Australia just squeezed home by one wicket. There were also personal duels. Chris hit Michael Slater in the head, but next ball the gutsy little Ocker hooked him for six. Slater went on to compile 196. There was a gulf in class. The Australians with their marvellous Sports Academy seemed like they would dominate test cricket in the '90s.

Soon enough Chris was back in Nottingham, boarding with Barry and Janet Newell and experiencing the great English summer — one morning he went to cricket practice through several inches of snow! His former flatmate Franklyn Stephenson was still first choice in the first team but Chris bided his time in the second XI. After a month of county cricket, Franklyn decided to rest a plaguing hamstring and give Chris some airtime. Chris' first match was against Worcestershire at the City Ground with Worcester Cathedral's steeple looming over the pitch in all its Gothic glory. Opposing Notts was Chris' ND team-mate Graeme Hick, but overall it was a quiet match for the 18-year-old, who bowled a short, expensive spell. His indifferent bowling continued against Glamorgan and he was back as 12th man for the quarter-final of the Benson & Hedges Cup against Gloucestershire.

On the journey there Chris was catnapping in the back of the car when he was woken by the vehicle being shunted violently forward. They had been tailgated by a 38-tonne truck on the Severn Bridge. The police declared that Chris was lucky to be alive, as three huge cricket coffins were jammed in the boot! He had a sore neck from the accident but fielded courageously after Stephenson broke down. In the following Championship match, against the grand old county Yorkshire, Chris took 3-50 and scored 41. This earned him a place for the next match against Middlesex at Lord's.

Every cricket lover, no matter if they adore the electricity of Sabina Park or the history of the Sydney Cricket Ground or the beauty of Newlands or the chaos of Eden Gardens cannot help but be moved on their first acquaintance with Thomas Lord's ground in St John's Wood. Lord's possesses something so essential to cricket, something so ingrained in the game that it has a magnetism all its own. There is something in the vaults of the pavilion, in the rustling trees beyond, in the quietude of those who gather there, in its historic idiosyncrasies that tells of the game's permanence, of its ethics and its fascination.

There is a grainy photograph of Chris standing in front of the pavilion at Lord's. He is nine, and smiling merrily in his shorts. Just after Sue had clicked the shutter, Chris had pointed to the pitch and stated that one day he would play there. That prophecy came true in June 1989. He took 3-79 in the first innings then waited anxiously for his big moment with the bat. When Derek Randall was dismissed, Chris made the long descent through the labyrinth of the great building before emerging onto the hallowed turf. He took guard, then looked around at the great stadium, breathing deeply, remembering the moment for his mental scrapbook. Chris Cairns was batting at Lord's. Only 15 months before he had been playing for CBHS First XI. It was amazing to him. He looked up to see the bowler start his run-up, then moments later turned to see his stumps shattered. Angus Fraser had bowled him first ball — a golden duck.

It was enormously deflating but he picked up two more wickets in Middlesex's second innings, and avoided a pair at Lord's when he scored 3 in the second dig. He made another prophecy. He vowed to come back and add his name to the litany of greats who had performed wondrous feats there — names like Trott, Woolley, Donnelly and Massie.

His time in the first team finished with a home game against Kent, when he scored his first 50 for Notts, and a match against Cambridge University at Fenners. Overall his bowling had been disappointing, but he was averaging over 30 with the bat.

If Chris was playing second violin to the maestro Stephenson, then Notts also knew that Chris had another troupe to play for. In late July

The place hasn't changed much . . . but the boy has. Chris in front of the Lord's pavilion where he vowed he would return to play one day. CAIRNS FAMILY

the New Zealand Youth team arrived for a 15-match tour. Chris was vice-captain. The team included Blair Pocock, Chris Harris, Adam Parore, Matthew Hart and Mark Richardson. The captain was David Mills, an off-spinner from Canterbury. In several warm-up games against the London New Zealand club, county youth teams and English Schools, the Kiwis played well, and Chris kept up his batting form. The three-match one-day series against the England Youth team began at Edgbaston. The English side included Nick Knight, Dominic Cork and Wayne Noon, who was to play with Chris for both Notts and Canterbury. The side was captained by a chisel-chinned, hyper-confident batsman, Mark Ramprakash.

The Kiwis were well beaten in the first two matches. The third was to be played at Lord's. The night before the match, David Mills went to the coach, Geoff Howarth, and announced that he would withdraw himself from selection for the match at the shrine of cricket. It was a brave, selfless decision by the young Cantabrian, to give up the opportunity of a lifetime to lead his country onto the most famous ground in the world. It was his own form that was behind the decision. While he was leading well, and batting efficiently, he had a major problem with his speciality, bowling. He had 'the yips'.

The yips is a golfing phrase that refers to the problems middle-aged players can develop with their putting. The drives are fine, the approach shots good, but the green work is terrible. Something that was so instinctive, so natural and so important to the player's game becomes a torturous agony. Many players are forced to change their grips radically to continue to compete, others give up the game entirely. Baseball shortstops can also suffer the yips, again with the simplest task in the game — a throw to first base. Cricketers, in particular finger-spinners, can also suffer this 'brain fart'. They bowl half-trackers, or shank the ball down leg, or toss the ball waist high. It is cricketing hell. For a discipline that exists purely on accuracy it is a breakdown of career-threatening proportions. Nearly all great slow left-armers have suffered from this at some time in their careers. Daniel Vettori leaves the room when the yips are discussed. David Mills had reached this parlous state. The honour of leading the New Zealand team fell to the vice-captain, Chris Cairns.

Again captaincy seemed to raise Chris' play to another dimension. He took five wickets for 38. Chasing 203, the Kiwis fell short — by just 22 runs. The youngsters had lost the one-day series 3–0. Four three-day matches against minor teams followed without a win and Chris led the team into the first youth 'test' very much as underdogs.

Scarborough is an English seaside resort, of the type that sells smutty postcards, rents striped deck-chairs and serves mushy peas. The cricket ground is near the town centre, not far from the seashore. The ground is famous for festival cricket and the whole town has a holiday atmosphere. The New Zealanders who took the field against the England Youth XI were not there for a vacation in the sea air, Chris in particular. He disliked his opposite number, Mark Ramprakash, disliked his swagger to the wicket, his demeanour of superiority. He may have been a Middlesex regular but Chris was determined to take him.

On the first morning Chris took the new ball and bowled a sustained spell to Ramprakash that Chris Harris remembered as extraordinarily fast. The umpire, former test cricketer John Hampshire, thought it as quick as any bowling he'd seen, and he had faced Lillee and Thomson. The English skipper had no answer to such hostility and had his castle destroyed.

Penberthy, the first drop, was hit on the elbow and retired hurt, while Chris Adams was LBW, for single figures. England was eventually all out for 156. Chris had taken 5-26. Harris (125) and Parore (96) ballooned the lead to 295. In reply English wickets fell regularly. Chris took 5-61 to finish with a 10-wicket bag. The Kiwis had won by an innings and 16 runs. It was a magnificent victory that sounded a bright note for the future of New Zealand cricket.

To celebrate, the 14 young men organised an Island of Origin touch rugby match on the beach at Scarborough. Bewildered vacationers watched as the two teams performed a haka each, then pushed the definition of 'touch' with some huge tackles. The South Island won and the entire squad went out for a drink — the age limit in Great Britain was only 18, two years younger than New Zealand's.

The next match was a rain-shortened draw, but in the third and final contest, at Old Trafford, New Zealand got speed wobbles. England had a new captain, Nick Knight, as Ramprakash had stated that the series was beneath him and went off to play for Middlesex! New Zealand failed to reach the follow-on target with nearly a day and a half to bat, and Blair Pocock sick with a virus. Just as the openers were padding up to bat again, Chris realised that Knight had not performed the courtesy of informing the opposing captain about the follow-on. Chris instantly told the entirety of his side to dress in their whites, and ordered the keeper, Adam Parore, to glove up. As soon as the umpires walked onto the field, the Kiwis went out and Chris began marking his run-up. The England 11 also emerged and 22 players stood on the outfield staring at one another.

The farce was sorted out, and the follow-on politely enforced, but it had been a cunning bit of gamesmanship by Chris. New Zealand needed to sop up every minute they could to save the test. A sound vigil by the ailing Pocock (108 not out) with good support from Parore and Chris (55) saw the Kiwis limp to a draw and a series victory. Chris negotiated some testing overs from leg-spinner Ian Salisbury before the game was halved. The victory was big news back home. The series had been won because of solid batting from Pocock, Parore, Harris and Simon Wilson. And the bowling of Chris Cairns stood like the man himself, head and shoulders over the other bowlers from either side.

While in England he had taken a call from David Trist, the Canterbury coach, who had persuaded him to play for Canterbury in the forthcoming season — Northland encouraged him to go. It couldn't match the offer.

Before the season started, however, he had a few wonderful weeks in Christchurch, catching up with friends, doing a bit of casual training and filling up on Sue's home cooking. It was one of those wonderful breaks where responsibilities are far off and life is simply to be savoured. He didn't need nor want to see another cricket pitch for two months. It felt like the calm before the storm, the storm where he would play his way into the full New Zealand squad to return to England in June. Then, in early November, six months early, the phone rang one morning as Chris was eating Weet-Bix. It was chairman of selectors Don Neely. He was wanted immediately.

CAIRNS FAMILY

Chris Harris on his way to a match-winning 125 for the NZ Youth team against their English counterparts at Scarborough, 1989. The keeper is Wayne Noon, who would later become a team-mate and friend of Chris at Notts.

5

The big break

When Pakistan had to postpone their Australian tour at the end of 1989, the Australian Cricket Board hastily invited New Zealand on a stop-gap tour, culminating in a single test. The New Zealand team arrived short of match fitness and an injury jinx started to burn through the squad. Richard Hadlee had withdrawn before the team had even left the country, then Gary Robertson fell victim, as well as Andrew Jones. The seamers included Danny Morrison, Willie Watson and Martin Snedden. Brendon Bracewell, Chris' team-mate from Northern Districts, was also on the tour, a place he earned as top wicket-taker in the Shell Trophy the previous season.

New Zealand looked short of pace, so the selectors contacted Chris to replace Robertson. Chris was taken to the airport by his mother. It all seemed so familiar. Just like 1973, a Cairns was taking off from Christchurch airport on a cricket tour to Australia. This time it was her son. Chris was feverishly excited, but kept trying to pretend that it was just another tour. He met up with the team in Adelaide — with some players he'd known since he was in short pants. His first room-mate was John Bracewell, who had babysat him a decade earlier. Bracewell's first comment was 'Gidday, Chris. Congratulations. There's some ironing of mine for you to do.' The implication was obvious — no matter who he knew, he was on the lowest rung.

A couple of rituals followed. He received his black blazer, with the fern shining from the breast pocket, from the elder statesman of the side, skipper John Wright. The other ritual took place in Perth, one evening on the team bus. Every New Zealand debutant must give a 'First Tour Speech'. A subject is drawn randomly from the pooled suggestions and the fresher must speak for two minutes on said topic. Chris' was entitled 'How I seduced the manager's wife'.

Chris' first match was at the Adelaide Oval against South Australia. It was where Lance had made his test debut. It is ironic that some of the most important cricketing venues for both father and son have been the same — Old Trafford, Adelaide, Perth, Eden Park. Chris always felt the heritage keenly. These were places Lance had been during those long absences from the family. These were the ovals that Chris had heard described over the transistor radio. In some way coming to these places, playing cricket at Lord's, Carisbrook or the MCG, gave the two a shared experience separated only by time.

The game against South Australia saw Chris bowling very quickly, quicker even than Danny Morrison and the other seamers available. He took 2-108 in 31 overs of hard work and looked up to the job on a flat, true Adelaide wicket. (Martin Crowe always used to say there were three certainties in life — death, taxes and a century at Adelaide.) Then with bat in hand he scored a solid 39.

Something that Chris couldn't help but notice was that after the slick efficiency of the Nottinghamshire county set-up, the national team didn't seem much better organised than any of the youth tours he had been on. There were hassles about

A look of apprehension from 19-year-old Chris Cairns as he prepares for his first test, Perth, 1989. The Aussies pictured are Carl Rackemann, Merv Hughes and 12th man Greg Campbell.

practice wickets, hotels, transport. Bob Cunis, a good bowling coach, for sure, would often stay in the dressing room while the side were batting, so little did the art of waving willow concern him. The senior batsmen were in charge of improving the batting techniques. He also had an old-school mentality concerning practice and the day before the Perth test the bowlers delivered well over twenty overs each in the bouncy WACA (Western Australia Cricket Association) nets.

New Zealand may have become one of the most successful test teams of the '80s but the administration seemed stuck in the brylcreemed, blazered past. Sixteen years after Lance had witnessed amateurish shambles at Hagley Park, it seemed that little had changed.

It was an injury to Brendon Bracewell that allowed Chris into the test side. Bracewell pulled up lame at a prolonged net practice and the matter was settled. Chris would play in the Perth test. The day before the test Chris went to a hairdresser to get his bouffant '80s haircut a little more bouffant. He then went to bed early and slept like a sloth, as he always did.

The WACA Ground is famed for two things. It is often bullied by a wind directly off the sea, the Fremantle Doctor, and it has the hardest and fastest pitch in world cricket. The Perth wicket has the consistency of asphalt. The ball rises steeply and loses little velocity kissing the pitch. No surprises then that Perth is the home town of Dennis Lillee.

On 12 November 1989, John Wright won the toss, and, trusting in his four seamers, elected to bowl. Thirty minutes later, Chris was walking onto the ground a test cricketer. To this day he has no memory of the hours before the test — breakfast, the trip to the ground, warm-ups, all gone in an oblivion of nervous amnesia.

New Zealand debut at the WACA, Perth, 1989. This match presented Chris with many firsts, including a test cap . . . and his first serious injury, a stress fracture of his back.

Martin Crowe remembers Chris looking like a zombie that morning.

Chris set a record before a ball had even been bowled. It was just three years and 356 days since Lance had left the international arena. Never among the 29 father-son combinations that had played test cricket had there been such a short time between test appearances. The Cairnses easily expunged the previous record (10 years) set by the Cowdreys. Even stranger was the fact that John Wright, Ian Smith, Martin Snedden and Jeff Crowe had played in both tests. Lance and Chris even looked similar and as the latter stood at the top of his run-up the keeper Smith felt odd, a little haunted, as generations crossed paths so closely in time.

Chris and Lance were just the fourth father-son pair to play test cricket for New Zealand, following the Vivians (Giff and Graham), the Andersons (Mac and Robert) and the Hadlee trifecta (Walter and Dayle & Richard). Chris was the ninth-youngest player to play test cricket for New Zealand, just a few days older than Martin Crowe and Ken Rutherford had been on debut.

Danny Morrison opened the bowling at the Northern End then Chris was to bowl to Mark Taylor. Perhaps it was the nervousness, or perhaps he was just pushing the definition of the word 'loosener', but his first ball was a shocker, a shin-high full toss that went flying past Taylor and bounced in front of first slip. Ian Smith leaped to try and stop the ball, but it would have taken a Greg Louganis-type dive to retrieve it. The batsmen scampered a single, and the umpire, Peter McConnell, signalled a bye. When the over was over Smith went to the umpire, fuming that he had already conceded a 'bye' in just the second over of the test. Surely that was a wide, not a bye? The umpire replied that he didn't want the young fellow to remember his first ball in test cricket as a rank wide, going wider.

Chris' brief was easy — to bowl hard and fast, as fast as he could. He did hurry a couple of strokes, did bowl some challenging balls, but also dragged a few short that David Boon dealt with ruthlessly. He lacked consistency and all too often direction.

Then, in his second spell, bowling to big Tom Moody (who was also making his debut), something happened. As he pounded along the pitch in his follow-through he felt a 'clunk' in his back. As he bowled the next ball it was as if there was a ball-bearing somewhere in his spine. Chris was scared. He told his skipper that something had happened, that he didn't think he could bowl any more. The senior players didn't ask the young bowler to cross the pain threshold. He was sent directly off the field to the physio.

Initially it was thought to be just a chill, a pinched nerve, but Chris couldn't bowl again that innings as he lay on the physio's table, receiving manipulation. Brendon Bracewell was instantly suspicious and encouraged Chris to get it checked immediately. He was sent to the hospital for an exploratory scan, but the results showed nothing. It wasn't yet obvious in the plates that, just like Bracewell, he had bowled so hard that he had literally broken his back.

Chris' figures of 12-0-57-0 had hardly been impressive, and Chris was hugely disappointed, even more disappointed as the weakened attack had struggled. Boon got a double-century, and Australia rattled up 500. But he was an all-rounder and had another chance. Mid-afternoon on the third day New Zealand were limping at 6-206, trying to get to 321 to save the follow-on, when Chris came to the wicket to join Jeff Crowe. Carl Rackemann, the tall blond Queenslander, was to bowl.

Chris moved forward to the pitch of the ball, but the leather spat quickly off the pitch and collided with the bat. The sheer force of the ball surprised him. It was as if Rackemann was bowling with a heavier ball. A couple of balls later the leather again collided with the bat and the ball rolled towards mid-off, who misfielded. Chris had his first run. It had seemed like a misfield was the only way he was ever going to score.

The experience was all over seconds later as he nicked a missile from big Merv Hughes to Ian Healy. The whole experience had lasted just seven minutes.

The Kiwis failed to pass the follow-on total and the openers were batting early the next morning. When Bert Vance was out early, Mark Greatbatch came in and began to play one of the great defensive innings of all time. Playing with a perpendicular bat to the rising deliveries, he defended for the rest of the day, leaving the ball with pinpoint discretion. On the last day the Kiwis were 168 for 4, still 122 runs away from even making the Australians put their pads on again. Jeff Crowe and 'Paddy' Greatbatch were together and both batting solidly. Then in mid-morning Crowe was out and Ian Smith wandered out to bat. He was out first ball, and cricket's mountainous tribute to the Hell's Angels, Merv Hughes, was on a hat-trick.

Suddenly, after hours of stasis, there was panic in the dressing room. The captain, John Wright, told Chris, who was padded up, to wait — nothing much had gone his way he said. Snedden would go in first to face the hat-trick ball. But at the crucial time Snedds couldn't get ready in time. Smith was already off the field. The umpires were waiting and in two more minutes someone would be timed out. Finally Wright, in desperation, sent the youngster in to face the ball with Merv scarlet with excitement. As Chris walked out to the torment of the middle, John Wright put his head in his hands and started saying over and over 'I've ruined his career'.

If Hughes had got the ball anywhere near straight he might have had Chris, but

'Take that, young fella'. Rackemann tries a bouncer to Chris during the last day of the Perth test in 1989. Chris hung around with Mark Greatbatch for a crucial partnership to help New Zealand draw the match.

the ball was wide and a determination started to grow in the youngster's mind — to make some kind of mark on the test. He decided to keep Greatbatch company. As unlikely as it seemed he was going to try to save the game.

There must be few more intimidating sights in test history than Merv Hughes, with handlebar moustache and a glare that would melt marble, running in to bowl with his overweight frame being pushed by the Fremantle Doctor like a spinnaker, with the asphalt of the WACA pitch waiting to receive the ball. Now Chris had to renew the steel every ball, to concentrate and parry the bowling attack. And this was no ordinary attack — Hughes, Rackemann, Terry Alderman and Geoff Lawson were virtually the attack that had won the Ashes only months earlier, a foursome that offered pace, swing, bounce and variation. The balls kept coming and the two Kiwis, urging each other on, kept displaying straight bats.

Chris scored his runs behind the wicket, down to third man and fine leg, but it wasn't about runs. To salvage a draw it was all about sands slipping through an hourglass. Both batsmen kept concentration by uttering little mantras. Greatbatch was audibly reciting, 'Watch the ball, watch the ball'. At the other end Chris was saying to himself 'Don't get out, don't get out'. The two followed familiar routines around the crease — tapping the pitch, walking towards square leg, whatever, then focusing with intensity on the next delivery, and then the next, and the one after that.

Massive cracks had opened on the WACA wicket and the ball deviated towards Chris' body several times. He was hit in the chest and ducked huge bouncers. It was a siege, and it was repulsed until 30 minutes after lunch. Chris, concentrating on back-foot play, was caught shuffling on the crease by a full ball from Hughes. The umpire raised his finger and the vigil was over. Chris Cairns LBW for 28. He had faced 67 balls, and five fours had deflected from his bat. The partnership had realised 43 valuable runs.

Chris was angry at himself for his one terminal lapse, but he had at least contributed, and significantly. Martin Snedden continued the good work, batting on through the middle session. It may have been the cricketing equivalent of reading a telephone directory, but it was undeniably compelling. Snedds spent an hour on the same score, while Greatbatch again and again got his bat behind the ball, ad nauseam. The deficit was cleared and Australia would have to bat again. Every run almost counted twice. Suddenly it was over, with a whimper rather than a bang, and it was the vaunted Australian attack that was whimpering.

The umpires called stumps, the game was drawn. It had been a brilliant rearguard action. Jeff Crowe had batted for over 2 hours, Martin Snedden for 3 hours 20 minutes, Chris for an hour and a half. Mark Greatbatch had been at the other end with all three batsmen. He had scored 143 not out. He had batted for 10 hours 50 minutes in the greatest display of discipline Chris has ever witnessed.

It may have been just a draw but the Kiwis celebrated like it was a victory, and it was of sorts. Sheer guts and determination, discipline and concentration had matched the team of all talents. He had been raised to the highest grade and competed. People congratulated Chris and the team went out that night and Chris eventually forgot about the ache in the small of his back.

You can't talk about Chris Cairns' cricket career without having a copy of *Gray's Anatomy* close by. From that first injury in Perth, Chris has missed cricket because of the following:

- Stress fracture
- Intercostal strains
- Pulled hamstring
- Kidney problem
- Torn calf muscle
- Bruised heel
- Damaged patellar tendon (left knee)
- Damaged patellar tendon (right knee)
- Ruptured spleen
- Bruised knee
- Shoulder strain
- Groin strain
- Sacroiliac joint trouble
- Damaged wrist
- Sprained ankle
- Bone spur on heel

There are few cricketers in the entire history of the game who have had such consistently bad luck. At one time or another it seems that every part of this cricketing machine has been damaged.

Perhaps the maxim about making your own luck is true. Chris always played hard, always drove his body to achieve greater things on the cricket field. Driving that hard occasionally meant something blew. It was not for Chris to pull out of a dive in the outfield, merely roll his arm over, or turn down a tight single.

Fast bowling is inevitably a high-impact activity. The human body was never designed to undergo the stresses that result from attempting to hurl a projectile as fast as possible and with a straight arm. The full weight of Chris' 90 kg frame, running in at 15 km/h, would fall first on his right ankle then, as his left leg extended a full metre in the delivery stride, would transfer across his lower back and hammer the left knee joint. The pressures were huge, and injuries inevitable.

In the two years before the Perth test, Chris had had a programme of cricket that would have exhausted calloused professionals. He had had four seasons of cricket in two years. He had toured Australia three times, England and Zimbabwe once. He had played nine youth 'tests' and 19 one-day internationals. He had played the national under-18 tournament, the under-20 tournament and a Hawke Cup challenge, seven senior (provincial or county) one-dayers in both hemispheres and 13 Second XI matches for Notts.

There were also all the minor tour matches, the university and benefit matches, and cricket for Lancaster Park, Te Puke, Onerahi, Blidworth and CBHS. He had also played 19 first-class matches, bowling 2523 deliveries (let alone wides and no balls). And he wasn't yet 20.

It wasn't just quantity it was quality. He had bowled at the best of his own generation and then at the full international sides of the West Indies, Sri Lanka, Zimbabwe, Pakistan and Australia. And he'd bowled fast, literally putting his back into it.

Chris believes that the workload put too much strain on joints and ligaments at a time when he was still developing. His body stored up the problems and breakdowns were queuing up. Quite simply it was too much, too soon — just as his father had feared.

When Chris returned home from Perth he kept going to the physio, trying to come back, but the pain persisted. Everybody thought it was a disc problem, that it would right itself. He was desperate to play. He even tried a cure suggested by a New Ager — he drank an infusion of dock leaves and slept with the leaves plastered to his back! Mostly he wanted to play alongside Richard Hadlee, and learn from the great man. But finally in February he had a bone scan, and the dark smudge on the slide, a hot spot, indicated an accumulation of blood around the area. He had a stress fracture.

A six-month rest was the only cure, so he began what would become a familiar routine, recovery in increments. He started by exercising lightly, retaining the fitness that he had considered his birthright.

These downtimes allowed him to keep in touch with his old Christchurch school friends, friends beyond cricket, friends who knew him before the recognition and autograph-hunters and sound-bites. Important people that gave Chris perspective and always reminded him that there is another world beyond the advertising hoardings and boundary rope, and also that he couldn't make a tackle in the First XV to save himself.

He also went up to Whangarei to spend time in the Far North. But it wasn't always the best environment for getting better. One afternoon Chris arrived at a match Lance was playing looking quite sheepish and shaken. A confession followed soon after. He had been heading off to one of the Pacific beaches when he had lost control of the car, writing it off.

Chris decided to develop a contingency plan. If this injury proved to be permanently debilitating then perhaps that would end his career. Within a week he had bought several books on marketing, management and business. He enrolled in a Business Communications course at Christchurch Polytechnic. It was to be a useful subject but at that time in his life it reminded him of school. While he studied he would dream of getting back onto the oval field. He also did some casual labour at a factory putting domes on jackets — the glamorous life of a test cricketer!

One thing Chris Cairns has in spades is determination and a desire to play that has brought him back from the brink so consistently. Even in the darkest moments when the injury seems to be regressing, or healing at a glacial pace, it is his passion for the game that keeps the cynicism and self-doubt at bay. Realism is important. A reasonable grasp of the optimum recuperation time is vital. To hurry back, fuelled by enthusiasm and delusions of immortality, is a great mistake, risking permanent damage. Chris had a focus. November 1990 he would be back. A rebuilding season and the year after that he would be ready for the World Cup.

In September, Chris began bowling lightly, then by October he bowled in the nets and for Lancaster Park when the season began. By the time the Canterbury trials began Chris was bowling almost at full pace, in short bursts. He was a shoo-in for the Shell Trophy squad. Lee Germon was captaining for the first time.

The New Zealand team to compete for the World Series Cup were to be announced in late November. Chris thought he might even have a chance of making that squad. After all, in limited-over cricket, a bowler only has to get through 10 overs, 60 balls — hardly excessive. Nevertheless, the selectors ignored Chris. Chris' Canterbury team-mates Richard Petrie and Chris Harris went to Australia instead.

So began the summer of the Young Guns. Hadlee, Snedden and both Bracewells had retired six months earlier. The new breed — players like Pringle, Petrie, Bryan Young and Rod Latham — were coming through, along with Harris and Grant Bradburn (who also both had test-playing fathers). Of course the term 'Young Guns' was a marketer's concoction and the truth was that players like Ian Smith, Andrew Jones and even late-starter Latham weren't strictly young. John Wright, meanwhile, was simply Jurassic.

The team performed well, and progressed through to the finals. With Willie Watson injured, Chris, ever the optimist, thought he had a chance of being selected as a replacement but in truth his domestic form had not been good enough.

Chris had started the summer well — one of his first brace of comeback wickets was the portly 42-year-old Wayne Blair, a former Otago team-mate of his father. At Queen's Park, Invercargill, Chris pitched a ball short and knocked the helmet right off Blair's head. The headgear tumbled onto the stumps. Blair hit wicket, bowled Cairns 2.

In the next game, against his former team-mates Northern Districts, he recorded his best figures yet in first-class cricket, 4-57, his wickets including his youth team colleagues Craig Ross, Kyle Wealleans and rival Shane Thomson for a very uncomfortable 27-ball duck.

The journalists watching this phoenix rise again couldn't get past the expression 'fiery' to describe Chris' bowling for most of that early season. Unfortunately that 'fire' wasn't always picking up wickets — he took only three in the next three games. His Shell Cup season was equally subdued — two wickets in five games. His batting

RON PALENSKI COLLECTION

Back in action for Canterbury during the 1990–91 season. Having missed almost a year to the back injury, Chris was keen to regain his spot back in the national side.

looked all right — a 29 not out helped win the match against Otago — but in the end his form never demanded selection as he would have wished. Then, just as the Sri Lankans began their tour the hex, the bad luck that had begun to dog him, occurred again. He strained his side and was out again. For two weeks.

In the middle of the Sri Lankan tour, the England squad came to New Zealand for a brief sojourn — three one-dayers before the long haul home. The English were an exhausted side, having just lost the Ashes series. They met the Young Guns at Lancaster Park first up. New Zealand had lost Danny Morrison with injury, and their bowling seemed to lack bite. The day before the game Chris was given a secret fitness test to assess his injuries, but he wasn't considered for the Christchurch match. Instead he'd go onto the bank under the old scoreboard with a couple of friends and a couple of beers like he usually did when he wasn't playing. Late in the day, as Chris was sitting on the concrete terraces, with the game leaning England's way, a voice rang out over the throng. Chris' girlfriend of the time, Rachel, was moving through the crowd towards him yelling, 'You're in the team. You're in the team'.

Things were just not computing. What team? People around Chris started looking around.

'What are you talking about?'

'Chris, you're in the team for the next one-dayer. I just heard it on the radio!'

People were now looking at Chris, some recognising him, and then strangers started to shake his hand, shout their congratulations and clap him on the back. It was as if the selectors had chosen someone randomly from the crowd, given some ordinary Joe Bloggs the chance. Chris was ecstatic and loved sharing the euphoria with the cricket public around him. It was an unforgettable moment. The feeling dissolved a little later, after England completed the win. When he got back to his car Chris discovered that his car had been broken into — and his cricket boots stolen.

On a sunny Wednesday in February, with the Basin Reserve packed, Chris made his one-day international debut, wearing brand-new boots. The bank was boisterous, abusing Phil Tufnell's fielding, creating long pythons of used drink-cups and yelling at passing businessmen to take their ties off.

New Zealand's batting effort was poor and England were only chasing 193. This seemed like a cakewalk, particularly as Robin Smith and Allan Lamb calmly pushed towards the target. This was an education for Chris. The two African expats seemed to have so much time to play the ball. In his early career Lamb always seemed to collar Chris. It was as if he would be asking the opposing captain when he was going to give Chris the ball! Smith, meanwhile, hit the ball frighteningly hard. There was a something — reputation or mana or self-confidence — that set these two batsmen apart from the players he'd encountered previously. Chris was not overwhelmed, but certainly more 'whelmed' than he had ever been before. The crowd fell quiet, lying back in the sun. It was 147 for 3. The day and the game were slipping by. But this was an English team that some journalists claimed were 'capable of losing any match from anywhere'.

Chris, more determined to raise his ability to the level of the two batsmen, bowled a very quick short ball that beat the batsman's pull shot and tenderised Lamb around his ribs. The next ball was fast and full, the classic one-two combination. The bails were launched, the stumps asunder and 20,000 people were celebrating. The game wasn't over and the crowd didn't lie down again. Wicket after wicket fell — to namesakes Pringle and Harris — and England fell short by just 9 runs. The game had been pickpocketed and Chris had begun it all with his deft poaching of Lamb.

The thieving continued the following Saturday. England were chasing 224 and at 171 for 3 Lamb and Smith were again cruising. Chris had bowled so loosely in the opening overs that the captain, Martin Crowe, wondered whether to bring him back for a second spell. But the partnership needed to be broken and Chris had the pace to do it. Twenty-seven balls later he had destroyed the English middle order, bowling Smith and Jack Russell and nicking out Lamb and Alec Stewart. It was a display of character and determination, a mature performance, to turn a match on its axis and win the series.

The clamorous press demanded his selection in the next match — the Hamilton test against Sri Lanka — but with Danny Morrison back the selectors made Chris 12th man. Test cricket was so close he could almost smell the new leather and linament. He was disappointed — but then again perhaps the selectors thought it was too soon to put the acid test on Chris' side. Finally on 3 March, Chris made it back into the test side for

After starting badly against the English at Eden Park in 1991, Chris came back to claim four wickets and help New Zealand to a series win.

the last match at Eden Park, replacing the dropped Chris Pringle. In the first two matches the Sri Lankans had proved adventurous opponents, batting freely and aggressively — Arjuna Ranatunga and Asanka Gurusinha were good batsmen while Aravinda de Silva was simply world-class. Injuries had weakened the Kiwi team — Martin Crowe was out and Ian Smith would captain for the first time.

Chris felt like he was making his debut for a second time. Having barely caused a ripple in first-class cricket since his return from injury he was back in the international arena. Just like Perth he would be opening the bowling with Morrison. Just like Perth it was exciting and nerve-racking in equal parts. And just like Perth he felt the weight of expectation on his shoulders.

If he was weighed down by emotional luggage he certainly didn't show it on the first morning. This time he would remain calm. He would not hare in and over-extend himself. He would play measured cricket, sensible cricket. He would bowl down the corridor of uncertainty, the alley of unease, and take wickets with guile rather than pace.

Charith Senanayake, an aggressive left-hander, rushed to 20 off the first 19 balls he received. The twentieth ball pitched and moved and Senanayake wafted his bat towards the region of the ball and barely managed to touch it. The new skipper took the catch and Chris, 15 months since making his test debut, had his first wicket. Chris leaped down the wicket as his team-mates crowded round him. The months of recuperation, effort, focus and pain seeped away.

Chris took another three wickets that day, but they didn't all come so easily. Gurusinha fell LBW, Ranatunga was caught behind, as was de Silva, though the brilliant right-hander had stroked seven boundaries off Chris' bowling before he was out. The tail-enders batted freely and inflated the total to nearly 400. Chris had taken an expensive 4 wickets. He had bowled more balls than the other bowlers, and in fact had bowled more overs than he had ever bowled before in an innings. He was both workhorse and charger. But he knew that he had been too loose and in the end had been so very close to taking a five-wicket bag — close but no Macanudo.

The newly knighted Sir Richard Hadlee had come up to Chris between innings and said simply: 'Test cricket was not meant to be easy.' The message was clear. He couldn't expect his talent would simply convert itself into success without some perspiration and concentration. Line-and-length bowling and untrammelled maidens would pressure the batsmen into mistakes.

In the New Zealand reply, Chris scored 17, batting for the third time in three innings with Mark Greatbatch. Then in the gloaming of the third day, Chris' pace again proved too much for Senanayke and Gurusinha. The next day, he bowled much tighter than the first innings. He was treated with considerable respect by de Silva, even as the little Sri Lankan tore the other bowlers apart. Chris then picked up two more top-order wickets. When Graeme Labrooy mistimed a hook and was caught at mid-on Chris had five wickets in an innings for the first time. He had bowled valiantly, with complete control and a determination to get a 'five for'. He had been New Zealand's star with the ball — nine wickets and his best figures in first-class cricket. The match was drawn but Ian Smith and coach Warren Lees praised his performance. Chris had proved that he belonged. He was there to stay.

After that success the dam burst. His next match was for his province against Central Districts. It was a tsunami of wickets. Chris took 7-39 in the first innings and

The 1990–91 season just kept getting better for Chris. In this match against Sri Lanka at Eden Park —
the third test of the series — Chris bagged a nine-wicket haul.

RON PALENSKI COLLECTION

4-66 in the second. Eleven wickets in a match! It seemed like he was becoming the world-beater that everybody had hoped. The sketchy silhouette of his promise was being filled with the inky certainty of his performances.

That victory meant that Canterbury were to play Auckland in what was effectively a Shell Trophy final. It was an elite match — 11 of the players involved were New Zealand reps, and Chris was always hyped for a match against the foes from the Big Smoke. Unfortunately there was little help from the flat Lancaster Park track and Auckland made 485 (Chris 3-124). Chasing first-innings points Chris scored 66 but the Mainlanders fell short and the trophy was lost.

Overall, however, the summer had been a triumph. Chris had taken 36 wickets — easily the best aggregate in first-class cricket that season. He had scored three half-centuries. He had fought his way into the Young Guns and he had enhanced their arsenal. However, the real victory of those balmy months was over his body. Chris had conquered injury — he had healed himself and come back stronger.

6

Of mice and men

Martin Crowe is arguably the best batsman New Zealand has produced, a player whose technique was admired the world over, a template for the art of batting. He was always a demanding batsman, demanding perfection of himself, yet only ever achieving excellence. The frustration that arose from chasing that chimera meant that he would often retreat within himself, to his affirmations and beliefs, to his tactical and analytic mind.

The press found him aloof, the public found him intense, yet the players who played with him found him wise and generous.

Chris had known Martin since he had first come into the New Zealand team, and had watched as records tumbled to his brilliance. He had later played against Martin, then later still became a team-mate. Now in late 1991 he was in a squad to train for the World Cup. Martin Crowe was captain.

Crowe's singular, undisturbed vision was that New Zealand could win the World Cup. Well over a year before the bunting was unfurled and the competition began, Crowe was talking of the potential of the side he was captaining. He knew if the Kiwis could get into the semi-finals of the Cup, then anything could happen.

For the first 18 months of his captaincy every tour, every match was not viewed as an isolated event, but as a build-up to the Cup. Fitness and focus were the buzz-words and a series of camps was organised for the winter of 1991. Commitment was another buzz-word — when Chris asked if he could miss one of the camps he was advised by New Zealand Cricket that his absence would threaten his place in the squad.

During the winter months, Chris had decided he needed some cricket so he went to England in June for a half-season with the Cockfosters club. It was while he was there that John Birch, from Nottingham, contacted him. He told him that they were going to release Franklyn Stephenson at the end of the season. They were looking for a replacement professional, and Chris was the obvious choice. Chris had missed the chance of playing for Notts in 1990 because of his back, and was rapt to get another opportunity.

The World Cup season kicked off in October with a trip to Australia for many of the hopefuls. The idea was to build a team ethic, to bond, commune and plan.

Chris bowled very well in the games against South Australia and looked the most likely new-ball bowler — the probable pace attack was Watson, Morrison, Pringle and Cairns, with Chris Harris and Gavin Larsen to bowl the slower stuff. It was a relatively inexperienced line-up. They needed all the exposure they could get.

One experience that the Kiwis could have done without occurred at the end of practice. Chris Harris was driving a van full of tired cricketers back to their Adelaide hotel. A large gas-guzzling car cruised up next to the van at an intersection. Chris Cairns looked over at the vehicle, heard the steady throb of the idling engine. Maybe he was thinking of his days as a teenage boy-racer on the flat avenues of Christchurch or what his Vauxhall Victor would sound like with a V8 engine — but he smiled and waved at the occupants. Harry, always the most aggressive driver, may even have revved the van in a comic way. However innocent the touchstone, the powder keg was ignited.

Several hundred metres down the road Chris eased the van into the hotel driveway — followed by the Aussie tank. The driver and a passenger leaped out and approached the van angrily while a third went to the boot of the car and extracted a piece of four-by-two. One assailant, red with rage or the excitement of the confrontation, pulled open the side door of the van and waved a knife at the player nearest to the door, Chris Pringle. Pringle suddenly found himself facing the sharp edges of Sheffield steel. The man yelled and waved the knife at Pringle's throat.

The other attackers started battering the van. They wanted a fracas. People in the lobby of the hotel were astounded at the scene. But suddenly it was all over. The knife-wielder punched Pringle and the three hoods sprinted back to the car and sped off. Everybody in the New Zealand side was shaken, especially Pringle. He wanted a cigarette but his hands were shaking so much that someone else had to light it for him.

Back in peaceful New Zealand the season started buoyantly — Chris took five wickets against Wellington, eight against Central Districts on a green top and three against Otago. The Shell Cup began on Boxing Day and Chris played as if Christmas had been cancelled. At Carisbrook he hit his highest score yet — 62 off 44 deliveries (three sixes, four fours) then bowled tightly to earn the Man of the Match award. Canterbury won, then beat both Districts sides to ease into the semi-final where they dismissed CD for 'nelson', 111. Chris had been a revelation — he was averaging mid-20s with the bat and was conceding just over three runs per over when bowling.

In a Shell Trophy game against Central, at New Plymouth, Chris again tore the hapless batting line-up apart, taking 4-66 in the first innings and 7-34 in the second innings. He had bowled in short furious spells to register his best figures in first-class cricket yet.

Before the Shell Cup semi-final, Chris had shown a gift for marketing. He suggested to Canterbury Cricket that the team have a mascot like most American sports teams and the Waikato (Mooloo) and Hawke's Bay (Magpie) rugby unions. His creation was Baaarney the Ram, a glowering sheep with bat and pads, who developed a rapport with the young urchins of Lancaster Park. This was the first time Chris had delved into corporate image and business innovations. He clearly had the knack. It had been fun and successful and for the first time the 21-year-old considered a career after cricket.

The England team arrived to prepare for the World Cup with three one-dayers and three tests. It would be a good work-out on New Zealand pitches. With one-day specialists like Dermot Reeve, Derek Pringle and Neil Fairbrother and talented players like Gooch, Lamb and Chris Lewis, they seemed likely candidates for the Cup. They had been finalists the previous tournament and had never failed to make the semis.

The first one-dayer was at Eden Park and New Zealand was humbled — losing by six wickets. Only Chris Cairns and Harris, with a partnership of 84 (Cairns top-scoring with 42), made the Young Guns' total respectable. But New Zealand was often rusty in the season's curtain-raisers and maybe a majority of the players had another match on their minds. The Shell Cup Final.

Canterbury were to meet the defending champions, Wellington, in the final at Lancaster Park. The team from the capital boasted the Shell Cup's most dynamic opening pair and many people's tip for New Zealand's vanguard in the World Cup — Martin Crowe and Richard Reid. Reid, son of John Richard Reid, the great all-rounder, hit the ball with the same power as his father. He was one of the few batsmen who could make Martin Crowe seem inert.

When one of them went out, Andrew Jones came in. Three other New Zealand reps were in the team. Canterbury had five internationals — Latham, Harris, Priest, Petrie and Cairns — but had five players who would also, one day, play for New Zealand (Hartland, Howell, Germon, Owens and young Nathan Astle). It was a match of two one-day titans and the struggle was to prove titanic, both in size and catastrophe. The Wellington juggernaut was at full steam while a red and black iceberg bobbed in their path.

Hartland and Latham started the match furiously, scoring 93 off 13 overs but the Cantabs found the Wellington spinners harder to get away and were all out for 252 (Cairns 24). Gavin Larsen required stitches in his hand after damaging it while fielding. He wouldn't be able to bat.

Crowe and Reid had started their reply aggressively then Reid connected with a ball from Petrie. It flew in a low arc and looked for all money as if it was going for six, but standing on the boundary rope Peter Kennedy leaped and took an astounding one-handed catch.

The Wellington innings didn't falter much. Jones and Graham Burnett, followed by some slogging from Derek Stirling and Lincoln Doull, seemed to have won the game for the capital. But Doull was out in the penultimate over and Wellington was still six short.

If David Attenborough were doing a programme about the natural habitat of Chris Cairns he would no doubt describe this scene — a crowded Lancaster Park, the last over of a final, six to win, two wickets to fall, Chris with the ball. Chris pitched the first ball well up to Michael Sears, who, clearly thinking of finishing the match asap, failed to connect with a big swing. The stumps exploded. Last man in was Gavin Larsen, with his arm bandaged and underneath his jersey. He would bat one-handed. But there was a bigger surprise — as the right-handed Larsen took guard it became clear he was, in fact, going to bat *left*-handed with his good hand, the right, acting as the top hand. This seemed like a game of chess gone wrong. The rules had been changed — but Chris knew that if he kept the ball on the stumps, the unfamiliar angle would trouble the Wellingtonian. He ran in again, bowled full, but with a confident stride forward, and a straight bat, Larsen pushed the ball into the off side and the batsmen swapped ends.

Four balls, five runs needed. Brett Williams pushed another single. Three balls, just a boundary needed to claim the Cup for the capital. Lancaster Park was fevered, the chant of 'Cairnsy' rolling across the terraces and under the grandstand. Cairns powered his legs forward with the three sticks his only focus. Fast and full — and Gavin Larsen's margin of error would be so small.

In the end it was always going to be an unfair contest. The ball pitched and moved slightly and Larsen's bat wasn't ever really close to the ball as it shot through to the stumps. Chris had won the match. He was ecstatic, the team were ecstatic, the Canterbury crowd was ecstatic. They had all witnessed the greatest Shell Cup match of all time. And it had been the final. The Cup was won, Chris' first top-class honour. Later, in the dressing room, the trophy was filled with champagne and Chris drank his fill.

Chris was on form. Most of the New Zealand reps were on form. The team was fit and focused. The country hyped and ready. This would surely be New Zealand's best tilt at the World Cup. Then just as the Kiwi cricketing machine seemed to be running on oiled rails, the wheels fell off.

Dave 'Syd' Lawrence, a fast bowler the size of a Belgian blue, started New Zealand's downward spiral by breaking Trevor Franklin's arm with a short-pitched delivery in one of England's tour matches. When Richard Reid unexpectedly retired a few weeks later, New Zealand suddenly had an opening crisis. More cracks kept appearing — Willie Watson went down injured and the in-form Ken Rutherford was again ignored, much to the chagrin of journalists up and down the country.

New Zealand hadn't lost a series on home turf for 13 years. On the seamer's wickets, where accuracy works better than pace, Kiwi bowlers had dominated. Since 1980 New Zealand had won home test series against every other test-playing nation. Even when they had struggled against stronger opposition the Kiwis had managed to hold on to draw series. No one, not the brilliant Windies, not the erratic Pakistanis, not teams containing Greg Chappell, David Gower or Kapil Dev, had been able to sway the outcome towards the tourists. It was an enviable record, a source of pride. It was all to be lost in five traumatic days in Christchurch.

Forcing off the back foot against England at Lancaster Park, 1992. This was Chris' first test 50.

PHOTOSPORT

Chris was selected to make his first appearance for his country in his home town. Another Christchurchian, Blair Hartland, Chris' old schoolmate, was selected to make his test debut. He would open the batting. In fact Hartland didn't get to bat until the sun was sinking late on the second day. England batted for nearly two days.

New Zealand got Gooch early, then just before lunch Chris bowled a sustained spell of short bowling at Graeme Hick. His old ND team-mate had not had the expected impact since his test debut against the West Indies six months earlier. He seemed to lose confidence when he put on a jersey with three lions on the front. The Caribbeans had greeted him with a hail of bouncers, and for the first time in his career Hick seemed vulnerable. The pressure on him to succeed seemed to stop his feet from moving and hinder his shots.

Test cricket is no time for therapy and Chris first unnerved Hick, pushing him onto the back foot, then trapped him LBW. It was a brilliant finesse. It was also the last time New Zealand had any advantage. England had scored 580 — the second-highest total the English had ever scored against New Zealand. Chris took just the one wicket. The New Zealand effort was marked by dropped catches and loose bowling.

Chris wanted to impress though. The British media was there, armed with the knowledge that he had just signed for Notts. He wanted to justify the county's faith. When he came to the crease 'the Young Guns' were wilting at 135 for 6. Dipak Patel was looking comfortable facing the only threatening bowler, left-arm spinner Phil Tufnell. Patel attacked Tufnell and scored with ease, so Chris decided to support him.

Many people probably think of Chris as a purely attacking batsman, which ignores the fact that some of his greatest innings have been works of graft and discipline. This innings was to be one of those. Chris had scored just 3 by stumps — the partnership already worth 30. The next morning he continued to bat circumspectly, facing more than 70 balls before he passed double figures. Patel was still batting fluently, then Chris joined in, driving Phillip DeFreitas for a couple of boundaries before taking 14 off an over from Derek Pringle.

The Kiwis had almost wrested the initiative from the English, but cricket swings like a metronome. Patel on 97, closing in on a maiden century, pulled a ball towards the boundary with Pringle, one of the more ambulatory fielders, in lukewarm pursuit. Patel hared down and back intent on three from the moment he set off. Chris heard the call for a third but even he had reservations about the last run. He responded but could only cross his fingers for Dipak. Even though Pringle had an unusual style of 'bowling' rather than throwing the ball, Patel never seemed likely to get to safety and a century. In the end he was remarkably close — just a metre shy — but was out for 99. Even now Chris wonders whether he should have sent Patel back.

The partnership had however broken records — at 117 runs it was the highest seventh-wicket partnership against England. Chris made his first test 50 just before lunch and saluted his home crowd. His mother was there, and some of his mates from school. He was bursting with pride but there was work to do. Chris was determined to save the follow-on. But 11 runs later he fell to an innocuous ball from debutant Dermot Reeve.

New Zealand followed on but there seemed no real danger as the Kiwi top order batted out most of the last day. There was no sense that they could lose the match as the afternoon wore on. The team joked with broadcasters and even put messages up on the big screen. Wright was also on 99 when a second rush of blood sent the metronome back towards England. Frustrated at a string of dot balls, Wright rushed far down the wicket to Tufnell and was stumped.

Then the middle order collapsed limply to Tufnell's flight as Greatbatch, Thomson and Patel were sent back. And Cairns. Surprised at even being required to bat after the game had been meandering so meaninglessly, Chris was suddenly forced to reconnect his concentration and move his feet to the pitch of the ball. He lasted only a few balls before one of Tufnell's deliveries feather-touched his bat, and popped off his pads to the helmeted Robin Smith.

The team had folded. Chris batted ninth. Two more wickets and the game was lost. England had used the advantage of surprise to devastating effect.

It might have been all right even then, but for the third time a Kiwi batsman had a rush of blood. With four needed to make the Poms bat again, this batsman sought to lob the ball over the congregated fielders. Four runs and it was all over. But the shot was poorly executed, the catch was made, the game lost. The batsman was Martin Crowe.

There was uproar around the country. The Rutherford fan club demanded his inclusion at the expense of Greatbatch and there were calls for Pringle, Thomson and Smith to go. Most disturbingly the bone was pointed at the captain for choosing to bat, for batting down the order in the first innings and for the final fatal shot.

The selectors went radical. All of the above were missing from the side for the next test in Auckland, except Crowe. Even Chris Harris was dropped and he had only been

Keeping an eye on the game while autographing for the fans, v England, 1992.

twelfth man! Rutherford was selected, as was Rod Latham, Adam Parore and Murphy Su'a, the Samoan swinger, who had been playing Second XI cricket weeks before. Su'a had looked good against England in a tour match and it seemed that with him alongside Cairns, Morrison, Watson and Patel that New Zealand had selected a team that could bowl England out twice. And they had.

The pitch for the Eden Park test was a shocker — it was prepared in order to help pace bowlers from the outset. One English official said that if a county had prepared such a pitch they would have been fined. With England's paucity of pace the state of the pitch could only be a good thing for the home team, so when Martin Crowe won the toss he naturally chose to bowl.

Morrison and Cairns instantly exploited the assistance the pitch offered. Morrison dismissed Gooch, then Chris picked up Stewart and Smith in consecutive balls both caught by Adam Parore.

Chris thinks the second was one of the finest catches of Parore's career. Lamb survived the hat-trick ball but fell to Su'a, then Chris bowled another furious spell at Hick. The Zimbabwean never looked comfortable and Chris again had him LBW. But Chris wasn't finished — when Chris Lewis slashed at a ball from Willie Watson, Chris leaped gymnastically to his right to take a great gully catch. It was reminiscent of the great gully fielders — Bruce Yardley and inevitably Richard Hadlee. At the end of a foreshortened day England were 146 for 7 and could have been in a worse position had more catches not been grassed.

The next day the tail-enders were allowed too many soft runs, but Chris returned to get the last three wickets. His figures were 21-4-52-6. Many years later Martin Crowe remembered that innings as the best he had seen Chris bowl. It had been an exhibition of fury and focus.

By the end of the second day, however, the gloss had gone from the performance. New Zealand were 91 for 2 before seven wickets fell for 50 runs. One of those was Chris, who middled a ball from Phil Tufnell, only to see it fly off the ankle of a close-in fieldsman to be caught at cover. He had been unlucky in the extreme.

The 61-run lead was huge, on a pitch of this quality, and the English prised the gap wider with positive batting. Gooch began the process with an innings of intense discipline. He was beaten time and again, outside off stump, but never once wavered, or acknowledged the fact.

Then Allan Lamb slammed the fourth-fastest half-century of all time, off 34 balls. He was particularly severe off Chris. It was both awesome and awful as Chris watched his bowling fly off Lamb's bat with such brutal force. Chris would stand halfway down the pitch watching the ball careering off the billboards, wondering how to stop this, wondering how to get a wicket.

New Zealand were left with an impossible target. Martin Crowe put a positive spin on the loss. They had improved from Christchurch, he stated, but as journalist John Coffey wrote, 'In racing parlance, a horse which finishes last by 10 lengths is just as much an also-ran as a horse which trails the field home by nine.'

Personal milestones have never been motivation for Chris Cairns in the same way they were for the 'statos' of world cricket like Richard Hadlee and Geoffrey Boycott. But a record like the 'unbeaten' status that New Zealand had enjoyed until then was a huge factor in his mental preparation. To have lost that record, a record his father had helped fashion, was disastrous. Chris was gutted at his own efforts. He had bowled poorly in the second innings. He had dropped a catch (one of six the Kiwis put down). He had gone out twice to Tufnell's slow left-armers.

The press meanwhile had cranked up the barometer on Crowe's captaincy — after all, the journos wrote, didn't the team seem more relaxed when Crowe was off the field receiving treatment?

Chris didn't know what the fuss was all about. He recognised in the skipper the same kind of focus and ambition that he had himself. Martin Crowe had a great cricket brain, a deep understanding of motivation and a pride in wearing the jersey with a black fern on it. Martin Crowe simply loved leading his country. And, after all, the World Cup was the real goal.

The Basin Reserve test was a draw. After four days New Zealand batted their way to an advantage, but another Lamb century torpedoed the Kiwi surge. Chris bowled well but the breaks that would have changed a good position into a victory never happened. He claimed only two wickets. He troubled the English and worked over Graham Gooch like it was a cruiserweight bout, but two catches were dropped off his bowling and a third, off Lamb, was claimed by Crowe before the batsman was called back when Ian Smith confirmed that it had touched the grass. Lady Luck, it seemed, had taken a sabbatical with Richard Reid.

There were three occurrences of note in the third test. The first was a tragic one — Dave 'Syd' Lawrence fell in his delivery stride and collapsed to the ground like he'd been shot. A noise filled the near-empty stadium that chilled every spectator and made Chris wince in sympathy. It was Syd screaming in pain. His action had blown his kneecap apart like it had been balsa wood. It was a haunting lesson to Chris about the fragility of a cricketer's career.

The second was Chris' encounter with another of the 'big four', the great all-rounders of the '80s. His idol, Ian Botham. Botham was playing his one hundredth test match. Chris was up for the battle — it scarcely seemed believable that he was getting the opportunity to play 'Beefy'. Chris wanted to test his skills against the old gladiator, wanted a clash of generations. However, Botham had been acting in a pantomime over Christmas and was rusty. The older man was caught by Chris at mid-on off the bowling of Murphy Su'a. Then Botham took just one wicket — Chris Cairns caught by the keeper off a tickle. Down leg side. Sometimes cricket tramples on sentiment like it's a doormat, but Chris is still proud of his small part in Botham's record-breaking statistics.

The last major occurrence was the most sensational. On the evening of the fourth day Martin Crowe was asked by the selectorial junta to stand down from the captaincy. In their mind the captaincy was the root cause of New Zealand's

The Basin Reserve crowd forms the backdrop as Chris appeals in the third test against England in 1992. Umpire Steve Dunne is unmoved. PHOTOSPORT

One of Chris' cricketing idols, Ian Botham was the epitome of self-belief . . . Chris loved watching him play.

problem. Crowe was livid and threatened to quit altogether. When Chris heard of the events he couldn't believe it. Why did they feel they needed to change things? Particularly so close to the Cup. It would ruin everything, all the planning, all the team spirit.

In the end, Crowe called the selectors' bluff and both he and Chris were selected in the World Cup squad announced the next day. There were no real surprises, though Su'a had played himself in, at the expense of Chris Pringle. Two more one-dayers against England followed, but they were both lost, the second by a big margin.

The Young Guns had lost five out of six matches over the summer. The only thing peaking was pessimism. At the press conference after the last match Ian Botham gave a rousing speech — he was confident, he said, of playing the World Cup Final at the MCG 'in front of 100,00 convicts'. When Martin Crowe said he thought the Kiwis could make the semi-finals, it sounded emptier than the trophy cabinet.

7

MCG or bust

Eden Park may be a rugby ground. It may be more oblong than oval. And it may often be tomb-like even during big matches, but when it is full, when tens of thousands of Aucklanders have arrived with a full chilly bin and a litre of sunscreen, then Eden Park has an energy that no other ground in the country can quite match. It is something perhaps to do with its width, with its high sides or the angle of the stands.

A wall of sound greeted the New Zealanders on 19 February 1992 as they trooped out for the national anthem. There was a surge of adrenalin and emotion through the team. Stark reality hit Chris Cairns. This was it — the World Cup. What he had dreamed about, aimed for, trained those long hours for. What had buoyed him when injury laid him flat, what had inspired him when he played. The culmination.

New Zealand were playing the reigning champions, Allan Border's great Australians. It was rumoured that the Aussie tail-enders had not even brought their pads over the Tasman so confident were they of victory! Not even a Kiwi with the most deluded 'she'll be right' attitude could envisage a positive result. New Zealand cricket seemed divided, the team off the boil, key players out of form. When John Wright was bowled by the first legitimate delivery of the tournament it seemed like all cynics and soothsayers were right.

But something happened that gave the Kiwis hope. Tom Moody dropped Rod Latham at slip. It was just a small error, but it suggested that maybe they weren't infallible *ubermenschen*. Then there was Martin Crowe who had been stung by the swarm of criticism that surrounded him. He came to the wicket, and after a stuttering start, began to find first footwork, then the middle of the bat, then the boundary. Profiting from some poor fielding, he and Rutherford added a century in even time. When Chris Cairns was called to the wicket, New Zealand were 215 for 6 with Crowe in his 80s, and playing brilliantly.

Chris was there to own the place. This was his destiny. He initially fed the strike to his skipper but suddenly it was the last over. Crowe was on 99. The mission was clear — Chris had to get Martin on strike and score as many runs as possible. What transpired was almost too perfect. Chris hit a couple then a boundary. The crowd went berserk. The Australians started commenting, trying to rattle the youngster. But this was his day. No lippy Ocker was going to get into his comfort zone.

To his captain's surprise, he started to answer the Aussies back. The fourth ball he hit deep and ran three in order to get Crowe on strike. Then Crowe dabbed the ball directly to Marsh at point. Chris sprinted down the pitch to give Martin his century, diving full-length to make sure he was home. There should never have been a single and Chris claims Martin owes him a lifetime of free drinks for the run! The crowd danced and cheered the three figures. Chris had faced just 11 balls, for 16 runs. His appearance had only been a cameo, but it had been a memorable supporting role. As the pair walked off they were surrounded by Kiwi kids sprinting towards their heroes.

The opening game of the 1992 World Cup and Martin Crowe is on his way to a sublime century against the Aussies. He led his men on a five-week journey which the whole of New Zealand would embrace.

The adults in the stands rose to their feet. It was Martin's ovation but Chris had been there at the other end. He had done the hard work when required. He felt fulfilled.

The Australians, as battlers do, came out swinging, and they swung mainly at Chris. Chris shared the new ball with off-spinner Dipak Patel. This had been decided the night before as a strategy to rush through the spinner's overs before the openers had settled. It was Crowe's masterstroke. Patel bowled beautifully and trussed up Marsh and Boon. Unfortunately for Chris, the Australians took out their frustrations on the quick bowler. His four overs went for 30 runs and he was banished to the outfield.

As he stood on the boundary with his back to the seething masses he was filled with disappointment. He had bowled terribly. He was in the side as a bowler, but he had not done his job. He went back to that word 'contribute'. He had to contribute in some way.

Geoff Marsh was out to Gavin Larsen and Boon was joined by one of the greatest one-day players the world has seen, a player of perpetual motion, Dean Jones. Instantly Jones upped the tempo, getting the Baggy Greens closer to the run rate required. When he was on 20 he pushed the ball towards square leg and sprinted down the pitch. Jones was a whippet between wickets who could turn ones into twos and twos into threes. He was out to steal another base.

This was Chris' chance. He got to the ball a bit slowly — Jones had already turned — but Chris had a great arm. This time he unleashed an Exocet of a throw, fast, low and destructive, a throw that only a few cricketers in the history of the game could

PHOTOSPORT

have cast — Colin Bland, George Bonnor, Roger Harper and Dean Jones himself would have been proud of the feat. The ball thudded into Ian Smith's gloves right over the bails, which were removed within split seconds. Jones was given out. Chris was ecstatic as the team rushed towards him. If he couldn't contribute with the ball then he'd field like a kestrel. Recently Jones has been working with the New Zealand team and still reminds Chris that he was in by a foot. Chris concedes that his bat may have been an inch or two over the line. Luck is always important in cricket and the home team had it that day.

A few runs later Allan Border swept Patel and Chris made a lot of ground from deep midwicket to deep square leg to take the catch. The Aussies began to fold. Later when centurion David Boon was run out brilliantly by Chris Harris the game was effectively over. The Young Guns had pulled off the coup of the tournament in the very first match. They had beaten the invincibles by 37 runs.

The feeling in the dressing room was one not only of triumph but of relief and release — they had finally won a match — and not just any match. They all felt that this was the turning point. They had beaten the world's best. Surely now they could beat anybody. The doubting was gone. For one player the belief was personalised. Martin Crowe's century had given him self-belief. His captaincy was vindicated. This was going to be his tournament.

New Zealand's triumph had been based around slow bowling. Patel's opening spell had been followed by a trio of medium-pacers, Latham, Larsen, and Harris, who bowled accurately at little more and often considerably less than military medium-pace. On sluggish New Zealand pitches (like Carisbrook which Botham had described as 'where the ball hit the wicket and went backwards'), these pop-guns became serious artillery. Willie Watson's accuracy guaranteed him a place, but it seemed likely that the quicks, Morrison, Su'a and Chris, would be competing for one vacancy.

Chris was dropped for the next match (another win) against Sri Lanka, but was back for the encore at Eden Park against South Africa. This was the first international match between New Zealand and South Africa for 28 years. The Springboks had been welcomed back from isolation after the collapse of the republic's apartheid regime just months earlier. Due to the negative connotations of their old nickname, they changed it to the Proteas and with this new image they had kicked off the World Cup pretty well — with a victory over Australia.

South Africa had some talent — young players like fielding wizard Jonty Rhodes joined old heads like Peter Kirsten and Kepler Wessels, but they were no match for the Kiwi steam-roller. South Africa were 29 for 3 but recovered to 108 before Chris took the wicket of Dave Richardson, mistiming a drive. Kuiper was caught off a Cairns no ball and run out as he ambled off the park, then Rhodes was caught brilliantly by Martin Crowe at short midwicket. Chris had taken his first two World Cup wickets. He followed that up with yet another catch in the outfield and the Young Guns were chasing 190.

If the victory over Australia had caught the public's imagination then the next partnership harnessed it, shoved it in a cell and fed it bread and water. It was late on a sunny Saturday afternoon and a lot of New Zealanders watched in disbelief as Mark Greatbatch, only in the side due to an injury to John Wright, and Rod Latham treated the South Africans as though it was backyard cricket. They recorded a century partnership in just 16 overs. It was exuberant play and for many a realisation that New Zealand could go all the way. The Australian game wasn't just a fluke. Chris and Gavin Larsen sat in the viewing room watching the otherworldly events unfold. All they could do was laugh — and they dared not move in case the spell was broken. For the rest of the tournament the pair would sit in the same chairs for every match at Eden Park.

The Kiwis swept Zimbabwe aside, but Chris made way for Danny Morrison for the next match — against the West Indies. It was understandable — he had been the most expensive bowler in all three of the games he'd played in. But while he was personally disappointed, the team were gulping the rarefied air at the top of the round-robin table. There was a buzz about the team — in the media, from the general public, from friends and relatives. When the assembled black pinstriped blazers were seen passing through airports, cheers rang around the terminals. Messages and telegrams of support piled high. This team that had been accused of acting like 'Gucci cricketers' without getting the results were suddenly folk heroes. When they had arrived at Napier what seemed like half of Hawke's Bay turned up at the airport to greet them.

The joie de vivre in the team was the same. Even the wizened old professionals thought that this was the best team spirit they had experienced. The 14 players with Warren Lees, manager Ian Taylor and physio Mark Plummer were probably as closely knit as any cricket team have ever been. They were on a crusade. The engraver for the cup would be practising his capital Ns and Zs.

In Dunedin, home town for Lees and Rutherford, and where Andrew Jones and John Wright had gone to university, another win, over India, was celebrated long into the night. The team hit the scarfie pubs — the Cook, the Bowler and the Gardies, Wright and Jones revelling in the memories of their alma mater, the rest loving the reception they got from the students. This night was one of the few occasions that the cricketers and the cricketing public were celebrating as one, together. The good feeling was communal and tangible. Heroes and fans dancing, singing and drinking Speight's. Chris and several members of the team sang a karaoke version of 'Suspicious Minds' at a packed Captain Cook, with John Wright being 'Elvis'. Then to finish the night Wright led the entire pub in a cappella version of 'The Banana Boat Song'. Wright would sing the 'six foot seven foot eight foot bunch' and the patrons would respond with the 'day-o' chorus. It was great to be a cricketer.

The winning continued in Wellington the week after, when the Young Guns finally beat bogey team England at the seventh attempt that summer. Chris played but was marginalised — the pitch was so slow that Chris Harris and Dipak Patel opened the bowling, and even Andrew Jones' occasional off-spin got an airing. In reply Chris didn't even need to pad up as Crowe completed a seven-wicket win.

In spite of a loss to Pakistan in the last group game, New Zealand progressed to the semi-finals top of the table and wild favourites. They were to face Imran Khan's 'caged tigers' at Eden Park. Danny Morrison had bowled well in the last game and was preferred to Chris. Whether injured or twelfth man, Chris has always felt frustrated watching New Zealand play when he isn't on the team sheet. He wanted with all his heart to be waiting to bat, as the Kiwis began their innings.

Another brilliant partnership between the odd couple, Crowe and Rutherford, left Pakistan 264 to win on a snail-paced wicket. However, Crowe had torn a hamstring during his innings and would not be directing the proceedings, in his Napoleonic way, on the field. He was crocked on the sidelines.

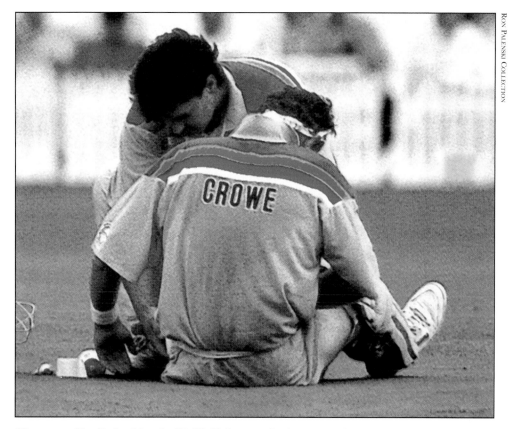

The moment New Zealand lost the '92 World Cup semi-final against Pakistan. Having torn a hamstring, Martin Crowe would be unable to captain on the field. The reins were handed to John Wright, who did not possess Crowe's Midas touch.

Chris and Martin watched from afar as the Pakistanis fell well behind the run rate. Chris then decided to get some bowling practice. The Kiwis seemed certain to be in the final, and the MCG was a pacey wicket. Seam bowlers would be needed. But while he worked out in the nets he heard the sighs and groans of the crowd and started to worry. Something sounded wrong. Miandad and Khan were winding up. Then the unwieldy Inzamam-ul-Haq, the couch potato of international cricket, came to the crease and began to smite the New Zealand attack. John Wright, the on-field captain, did not have the same instinct with bowling changes that Crowe had. It had, after all, been two years since he'd captained the side. The bowlers also struggled to find an Achilles heel in Inzamam's technique. Chris went out to field and it felt like the team were playing on quicksand. They were trapped in a situation totally out of their control, just like every Kiwi glued to their television set throughout the country, wanting something to change. But it didn't. A couple of late wickets fell, but the damage was done and Pakistan won with an over to spare.

The bubble, the most fantastic multi-coloured bubble, grey with four coloured stripes, had burst. Emotions and tears spilled readily. Crowe gathered his team and led them around the Eden Park boundary. It was a lap of commiseration but nobody could begrudge the Kiwis this. The country and this score of men had surfed a wave of fantasy and it so very nearly became reality.

RON PALENSKI COLLECTION

The players did a lap of honour after the semi-final loss to Pakistan to thank New Zealand and the Eden Park crowd for their support during the '92 Cup campaign. It was a magical time for everyone involved . . . a special piece of New Zealand cricket history.

Chris was close to tears as the Auckland crowd saluted the team and his team-mates replied in kind. Twenty thousand people in the stands, and 15 on the field all felt the same weight in the stomach, the same tightening of the jaw. Everybody was in pain.

Back in the dressing room, everybody sat in a heavy silence repeating over and over mistakes they had made, little moments that could have changed the outcome. But the outcome was the same whenever they returned to reality. They would not be playing in the World Cup final.

Partners and beer arrived but the atmosphere was still sombre. Levity was needed. Chris began cutting up his boots dramatically then burned them in the middle of the floor, blaming them for his inept bowling form. The room filled with laughter for the first time since the loss. The little bonfire on the dressing-room floor cauterised the open wound.

The whole team were invited to the final at the MCG but Chris didn't want to go. He couldn't have sat in the stands thinking of what might have been. The World Cup had finished for him.

In spite of his quiet World Cup, he had had a solid season. He had taken 42 first-class wickets, second only to Otago's Neil Mallender. He had won the Shell Cup with Canterbury. He had proved himself in test cricket with both bat and ball. And in late March he was awarded the Winsor Cup for the bowler who had had the greatest impact in the 1991–92 season. This symbol of bowling excellence had many great names on it — Cowie, Collinge, Motz, Blair — but it had never had the name Cairns inscribed upon it. Chris was carving his own history.

8

The county drudge

Chris was not in the country to pick up the Winsor Cup. He had flown directly to England after the semi-final defeat to take up his position as the new overseas professional for Nottinghamshire.

Notts had also acquired Chris Lewis, on his day the best cricketer in the world, thinking that signing another young all-rounder might give the county the same edge they had enjoyed in the '80s with Hadlee and Rice.

Chris had no unrealistic expectations of the season. His few games in the first team had hinted at the reality. Everybody told him of the daily grind of county cricket, where the game was played six days a week, punctuated only with journeys up and down the M1. As Chris described it, you would bowl for two days then directly after the match drive from Somerset all the way to Durham to be ready for a game starting the next morning. The captain would promptly lose the toss and you'd be bowling again. A game finishing in two days was considered a luxury.

As the sole overseas professional, he would also be expected to perform, to win games. It would be a cricket immersion course like nothing he had experienced. He certainly wasn't there just for the money — like Turner, Howarth, Wright and Hadlee, he was there to learn about the game, to polish his ability and mine for new skills. After all, with his experience it was easy to forget that he was only 21 years old.

Nottingham is a very pleasant, middle-sized English city. It is not so small as to feel like a town, yet it isn't an endless conurbation like Birmingham, London or Manchester. It is famous for its lace, Sherwood Forest and Raleigh bicycles. It's an industrial centre without the uncompromising grimness and crop of chimneys of the northern cities. There's a stately manor and a pretty abbey and the River Trent passes through. Nottingham also has a great nightlife with olde taverns and slick nightclubs.

Trent Bridge is at the heart of Nottingham. Its old pavilion is modest and attractive with 19th-century gables and wrought-iron trimmings reminding people that Notts was one of the original heartlands of cricket.

But Trent Bridge is different from other grounds like Edgbaston and Lord's. The lower stands allow views into a functioning city, to brick houses with bay windows, to the tops of double-decker buses travelling along Bridgford and Fox Roads, to the floodlights of the football grounds nearby. You are not in a hermetically sealed cricket world here, separated from the outside world. Trent Bridge is part of Nottingham's being.

Chris' accommodation was not the best. The one-bedroom flat was literally on the wrong side of the tracks in a feral part of Nottingham. It had a power-meter that required a coded card to be bought from the power supplier in town. He returned late one night to find the power had run out, but it was a long weekend and the shop was closed for the duration. Chris lived on cold showers, candlelight and takeaways for the next four days.

Notts had done well the previous season, coming fourth in the County Championship and winning the Sunday League 40-over bashathon. With Lewis and

Relaxing 'at home' in England on a rare day off, Chris makes a brave attempt on the world bubble-making record.

Cairns spearheading its tilt at the championship it seemed that the county could do even better in 1992. Lewis was one of the greatest athletes that Chris played with — a fluent batsman who could flail any attack, a rhythmical bowler and a balletic fielder. Chris Cairns freely admitted that Lewis was a better cricketer.

Chris enjoyed Lewis' company but never really got to know him. They lived very different lifestyles. After a match Chris would go drinking — initially at the tavern attached to Trent Bridge, then in the pubs of Old Market Square. About the time Chris Cairns would be heading home, Chris Lewis, a teetotaller, would be heading out to nightclubs. Lewis always seemed very pleasant, but there was resentment from the rest of the squad about the size of his wage packet.

The kind of impact the two could have had was shown in the second game of the season against Warwickshire when Lewis hit 134 and joined in a quickfire 80-run partnership with Chris. The two all-rounders batting aggressively in tandem was a dream image but it occurred too infrequently. Neither did they form the two-pronged attack that the Notts management envisaged. Injury to either of them and international commitments for Lewis meant that the pair rarely had a chance to appear together to any effect.

As the overseas professional, Chris often focused on doing battle with the opposing pro. Many counties had chosen West Indian quick bowlers and Chris thought it amazing to turn up for work and face the likes of Ian Bishop, Curtly Ambrose or extraneous Benjamins. Yorkshire had the very first foreigner in their long history, the young genius Sachin Tendulkar. Durham had Dean Jones, and 'White Lightning' Allan Donald had been employed by Warwickshire. These were the pros that Chris found himself jousting with.

There were other familiar faces around the county circuit. Graeme Hick was there, of course, along with other regulars from the New Zealand season — Warwickshire's Roger Twose (English but applying for Kiwi residency), Gloucestershire's Justin Vaughan (Kiwi but with a British passport) and a quartet of players with New Zealand connections at Somerset — Richard Harden, Neil Mallender, Roland Lefebvre and Andrew Caddick.

Lancashire meanwhile had hired Danny Morrison on a year-long contract. It was great for Chris to see Dan every so often and share a vino or two and some flattened vowels. But no matter who Chris socialised with, no matter how late the night went, no matter how many pints of lager or Somerset cider were drank, the next morning always offered freshly painted crease lines and hard leather.

Both Morrison and Cairns found the strain of playing day-in day-out tough. Morrison eventually broke down and missed the end-of-year tour to Zimbabwe and Sri Lanka. The difficulty for Chris, however, was not with biomechanics but with the tools of trade. In the '80s, with Hadlee and Rice sharing the new ball, the pitch at Trent Bridge had been seam-friendly, but since their joint retirement, with batsman Tim Robinson as county captain, the groundskeeper was told to develop a batsman's paradise of Nottingham marl. The demon was expelled from the strip.

It was the same type of strip that the great Notts batsman Arthur Shrewsbury used to be so confident batting upon that he would order a cup of tea at a certain time when he went out to bat. As Neville Cardus wrote: 'It was always 340-2 at Trent Bridge.' It certainly helped Chris' batting — he didn't get a single-figure score that season until the middle of June, but wickets were another story. They had to be earned through long spells at the crease.

Chris learned that county cricket was about discipline. He now understood the meticulousness that Richard Hadlee brought to the game. Tim Robinson was similar. He was always immaculately turned out, packed his gear the same way in his cricket coffin, with pre-match routines repeated ad tedium, and a mannered approach to batting. He was the ultimate professional — if the wicket was good he would almost certainly get a hundred.

Chris also learned more about the discipline of bowling. He couldn't rely on a generous pitch or on pace to blast out batsmen. Chris began to think about 'thinking' a batsman out, exploiting weaknesses or strengths. Chris started experimenting with different deliveries. He remembered Franklyn Stephenson's slower ball, a delivery which would loop so much that batsmen would think, initially, that it was heading skull-wise, only for it to drop like it was fashioned from lead.

The shape of an over became important. Dot balls were invaluable. Denial became a form of attack. The batsman's psyche became as important as his technique. It was all about pressure, expectation and confidence. It was little wonder that among the Kiwis who have played the county game are some of the most cerebral players in New Zealand's cricketing history — names like Crowe, Howarth, Turner, Hadlee, Donnelly and Lowry.

But there were many other things to learn about county cricket that were not, perhaps, as positive — things like managed results, feeding runs for a declaration and forfeiting innings. Yet this was the reality of the County Championship — wins were all-important.

Notts started the season well — in fact they didn't lose a first-class match until the start of July — but they fell out of contention in August when two matches were lost by paper-thin margins. Chris had played well in the single-innings win over Hampshire, and hit the winning runs at the Oval against Surrey but most of his best performances seemed to come in drawn matches or lost causes.

In his head-to-head with Danny Morrison's Lancashire he had come out on top — 6-70 and a second first-class century (102 not out and a 200-run partnership with the great Derek Randall) but the match finished a draw. A five-wicket bag against Kent was in a defeat. Two 50s and Tendulkar's wicket at Headingley only helped Notts square the match with Yorkshire. His third century (107 not out against Gloucestershire and Courtney Walsh at Worksop) was in a game Notts lost by 10 runs.

Notts' one-day form was terrible. The defending Sunday League champs failed to win a match for over two months and were lucky to finish second to last. In the knockout Benson & Hedges Cup, the Cairns curse struck again. He played spectacularly well in the second round — 77 and 12-2-38-2 — which meant that it was almost inevitable that the opposition, Glamorgan, won and went through to the next round.

Chris believed that Notts were suffering a hangover from the success of the previous decade. Many of his team-mates were good supporting players but few would produce the performances required to win matches. Chris thought that some of them were used to relying on fine professionals like Robinson, Hadlee, Rice and Stephenson rather than winning matches in their own stead. Then there was the 'Scarlett O'Hara syndrome' where a player would be relaxed about performing averagely, as 'tomorrow is another day'. There was so much cricket played that it was easy to become 'soft' about failure.

Overall it was a season of steady performances. Chris' batting (984 runs at 41.00) had been excellent — and better than other all-rounders like Ian Botham, Franklyn Stephenson (who had moved to Sussex), and Chris Lewis — but his bowling (56 wickets at 35.25) was expensive. Still, for his first full season he had done well — one of only four players (including his team-mate Lewis, also) who took 50 wickets and scored 500 runs. He signed up to return in 1993.

But before he could even think about the future he had another worry to sort out. One afternoon after practice a few of his team-mates were heading out for a drink. Chris declined. One of his colleagues, the late Mark Saxelby, asked why. Chris told him of a cramp, a pain that would frequently occur in his right side if he had a drink in the afternoon.

To Chris' astonishment, Saxelby described a whole list of other symptoms. He had had a similar problem — a kidney disorder. Chris had always assumed the pain was just the way he had been constructed and had never bothered to have it checked. Saxelby told him it could be fixed by an operation. Incredibly this amateur diagnosis was confirmed by a specialist the next day. A major operation, a kidney piloplast, was needed.

Chris missed the last couple of games for Notts to head home for surgery. It also meant that he would have to withdraw from the New Zealand tour to Zimbabwe and Sri Lanka. Instead surgeons would cut a huge crescent incision across his side and back and operate.

9

Sour times

The story of the last two decades of New Zealand cricket has one constant. Every time a sense of camaraderie has been built, every time team spirit begins to rise and bonds are formed within the squad, something has always come along and rent the team apart.

In 1986 it was an Alfa Romeo that caused a split through the heart of the team, that ended with the farce of captain and best player not talking to each other. (Ironically Chris' uncle Graeme Allport bought the car from Richard Hadlee, even though it appeared to need constant repairs. Chris told his uncle that the vehicle was cursed!) In 1990 the team were decimated by retirements. Five years later the team bonds unravelled in a haze of marijuana smoke and acrimony on a tour to South Africa. In 1992, the success and togetherness of the team were blown apart by a terrorist bomb in Sri Lanka. The team were riven apart and the élan of the World Cup replaced by mistrust.

Several members of the New Zealand team had witnessed the suicide bombing, and all the squad had felt a deep sense of unease in Colombo. A majority of players voted to return to New Zealand. But this decision was usurped by the arrival of New Zealand Cricket's chairman, Peter McDermott, who demanded that the contracted players stay, and then proceeded to convince others to remain on tour.

McDermott's actions had a financial and diplomatic rationale behind them, no doubt, but to cleave a squad in two as he did was a misjudged disaster. The 'all for one, one for all' attitude evaporated. There was resentment from players towards New Zealand Cricket, and bitterness between some who chose to leave and those who had changed their mind. The squad was shrouded with unhappiness. The sunny days of the World Cup seemed like they had occurred years, not months previously.

Chris was a million miles away from these tragic concerns. His biggest worries were recovering from his operation and wondering if Richard Petrie had arrived later than him to training. Petrie and Cairns each owned cars that had been bought for three-figure sums — an Anglia and a 1960 Vauxhall Victor (a solid beast of a car according to its owner) respectively — cars with more grey patches than original chassis. If Petrie's car was in the Lancaster Park carpark when he arrived, Chris would leave a few bumps in the fender to remind him who was the new-ball bowler. Likewise if Petrie arrived second, Chris would later find dents in the Victor's rear and chips of chrome on the ground.

Six weeks after the operation, Chris decided to put his kidneys to the test. He organised an afternoon drink with his good friend Brendon Charteris. In a café the pair ordered what used to be his nemesis at midday — a bottle of red wine. But after a couple of hours there was no pain. The operation was a success, his quality of life enhanced and to celebrate the recovery the two friends laughed and ordered a couple more bottles of wine.

The Canterbury team were also in good spirits. With Michael Owens being selected

Chris' first car . . . and what a beauty it was. The 1960 Vauxhall Victor.

as a replacement for Sri Lanka, the team could boast five bowlers who had played for New Zealand in recent years. As well as Petrie, Owens and Cairns, there was Stu Roberts and Mark Priest. Canterbury looked great on paper but, as the old adage goes, they don't play cricket on paper.

Chris knew he would miss the first few games of the season but the frustration of watching from afar was powerful medicine and finally he convinced the Canterbury selectors to play him in the third Shell Trophy match in mid-December. It had only been two months since the op. He concentrated on being steady rather than pacey in the first innings (12-6-12-1) but in the second innings he would change up a gear and bowl the occasional very fast ball. Thirty-two overs represented a good work-out. Results, however, were not forthcoming, just two wickets in his first match back were followed by only one in the next. In the New Year he confessed to a reporter that he was only 90 per cent fit.

Perhaps he had rushed back too quickly, perhaps enthusiasm and ambition had got the better of him. Coming back was always as hard mentally as physically. While the huge shark-bite across his back might have healed, there was psychological scar tissue.

However, two innings seemed to lubricate his aching joints and polish his confidence. Against Central on 5 January he smashed 79 runs before taking three wickets. He loved performing against CD because of their coach, Dermot Payton, who would fire up the team by calling the Cantabrians 'townies' and 'city slickers'! The innings also had special significance for the Cairns family. The game was played at Horton Park, Blenheim, a place that had been like a crèche to him when he was a child.

Then four days later in the Shell Cup, against Wellington, in a repeat of the sensational encounter of the year before, Chris was joined by Lee Germon with Canterbury punch-drunk at 27 for 4 in the 15th over. They started to revive the effort by pushing singles, and the first boundary of the innings didn't arrive until the 22nd over. It was sensible, mature batting from the two youngsters, marked by fluid running between the wickets. The pace quickened with Chris mixing innovative shots with intelligent straight-hitting. Then between the 40th and 50th overs, 93 runs were scored in exhilarating style.

Chris was out in the second-to-last over — for 115, a record for Canterbury in the Shell Cup. The fact that he scored just 6 fours and 2 sixes says everything about the discipline of the batting. Never reckless, Chris had imbued the knock with what he had learnt from his English experience. The partnership with Germon was worth 198 — just one short of the all-time Cup record. Bruce Taylor, the national selector, was in the stands to note the innings and the standing ovation. Incredibly, however, it was not enough to win the game. Martin Crowe and Martin Speight batted superbly to take the match.

This was typical of Canterbury that season. They drew five games in a row in the Shell Trophy and didn't record a victory all season. They finished last. As defending champions in the Shell Cup they scraped through to the semi-finals in fourth place, heading off Central Districts by a few hundredths of a 'net' run. The run rate calculation meant that if Canterbury had scored just four runs less in any group game they would have missed out.

They certainly decided to ride their luck. The semi-final against Wellington turned out to be a one-sided affair after a great innings by Rod Latham set up the win that Harris and Cairns converted. They were in the final again — this time without home advantage. They would have to visit the House of Pain, Carisbrook.

In 1990, friends of Chris had come to his flat in Riccarton. Chris' mates had brought a friend with them. The four went out on the town then came back to the flat for a few more. Late in the evening someone suggested a wrestling match. A couple of bouts followed until Chris was squaring up to this fellow from Dargaville. This bloke was shorter and lighter than Chris but very wiry and in the ensuing maul pinned Chris down. The victor leaped and yelped around the apartment. It was Chris' first encounter with one of the most competitive and talented cricket players of the '90s — Dion Nash.

It is obvious why Nash had enjoyed

Dion Nash, says Chris, is the most competitive man he has played with or against. Here he is pictured at his enthusiastic best against the West Indies. PHOTOSPORT

beating Chris so much. He was 18 months younger than Chris but also had a burning desire — to be the best all-rounder in New Zealand. This horseplay was just the first round of a long-term campaign. He wanted Chris' job.

The following season Nash played for Northern Districts and then in 1992 led the New Zealand youth team impressively on a tour to India. These performances got him selected for the tour to Zimbabwe and Sri Lanka, where he made his test debut. He had previously played just three first-class matches, for modest returns, but the selectors clearly regarded him as an investment.

Chris had had no real competitor for the title of 'best all-rounder'. Because of persistent injuries, Shane Thomson had chosen to concentrate on batting and trying to develop his off-spin. Otherwise, most of the players were batsmen who could bowl a bit, or bowlers who knew which end of the bat to use. There were very few genuine all-rounders around the provinces. Dion Nash's emergence threatened that. Even though he had an unexceptional Shell series with Otago he certainly looked the part — he could hurry the ball through, and he was a sterling hitter of the ball with a hint of the classical stroke-player about him. But his results and technique told only half the story. He was also an explosive character, aggressive and intelligent, who liked to intimidate and torment opponents. His habit was to follow short-pitch with short-pitch, to underpin a good ball with an assessment of the batsman's character and paternity, all delivered in a high-pitched voice as cutting as a switchblade.

There was also another new all-rounder who carried a different attitude — one of quiet confidence — a player who had played against England the year before while still a schoolboy. He was a player with the Midas touch, able to take wickets at crucial times or to hit far and wide. He averaged under 20 with his bowling, and hit a 99 against Central in the Shell Cup. He had also played rugby for Southland and had once scored 66 points for his First XV, in one game. His name was Jeff Wilson. He was 18 years old.

Nash and Wilson played for Otago and the Shell Cup final set the three young all-rounders against each other. Otago had some insider knowledge as well — the coach of the province was Lance Cairns.

A huge and excitable Dunedin crowd of 13,500 watched the Otago quicks restrict Canterbury to 186 on an inconsistent pitch. Nash bowled beautifully and when Chris came to the wicket he welcomed him with a trail of invective. There was no riposte from Chris' bat as he was dismissed cheaply by Neil Mallender. Round two to Nash. Chris was even more determined to succeed with the ball.

Jeff Wilson was out early in Otago's reply but then Ken Rutherford walked to the wicket, without a helmet. Chris saw red. This wasn't just a sign of disrespect for the Canterbury pace-bowling attack, but also plain naked arrogance on this type of pitch. Rutherford had pushed Chris' button, the one marked 'Wrath'.

Chris bowled short and fast, and the Otago skipper, late on the shot, ballooned the ball to Mark Priest at midwicket. Nash appeared in Rutherford's place and Chris again cranked up the velocity and delivered a barrage of equal parts abuse and hard white leather. It was an enthralling contest, two players locked in a contest, as gladiatorial as cricket gets.

Nash worked a few singles then hit a boundary but Chris bowled straight through his defence moments later. Chris sent his opponent away with an explanation of just who the best all-rounder in the country was. This was territorial pissing.

Just like the year before Chris came back to bowl in the closing overs to snuff out any resistance. He finished with 4-41 from his 10 overs. The Cup was retained. Ironically the Man of the Match performance didn't go to the stars Nash, Wilson or Cairns but to another all-rounder, a quiet player who bowled 10 placid overs and hit 28 off 15 balls at the end of the Canterbury innings. Nathan Astle won the award.

Chris' only other significant game of the domestic season also occurred at Carisbrook. Days of persistent rain meant that the outfield was sodden and the pitch unprepared. The first day was declared a washout but the second day saw the crease marks painted and the stumps banged into the ground. In between was 22 yards of lush grass that any dairy farmer would have been proud of.

Canterbury lost the toss and were all out seconds later for 42. It was the lowest score recorded in New Zealand since 1957. The ball was moving in random directions. Facing Gale, Mallender and Nash it was impossible batting. Chris scored the only boundary of the innings and top-scored with 12, an innings he still regards as one of his finest. Otago realised that attack was the only form of defence on such a lethal pitch and gathered a 60-run lead.

In the second innings Chris hit 58, easily the highest score of the entire match, before Otago limped to 95 for 7 to win. Chris had mixed feelings about the loss — his dad's team went through to the trophy final — but it certainly hadn't been ideal preparation for the games ahead. Australia were coming.

Overall the season had been disappointing, particularly with ball in hand, but Chris had been using the Shell Series as rehabilitation. His main aim had been to return to international cricket with all due haste. He needed it. Luckily the selectors needed him almost as much.

The Lancaster Park pitch had been hard and fast all summer. New Zealand — with Morrison, Su'a, new boy Michael Owens and Chris — finally had a quartet of bowlers of genuine pace. With Greatbatch's transformation into an opener there was also a vacancy in the middle order. Chris fitted the bill at number six. The mood was confident, while the hype surrounding the test focused on how the battle-weary Australians, fresh from the torments of Ambrose and Walsh and their compañeros, would handle the Kiwi speedsters.

When misty weather descended on Christchurch the night before the first test it seemed that the weather would 'juice up' the pitch, giving the bowlers even more assistance. Martin Crowe won the toss and chose to field. The bowling conditions were perfect, the Australians vulnerable — and the bowlers responded by being just plain awful. Perhaps they were psyched out by all the press, all the expectation — perhaps they simply tried too hard to bowl the unplayable ball — whatever the reason, all four bowlers failed to put the ball on the spot. With the situation screaming for someone to bowl a disciplined spell just outside off stump, they all bowled too short or too wide.

Mark Taylor, who had been in miserable form, played himself back into touch, and Crowe was forced to turn to the off-spin of Patel before lunch. At the break Warren Lees blasted the four young bowlers for wasting the gilt-edged opportunity before them.

The next day the Aussies carried on where they'd left off. By the time Chris got his only wicket, last man out Craig McDermott, Australia had scored 485. Ten of their batsmen had scored double figures, four half-centuries. In the mid-afternoon,

PHOTOSPORT

Above: An appeal against Merv Hughes at Lancaster Park, 1993. Inset: This match was the first time Chris encountered Shane Warne. The leg-spinner won the first of many duels between the two. Warne dismissed Chris in the second innings of this test.

Allan Border had hit a ball from Patel to the boundary and become the greatest-ever run-getter in tests. It had been a Baggy Green triumph.

New Zealand then missed the follow-on target, Chris recording the second duck of his test career. In the second innings he batted better, coming in at a crisis time and battling to 21. However, he encountered, for the first time, a leg-spinner, a solid blond bloke with a mullet, who could spin the ball prodigiously. Chris reached to smother one of Shane Warne's deliveries but it bit and turned and caught the edge. Again he had had trouble defending leg-spinners.

For the second season in a row, New Zealand lost the Lancaster Park test by an innings. It had been a private hell for Chris. He had waited a year to return to international cricket, but had under-performed in both areas of the game.

The Wellington test was a rain-affected match and the Kiwis batted much more competently in the first innings than they had in Christchurch, but Chris managed unlucky 13. He seemed tentative, lacking the assertiveness he had in provincial cricket.

With the ball, however, he was back to his best. His rhythm was good and he worried the Australian top order with his pace, but the ball never tickled the bat and the enthusiastic shouts for LBW were declined. In the middle session of the fourth day Danny Morrison bowled a great spell, taking 6-38, to bowl the Australians out.

The Kiwi batsmen secured the draw and then the bombshell — during the post-match drinks in the Aussie dressing room Chris was asked to go with Warren Lees. In the privacy of the dressing room Wally tearfully told the kid he had known for 15 years that he wasn't required for the next test. He had been dropped. Both of them sat crying.

On the bare statistics it was understandable — scores of 0,21,13 and 14 and only one wicket in the two games. But he felt that he had bowled well and quite quickly in Wellington without luck or wickets. Danny had reaped the rewards but Chris felt that it could easily have been him collecting the scalps instead. He had been good support for his new-ball partner.

His place in the team was taken by the out-of-form Chris Harris. The line was that the Eden Park pitch would suit Harry's bowling better, but a rumour circulated that Harry was selected in order to get him into some form for the one-day series. If there was any truth in this suggestion it would have to be one of the least valid rationales for discarding a player. While one-day cricket may have won over the populace, its older brother, test cricket, is still the pre-eminent form of the game.

No matter what reason lay behind it, the stark fact was that Chris had been dropped for the first time. It was the lowest point in his career. Help came from an unlikely source — that night Chris and his team-mates went to the Backbencher pub in Wellington, opposite Parliament Buildings. There they met up with some of the Australians. It was David Boon, the tiny Tasmanian, who gave him the biggest boost. He told Chris that the Australians rated him, that he shouldn't get downcast. Boon told Chris that he had taken four years to establish himself in the Australian side, a time when he was regularly in and out of the team. His advice was to keep focused, keep his eyes on the prize, to come back better. As he stood in the Backbencher, with its 'spitting image' puppets of politicians and sports stars staring down from the walls, Chris made a vow to himself. He would never be dropped again.

Chris was not included in the squad for the one-dayers either, his place being taken by the golden boy of the New Zealand sport, Jeff Wilson. Perhaps, as John Bracewell suggested in a newspaper column, Wilson's selection over Cairns had a little to do with politics — if he played cricket for New Zealand it could woo him away from the career in an All Black jersey that seemed inevitable, but in the end 'Goldie' performed miracles in the fourth one-day match and the selection was justified.

Chris flew out of New Zealand a few days later. It had been his worst season yet. He felt like he had to start all over again.

10

The shire

On the morning of 10 April 1993, only months before the first free and democratic elections in South Africa, in a quiet middle-class suburb in north Johannesburg, Chris Hani, a black politician, was approached outside his home by a white supremacist and shot several times with an automatic weapon. He died instantly.

The whole of South Africa tensed — Hani was the second most popular figure in the Republic, after Nelson Mandela. Many people considered him to be Mandela's successor. He had been a warrior, activist, and Greek scholar and was a vocal proponent of a peaceful transition to democracy. This hope seemed to drain away with the blood on Hani's driveway.

The country was gripped by fear. It seemed that this assassination would be the catalyst for a bloody chain reaction that could only lead to civil war. Mandela himself, the president-in-waiting, appealed for calm.

Chris was in Cape Town when Hani was shot. He had joined Nottinghamshire for a pre-season tour, but suddenly the tour had descended into chaos and uncertainty. The British Embassy was contacted and the tourists confined to their hotel for a few days until things calmed. There was concern throughout the squad.

In the end the apocalypse did not occur. Hani's funeral saw an outpouring of grief and some minor incidents and there were some riots in the townships, but the social structure never collapsed. This was Chris' first experience of the weird, beautiful, dynamic and dangerous place that he was to grow to love.

Back in England, the season started dramatically. The first game, against Worcestershire, was a tie, the first tied game in Notts' history, when they were all out for 248 (Chris 68), chasing 249 in the second innings. The feeling afterwards was odd, completely different from being involved in a draw, loss or win. There was exhilaration, of course, as the game had been so close, but there was also disappointment that one little moment could have changed the outcome. Chris, as usual, examined what more he could have done.

In the first couple of games Chris began to notice pain in his left knee that wasn't allowing him to run at full pace. This was to be his first experience of patellar tendonitis, a problem that was to blight his game for much of his later career.

With this ailment Chris experienced the brutality of English sports medicine first hand. He was examined by the Notts medical board, who recommended a cortisone injection directly into the tendon. Chris had this delicate procedure and was back playing within the week. It was only later, back in New Zealand, that he was advised how dangerous this treatment could be. To inject directly into a tendon risks rupturing the cord completely and causing irreparable damage.

But play he did, no longer in pain, and took five wickets at Lord's in the third county match of the season, then 6-52 in the Sunday league against Kent. That brought about the second victory over Kent in the same week. In the three-day match Notts was forced to follow on in spite of Chris' crisis-time innings of 93. The Cairns-

NOTTINGHAM POST

In action for Notts against Somerset during a NatWest Trophy match at Trent Bridge, 1993.

style attack was replicated by the entire Notts batting line-up in the second innings and an extraordinary victory was achieved. It was the first time Notts had won after following on since 1863! In June, Chris hit three half-centuries in a row in the County Championship. He was in a purple patch.

It was the kind of consistent performances that the Notts board had wanted when they had offered him the long-term contract. In all of the first 13 first-class fixtures that season, Chris either scored a half-century, or took four or more wickets.

As a cricketer Chris was constantly improving, but in cricket a few words can be worth a thousand throw-downs. Playing Glamorgan in Swansea in late June, Chris had bowled well, taking 4-66 in the first innings. At tea one afternoon he wandered over to the Welsh side's overseas professional, the great Viv Richards, and asked if he could chat with him after stumps. The Master Blaster, greying now, the sage of batting, agreed. For the price of a couple of rum and cokes Chris was to get an exclusive course in one thing — dominance.

Chris sat entranced as Richards talked about dominating an innings from the start. If a batsman could get the bowler to concentrate on bowling defensively, percentages went up. Instead of playing oneself in, being tentative and protective, prodding and plodding, Richards extolled taking the attack to the bowler early. If anybody other than an opener arrives at the crease the bowler and the fielding team will be on a high — a wicket has just fallen. Richards' idea was to wrest initiative, to puncture the morale of the side.

Of course that wasn't always possible. The great West Indian said he rated Lillee slightly over Hadlee as it was easier to knock Hadlee off that nagging length that he made his own. A couple of hits off Hadlee and the Kiwi might pitch one short, or try some variations. Lillee, however, would be back at the batsman, ball after ball, no matter what the batsman did. It was a lesson for Cairns the batsman and Cairns the bowler.

After that conversation he had consecutive scores of 53, 47, 71, 47, 73 and 126 not out in one-day competitions. That last innings was one of his finest. The night before, Chris, his girlfriend Ruth, Chris' schoolmate Mike Smith and his partner, Joanne, went to the Slug and Lettuce in Fulham. It was a big, joyous night that ended with Chris and Ruth dossing at a friend's place far across the other side of London.

The next morning Chris woke up and took the Northern Line to The Oval tube station. Sleep-deprived and hung-over, he fell asleep in the Notts dressing room. His team-mates let him snooze but, suddenly, Waqar Younis blew apart the top order and Chris was needed. He was shoved in the shower.

Chris had never faced Waqar before and was surprised at the Pakistani's pace. But in spite of the fact that he wasn't feeling his best he just started to move his feet and swing his bat; like an automaton he began to hit boundaries regularly. He had numerous mid-pitch conversations with his team-mate Paul Pollard, who had also been out the night before, but the suffering pair kept hitting.

He would never envisage pushing the boundaries of his professionalism like that in today's environment, but as a headstrong 23-year-old he played hard on and off the field. His remarkable unbeaten century, scored in self-induced pain, helped set the home side an incredible 314 to win. Equally incredibly, the Londoners got that with room to spare. Chris had now hit two centuries in limited-overs cricket within six months, and finished on the losing side each time.

In spite of the losses it was turning out to be a fabulous season. His girlfriend, Ruth, had come over with him and they were sharing a flat with the ever-dry Steve Bramhall, and long-time friend Graeme Archer, who were both on the Notts staff. The loneliness of the year before — coming home to an empty flat — was gone. When Danny Morrison and his new wife, Kim, came to visit one afternoon in August the four Kiwis chatted and joked and drank Marlborough wines to remind them of home. The two men cooked steaks on a barbie and talked about the upcoming tour to Australia and a thousand and one other things well into the midsummer evening. It was a beautiful time and the world seemed perfect.

Then in the chilly silence of pre-dawn a few days later Chris' world collapsed.

11

Louise

The Southerner train pulled out of Christchurch station around 8.30 a.m. on 25 August 1993 on its journey to Dunedin, then Invercargill. It slipped through the western suburbs and out into the plantations and hobby farms of the Selwyn district. The Main Trunk Line runs parallel just a few metres to the left of State Highway One as the two arteries move south. When the locomotive was approaching the small hamlet of Rolleston a truck, a concrete mixer with tonnes of wet concrete circulating in its vat, turned off the main road towards the railway line.

The vehicles collided. The nose of the lorry was struck by the train and the truck was spun like a coin on its axis. The huge vat of cement smashed into the left side of the first carriage. Three young female passengers were killed — including the young woman in seat 4D, Louise Cairns.

As soon as Sue Wilson heard of the accident she was filled with panic. When the police arranged to see her she knew something terrible had happened to Louise, but hoped against hope, in vain.

Lance was playing a round of golf at the Heriot course in west Otago. When he saw the blue uniformed figure of a police officer walking down a fairway he also knew that something had happened to his little girl.

Chris meanwhile was woken by one of those early morning phone calls that are harbingers of bad news. Initially he thought it would be one of his mates from home, maybe Smithy, in high spirits, wanting a chat and not bothering to check on Greenwich Mean Time. But it was Wayne Wilson. He asked for Ruth.

Chris, half-asleep, padded back up the stairs to the bedroom, woke her and got back into bed. Wayne had a brief conservation with Ruth, and told her to stay by Chris. When she rewoke Chris, he knew something was very wrong. They walked back down together and Chris picked up the receiver. The message was just eight words wide: 'There's been an accident. Louise has been killed.' The words seemed so stark and ordinary for such a momentous event. The pair sat on the stairs. The early morning was very cold.

Chris's sister, Rachel Louise Cairns — 1973–1993. Cairns Family

Chris went to Trent Bridge that morning to tell his coach, ex-England seamer Mike Hendrick, of the tragedy. But Hendrick was last to arrive that day and as Chris sat waiting for him his team-mates trooped by, firing off jokes and cheery greetings. When Hendrick finally arrived Chris broke down as he told him what had happened. Chris wept for long minutes.

Mike Hendrick quickly arranged things and Chris and Ruth flew back a couple of days later, thanks to Air New Zealand getting them seats on the first flight out. It was a long-haul flight in every sense, a journey marked by the tiredness of grief and memories of Louise.

Chris tried to collect the images he had of his little sister. He remembered setting her hair alight accidentally when they were kids. He remembered times when the family numbered just three, under the one roof. He remembered the last time they saw each other, just after she had moved up to Cheviot with her boyfriend, when she seemed really happy, putting troubled teenage years behind her. But already some memories had been wiped, maybe from the shock of it all.

Chris got more and more nervous as he moved over the globe towards Christchurch. Customs, the domestic leg, the pick-up from the airport were all a blur. The first thing he recalled was the door of his mum's house opening and there were Lance and Sue weeping. The family went to the funeral parlour and Chris saw Louise in her casket. Outside his father gave him an embrace, the length and strength of which he will never forget.

Chris' job was to sort out a photo montage for the funeral, but he kept putting it off until the very morning of the funeral. He woke up early and laughed and cried as he made the tribute.

Louise Cairns was a bubbly child. She worshipped her father and was deeply hurt when he left. While Chris was a stoic 10-year-old, Louise was just seven and probably unable to understand that it wasn't her fault that the family had unravelled. She never lost her vivaciousness but sought attention and approval. It only worsened when Lance rang. He would speak for two or three minutes to Louise about school and friends, and then he'd speak to Chris for 20 minutes about cricket.

When the family moved to Christchurch, Chris was closing in on his hormonal teens and Louise became just a bit of a nuisance, a little sister who annoyed him. They had shared the hard years of the divorce as children but Chris had grown up into a different world. Louise, in her turn, wanted to be like Chris, wanted to get attention from her mum, her brother or particularly her dad. She tried cricket, ballet and athletics but she never seemed able to stick at any one thing. Once she had a trial for a Canterbury age-group netball team, but even then no one was there to watch her — Chris was playing rugby across town.

After a couple of years at Papanui High School she moved to Christchurch Girls High, but her school marks were overshadowed by Chris'. In spite of all this she wasn't resentful but immensely proud of Chris' achievements.

During her teenage years, she clashed with authority on occasion. This included her head-teachers and her mum. She was an individual, trying to be viewed in her own right, not the 'daughter of' or 'sister of'. However, some of her choices as an individual weren't the right ones. She often got into some sort of mischief, usually involving parties, cigarettes and boys. But it wasn't as if she was a bad kid. Louise was more a lovable ratbag.

Her mother had seen it all before, for the simple reason that she had been a teenager just like Louise — headstrong, mischievous and cunning. Once when Louise was ordered to change into her school uniform, she threw her mufti clothes out the window to collect them later. Sue saw straight through the guise — she'd done the same things 20 years earlier. Mother and daughter were cut from the same cloth. But for all her misbehaviour she was just like her mum, thoughtful, generous and fun-loving.

Louise could also be hilarious. She could spin a wild yarn about some character, though her aunties or cousins or friends always suspected that the story may well have been about Louise herself. The audience would be in stitches and she would punctuate her tale with a wide smile.

The most tragic thing was that Louise, nearing her 20th birthday, had just started to find herself. She and Chris had started to develop a mature relationship — sibling revelry rather than rivalry. They had started to talk and understand each other. She had also started to find her feet. She had done some work experience at an old people's home and enjoyed the contact with another generation. She was also content in her relationship with Mark Righton.

Most importantly, she had really begun to connect with her father. After years of little contact she was seeing more of Lance — and had spent long periods with him in both Whangarei and Dunedin. She had been on her way to visit him when she was killed.

The family gathered for the funeral and were forced to mourn in public — glossy magazines and television showed the Cairnses grieving. Chris' most graphic memory of the ceremony was Sir Richard Hadlee hugging Lance and weeping deeply. For someone whom Chris always thought of as aloof it was a display of pure emotion from Sir Richard, grief for the loss of a little girl whom he'd also watched growing up.

Everybody grieves in different ways. Chris wanted to run away, the old Cairns impulse. He wanted to go back to England and finish the season, even though Notts had excused him. He wanted to get back to an environment that he could control, to routines that were familiar and comforting. He wanted to get away from the pain and sadness all around him. So he made the biggest mistake of his life. He left.

In retrospect, he realises he should have stayed with the family and worked his way through the stages of mourning, to reach a point of acceptance from where he could start healing. As it was, he arrived in England and played four games of cricket very much on autopilot. When he was at the crease he blanked the loss out of his head. But when he wasn't playing his mind played over things. How unfair it had all been. How freakish the accident had been. How fragile life was for everybody.

Chris would think these things over and he would be filled with rage. He would rage for five years.

12

His Achilles heel

When moments of high tragedy, like Louise's death, occur cricket seems like an irrelevancy, on the margins of real life. Perhaps that's why Chris sought refuge there. The plaudits and accolades and sympathy he received from the English cricket establishment buoyed him. Here was a place to stand, an area of order in what had become a world of chaos.

In October, Chris flew into Perth to begin a tour of Australia. He was on a mission. In spite of the tragedy, Chris had had a great English season, a season where his talent had flourished. Notts had finished seventh in all (and 17th again in the Sunday League). But Chris had been third in the Notts batting averages, and 28th in the batting averages for the whole country. His 43.72 (with nine half-centuries) was higher than David Gower, Alec Stewart, Allan Lamb, Desmond Haynes, Salim Malik, Graham Thorpe, Richie Richardson and Ian Botham.

He was Notts' top bowler with 53 wickets at 23.43, better than Courtney Walsh, Allan Donald, Dominic Cork, Malcolm Marshall, Paul Reiffel and, again, Ian Botham. Only veteran John Emburey had finished higher on both tables. It had been a triumph for Chris. He was a world-class player. Now he wanted to prove that on the international stage.

The Kiwis had a new coach, a familiar face to Chris, Geoff Howarth. Warren Lees had been replaced controversially over the winter. Chris was not the only one to suspect that that had had less to do with Lees' coaching ability and more to do with the fallout from the Sri Lanka debacle. Chris had known Geoff Howarth since he had been a boy. Howarth had even given the youngster his first adult-sized bat, in the early '80s. The former New Zealand skipper had coached Chris during his first season with ND and on the subsequent Youth tour to Australia back in 1989. Howarth certainly had the experience and knowledge to do the job and Chris enjoyed his company socially. But the new coach would rule over a New Zealand team that would reach their nadir.

The New Zealand team's performance in the opening weeks of the tour was embarrassing. The first match was a festival event at Lilac Hill, the opposition a mixture of veterans and up-and-comers. The tradition of the visiting side batting first against 'weaker' opposition, to ensure the crowd gets value for money, backfired. The top order were skittled by three players with a combined age of 130. Their limbs were less supple and their heads silvered but their names were among the greatest of players — Lillee, Thomson and Hadlee — and the desire to win still evident. Chris faced Sir Richard for a few balls (and the only time in his career) before slicing Dennis Lillee to point. The Kiwis wouldn't have made the 189 they did had the Invitation XI not let their wicketkeeper bowl. They still lost by six wickets.

When they faced the state sides it was even worse — Western Australia won by an innings, and the Kiwis could only draw against Tasmania though Chris bowled 32 overs on a placid pitch, and took five wickets. Sandwiched between those games was yet another loss, to the Australian Cricket Academy, and a morale-boosting win over New South Wales. Unfortunately Chris didn't play in the victory — he still had not won a first-class game in Kiwi colours!

The first test was at Perth, the scene of his debut four years earlier. There was a pungent sense of déjà vu. Again New Zealand fielded. Again he held the new ball. Again, after being dropped and injured the year before, he felt that he was at the beginning of his career. And yet again his first few overs were very fast and very wayward. He even sent one ball well over Tony Blain's head for four byes.

Nerves had got to him. He had been too caught up with the sense that he had something to prove. At fine leg he lectured himself. He had to stop trying so hard and concentrate on nothing more than enjoying himself and the favourable conditions.

Chris is a firm believer in the part fate plays in cricket. There are so many imponderables in cricket, so many things that can go wrong, that it sometimes seems unlikely that anything will run your way. Then suddenly a ball popped and Michael Slater pushed it into short-leg's hands. Next ball, a climbing delivery, took the shoulder of David Boon's bat. Chris was on a hat-trick, and even managed to get an edge off Mark Waugh that fell just short of the field. Late in the day, Chris bowled Mark Taylor for his third wicket. The déjà vu had evaporated.

The Australian tail wagged like a terrier's and New Zealand was solid in reply. By the time Chris came to the crease they were a little over 100 behind with five wickets remaining. For Chris it was an emotional moment. He had dedicated this performance to Louise, as she would have turned 20 on the second day. He began to bat appropriately.

Chris was looking to be more aggressive at the crease. He had always gone into his shell when batting in tests, and remembered Martin Crowe roasting him after one innings. Crowe criticised Chris for playing defensively and putting pressure on his skipper to score runs and keep the total ticking over.

There was another reason to attack. The New Zealanders had developed a plan of controlled aggression for Shane Warne, to knock the leg-spinner off his length. Warne had, only months before, rocked the English cricket establishment with the prodigious turn he imparted on the ball and tied the Poms in knots. Chris knew he would struggle if he tried to pad up to the leg-spinner. Early in his innings he hit Warne back over his bleached head. It was his first six in test cricket.

Chris had a rousing partnership with Tony Blain, dominating the tiring bowlers. He passed his half-century and with an all-run four he had his highest test score. When stumps were drawn he was on 66 not out. It seemed inevitable that he would post a great maiden century, but the next morning his bête noire, the leg-spinner Warne, managed to hurry a flipper through his defence. Chris had made 78.

The pitch had flattened out on the second day and Chris hurt his left heel when bowling. It was badly bruised. It didn't seem to affect his batting, but in the Australian second innings the pounding his long legs gave the heel as he ran in to bowl was unbearable. Three boundaries were hit off the only over Chris could manage. With Willie Watson and Martin Crowe also injured it was as if the Kiwi effort was only held together by band-aids and gauze. Chris cursed the ailment. It was so minor, yet so debilitating, and he had performed so very well in this test. As the Kiwis played out a draw with eight fit men he rested his discoloured foot.

Chris didn't play the next match, against South Australia, then the Kiwis returned to Tasmania for the second test. After a cortisone injection, the heel seemed better. He was duly selected.

But his self-doubt was as nagging as the pain in his foot. The day before the test he had bowled in the nets. It had been OK, but not more than that. He felt 60 to 70 per cent. That night Chris could not sleep. All he could think of was his test career. Not once had he grabbed a game by the scruff of the neck. Not once had he won a test. Now he was going to enter a tough contest considerably less than match-fit. At six in the morning, he rang his father in Gisborne (where Lance now lived) and they talked over the situation.

Lance's advice was to not play. An athlete knows his own body better than anyone else, he said, and Chris knew the mechanics weren't right. He couldn't give his all for his country, so it was better that he let someone else step up. As his room-mate snored lightly in the next bed, Chris decided to withdraw.

Chris told the management team first thing, and the news percolated through the team. It is always disappointing to lose someone with injury, and Chris was an 'impact' player, but most of the team understood. It seemed, however, that two members of the touring party in particular didn't have the same compassion. Unfortunately they were the coach and captain.

Howarth claimed later in a press conference that he was bemused by the late withdrawal, that it indicated Chris simply didn't want to play.

Not only did Chris have an injury, but now he also had a lot of mud sticking to him. Rutherford said in his biography, *A Hell of a Way to Make a Living*, that he was bewildered by the turnaround, and facetiously suggested that the only way he could have re-injured himself was in his sleep. Both tried to encourage Chris to play that morning, to play through the pain, ignoring the player's own assessment of his ability to perform. Then when New Zealand were outclassed by an innings and 222 runs, one senior player confronted Chris about his reasons for withdrawing as if his absence was the main cause of the whipping.

Mike Sandlant, the team manager, gave Chris an ultimatum — play in the next test, in Brisbane, or go home. The management were making very public insinuations about his commitment to the New Zealand side. But to doubt Chris Cairns' desire to represent his country shows a complete lack of knowledge of the man.

Chris played at the Gabba, and in the first innings Chris was facing Shane Warne when the spinner started limping as he ran in. Ian Healy, the Aussie keeper, stood up with a concerned look on his face.

'What's wrong, Warnie?' he inquired.

'Awww, mate it's my heel. It's really sore.'

'Awww, Warnie, you'd better have a couple of weeks off.'

This was typical Aussie sledging — patronising, comical and insulting.

There is an urban myth still current among New Zealand cricket followers that when Chris was batting during this series, close-in fielders started making train noises. It was suggested as a possible reason he didn't play in Hobart. This never happened. Sledging, particularly among a handful of test players, can be deeply insulting and chronically abusive, but referring to a family tragedy is in such extreme bad taste that it is inconceivable to imagine a player behaving in such a base manner. Yet even on the 1997 tour to Australia, newspapers — seeking to hype the contest — repeated this fable as fact, much to the distress of the Australian cricketers and their families.

Chris quickly came to their defence publicly to put an end to the accusations.

There is, however, a kernel of truth to this fiction. In Sydney during the one-day series that followed, a few boors on the Hill started taunting Chris by making train sounds but were quickly shouted down by the offended crowd around them. Danny Morrison remembers hearing a chant of 'Sook, sook' at the Adelaide Oval during the same competition. A small odious minority of Australians may not respect grief and lack common decency, but the Australian cricket team are not among them.

The Gabba test was a huge disappointment. Another innings defeat included two shocking batting efforts, and substandard bowling. Two Australians recorded centuries and four hit half-centuries. Chris bowled poorly but he was not alone in that regard. He was also given out dubiously in the first innings (caught and bowled by Warne for 5, straight off his front pad), then, to complete a really bad test, fell in the second dig to Glenn McGrath for the first of six times in test cricket.

The World Series Cup at least provided a clean slate. The Kiwis lost twice to Australia, but the losing margin of the second match was just three runs. Then, before the team headed back to New Zealand for the yuletide break, they beat South Africa. Chris scored 30 not out to nurse the team past the Africans' modest total. It was the start of a majestic month and a half for Chris.

Christmas was a sombre affair — the first without Louise — but the Roberts family gathered around for support. There was joking and laughing but everybody was a little tentative, avoiding the issue, not looking at the photos of the pretty blonde girl on the mantelpiece. Chris found the whole thing awkward.

He joined the Canterbury side on Boxing Day to defend the Shell Cup. Fuelled by turkey and Christmas pud, he hit form. A lucky 63 against Otago was followed by an 84 against Wellington. By the New Year, when Chris and the Young Guns returned to Australia for the second half of the World Series Cup, Canterbury had won four of the five matches played and had virtually guaranteed themselves a semi-final place.

First up was a return to the Gabba, against South Africa. Chris finally scored runs in a one-dayer. In some of the highest temperatures — over 40 degrees — Chris blazed like a bushfire. He scored 70 in just 55 balls, his first half-century in limited-overs internationals, hitting 4 fours and 3 sixes. The record-breaking partnership (111 in 96 balls) he had with his old mate Shane Thomson saw the two best young talents in New Zealand fighting exhaustion and spontaneous combustion. Sweat poured from the pair as they ran singles and twos and sucked hot air deep into their lungs.

When the third umpire was called for in a close run out decision, Chris didn't really mind which light showed. Green — he would keep batting in the sauna. Red — he could rehydrate and rest. Shane Thomson sat under a cold shower for a full hour after the innings. From 86 for 5, the two all-rounders had hauled New Zealand through to a final total of 256. Although near exhaustion, Chris took two wickets as the Proteas fell short.

The next game produced a remarkable ensemble effort from the Kiwis. Defending 198, all the Kiwis pulled their weight. There was aggressive fielding and tight bowling. Chris Pringle pulled off a George Best impression when he ran out Damien Martyn with a side foot kick. Richard de Groen (the only florist to play international cricket) bowled superbly and Shane Thomson cleaned out Allan Border. Chris Cairns produced a spell of accuracy that Robin Hood would have been proud of — 9-2-18-1. The win gave the Kiwis every chance of finals cricket. The equation was simple —

Good mates off the field, Shane Thomson and Chris shared a match-winning partnership — in 40-degree heat — against South Africa at the Gabba in 1994.

New Zealand had to win either of their last two matches, or South Africa had to lose.

What happened was hugely disappointing. On the Perth tarmac Allan Donald and the other quicks won both matches of a double-header for South Africa. Then New Zealand were well beaten by Australia in the final match. The Proteas and the Kiwis finished level on points but the two losses had dragged the latter's run rate well below the Africans.

Chris at least had the consolation of a final back home. In his absence, Germon's Canterbury team had been top of the group stage, and after a washed-out semi-final had qualified for a home final against Central Districts.

There was a problem however. Lancaster Park was being renovated and was declared unfit. Hagley Park was the option proposed by Canterbury Cricket but the ground was considered too small for a major match. Gate receipts would be reduced — so McLean Park in Napier was decreed the venue by New Zealand Cricket.

This would be a 'home' final only in name. The Mainlanders were disappointed for their fans and sponsors, but were determined to win, in spite of this setback. Canterbury Draught summed up the situation in its adverts saying: 'Their stadium, their crowd, their pitch, their weather, their advantage, our cup.'

Local knowledge certainly seemed to aid Central as Canterbury slid to 66-5 playing injudicious shots to good-length balls. Chris was then joined in the middle by young Stephen Fleming, the tall, languid strokeplayer, who seemed destined for higher honours. A total nearing 180 seemed like the best the pair could hope for, but the change of ground had one huge advantage for Chris Cairns. The Hawke's Bay sun had

PHOTOSPORT

Trying to come back for his 100th run in the 1994 Shell Cup final at Napier, Chris falls short and is run out. Canterbury beat Central Districts and Chris' four wickets and 99 runs earned him the Man of the Match award.

baked a pitch conducive to shot-making, as long as one took the time to assess the pace and conditions. It was, in many ways, just like the wickets he had been batting on successfully in Australia.

With Fleming feeding him the strike, Chris began gathering runs, regularly sweeping danger man Stu Duff, and pulling any short ball. It was a controlled and composed innings until the final 10 overs when both southerners upped the tempo — Chris played a reverse sweep off David Lamason one ball, then lofted him over long-on the next. It was by no means a chanceless innings — he was dropped on 78, should have been stumped when he was 86, and when he was on 59 he survived a rare appeal for 'obstructing the field' when he deliberately moved his body in front of the stumps to prevent a run out. He had used up all his luck. On 98 he attempted to squeeze two runs out of a situation that guaranteed only one and was run out by a couple of metres.

It had been a great knock, 99 off only 102 balls, the highest innings in the 13-year history of the Shell Cup final. The partnership with Fleming (142) was also a record for the final and Canterbury set CD an imposing 241 to win.

For a while Central looked in the hunt when Greatbatch and Twose kept up with the required run rate, but this was Chris' day. He bowled a perfectly executed slower ball to Mark Greatbatch, who popped up a catch to the off side field. Slower balls also accounted for two tail-end wickets and Chris finished with 4-44. It had been the complete all-rounder's display, the culmination of all the knowledge he had gleaned from long hours under English skies.

Chris was inevitably the Man of the Match. The 99 was frustrating but Canterbury's Shell Cup 'threepeat' — a hat-trick of triumphs — more than made up for it. He had topped the Shell Cup averages for both batting and bowling. In the World Series Cup, Chris' batting aggregate had been second only to David Boon and he had bowled very economically. Everybody from Allan Border to Geoff Howarth complimented his work rate and determination and, most of all, his maturity.

However, there was a dark cloud on the horizon of this halcyon summer. He was in some discomfort with his knee — the patellar tendonitis was back.

Bowling only 10 overs in a one-day match was fine but he wondered how the knee would hold up during the long spells required in test cricket. It was worsening as well — he had really begun to feel the stress during the final. He had a scan in Christchurch and rest or surgery was recommended. Pakistan, however, had arrived for a three-test tour and he was reluctant to withdraw from the national side again, after all the criticism he had received for his actions in Hobart. A compromise was arranged — another cortisone injection, this time around the tendon, would work as a stop-gap measure. He would play the first test.

The encounter at Eden Park was strange. Fifteen wickets fell on the first day, 16 on the next. Extravagant shots were played and runs came quickly, but it seemed that the New Zealanders couldn't extricate themselves from the limited-overs mentality, and that the Pakistanis considered attack the best form of defence.

In the first innings, Chris was again out to a spinner (Mushtaq Ahmed), who moved the ball away from the batsman, for the 7th time in 17 innings. The Kiwis took a wafer-thin lead into the second innings but batted very poorly. Only Chris and Simon Doull showed any purpose. Chris went out to bat at 40-5 and decided simply to survive, gathering runs rather than hunting them. Doull hit out effectively when he joined Chris, but the sorry event was soon all over in 32.1 overs. New Zealand were all out for 110. Chris top-scored with just 31.

Pakistan had an awkward total to get, but Chris bowled poorly in the second innings. Three overs was all he could handle on the third and last day as Pakistan won. The knee couldn't cope after all.

He wanted to play test cricket, but wanted to tour England in May even more. He decided to rest his knee and forgo the next two tests. He would come back for the one-day series. His knee would have time to heal. He could not have envisaged, even in his worst imaginings, that he wouldn't play test cricket again for almost two years.

This was the summer of Waqar Younis and Wasim Akram, and the one-dayers saw these great bowlers at their destructive peak. Waqar was very fast indeed — with a deadly yorker and a preternatural ability to swing the ball. Wasim was simply a genius, a player Chris considers the greatest cricketer he has played against. As a bowler he had everything. He could move the ball both ways in the air and off the pitch, and could bowl a string of slower balls followed by a bouncer at 145 km/h, as Lance knew all too well. His control was glorious and whether Chris was watching from afar, or at the sharp end of an Akram over, it was always educational. Wasim could bat too, though he neglected this side of his game as Pakistan always seemed to field a side replete with batting talent. He was to Chris what Imran Khan had been to Ian Botham — both a rival and an idol.

The Pakistanis (in general) and the two quicks (in particular) routed the Kiwis in the first three one-dayers. The fourth was leaning New Zealand's way thanks to

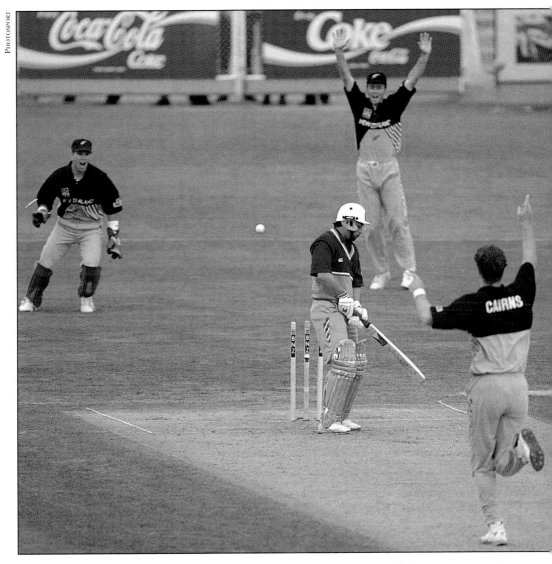

Asif Mujtaba is bowled by Chris during the New Zealanders' seven-wicket win over Pakistan at Christchurch in 1994. Despite this win, Pakistan took out the one-day series 3–1.

a patient innings by Chris (39 in 54 balls) and an impatient one from Ken Rutherford, then Waqar returned to pollard the tail and the game was tied. It was the first tie in New Zealand's one-day history. The last game, at Lancaster Park, witnessed the only New Zealand half-century of the series (Blair Hartland 54 not out) and finally the Kiwis won.

During the innings break, Chris had a run-in with Glenn Turner. Chris had announced that he would not be available for the forthcoming test against India. During the television wrap-up, Turner, who was commentating for TVNZ, said that he couldn't see much wrong with Chris, as he was running around aggressively in the field. Again the insinuation was that Chris was a 'reluctant' player, an absentee cricketer.

The live feed was being filmed just down the corridor and Chris went and stood behind the cameras waiting for Geoff Bryan and Turner to come off air. When the wrap-up finished, Chris asked Turner what was going on, why had he made such uninformed statements? Turner was evasive but Chris continued — after all, the commentator was suggesting the injury wasn't serious, sowing doubt in the mind of the public and putting Chris' integrity in question. Turner turned to Chris and said, 'You're only part of the equation.' What he meant by that enigmatic comment, Chris has never been able to divine.

In Christchurch, a second consultation with an orthopaedic surgeon gave Chris the bad news that he wouldn't be 100 per cent for the tour of England. The doctor said that the cricket Chris had played over February and March had only served to inflame the left knee. It is ironic that a player who was castigated for not wanting to play through pain in November was now going to miss several tests and a full Britannic tour, because he had played with an injury.

Chris was gutted. Just like 1990 he would miss cricket's hadj, the great pilgrimage, because of injury. He wanted so desperately to follow in his father's footsteps, and in the size 14 indents made by Sir Richard Hadlee. He wanted to play at Lord's and Trent Bridge for his country. It was the greatest disappointment yet in his cricket career, particularly coming at the end of such a golden season. Instead he faced a long winter of discontent, rest and recovery. Just days after the Pakistan series, Chris decided to have surgery on the knee.

It proved to be the right decision — debris was scattered around the joint causing discomfort and the tendon was, in fact, discovered to be torn. He had clearly been playing through pain for months.

13

The summer of
our discontent

With little to occupy his thoughts apart from building up strength in his knee, Chris indulged himself. He bought a house at Sumner in Christchurch, facing the beach and the Norfolk pines that line the esplanade. It was a small but comfortable bachelor pad. He flatted with his schoolmate Ciaran Hartley, a fine cricketer but more famous for his passionate support of Canterbury rugby and the red and black platform-soles he wore to every Canty match.

Chris spent hours on the exercycle musing about test cricket. He half-thought that he could be back for the South African tour at the end of the year, but he didn't push his rehabilitation. He simply enjoyed his first break from cricket in three years.

He was, in retrospect, to view this downtime as a major factor in elongating his career. Invasive surgery like he had suffered could shave years off a sporting life. He gave his body time to heal. He had his first ever holiday — in Fiji. He watched the progress of the Kiwis through England. He saw Dion Nash's remarkable all-round efforts at Lord's and the two peerless centuries of Martin Crowe.

Chris came back to cricket, as a batsman sole, in October 1994. He scored two centuries for his club side, Lancaster Park, and even had a light work-out with the ball. In the nets he worked to iron out some of the bad habits that had crept into his action over the previous seasons and to refine his technique. But coming back from injury is a gradual process. He was hoping to be back bowling competitively by Boxing Day. When the Canterbury squad was announced he was selected purely as a specialist batsman. He was also captain.

Lee Germon was on the tour to South Africa and Chris took the helm for the first matches in the Shell Trophy. He loved captaincy — the process of motivating, setting fields and working strategies. He loved having five things demanding attention at any one time. There were no breaks for the captain — it was more a lifestyle than an occupation, but it was a great honour to be chosen to lead.

This new challenge began in Oamaru in the Shell Cup opener against Otago. Canterbury won. The next match at Rangiora was not so successful as the game of human chess went a little awry. Chasing a large total, Chris' team foundered.

His first first-class match as captain was at Lancaster Park in early December against Auckland. Opposing seamer Danny Morrison was also on the recovery trail. He was bowling at a lively pace and hoping to get a call-up for the tour to South Africa. Canterbury took first innings points, but in the second innings the top order fell to the international attack of Morrison, Watson, Patel and Vaughan and only a patient captain's knock of 64 from Chris secured the draw.

At the tail-end of the match Morrison had been mucking around, changing his style on occasions as he bowled to his good friend. It was typical of Morrison to be the jester and Chris was amused at his antics. Morrison would bowl in imitation of

Malcolm Marshall then turn to his captain, Justin Vaughan, and ask in a comical West Indian accent for some close fielders. Or he would try out a ball he called the 'crab', where he ran in almost crouching before leaping high into his delivery stride and unfurling his limbs. While the techniques might be funny there was nothing jocular about the resulting balls — they were quick and skidded off the pitch. One of these short balls came onto Chris very fast. He swung over the ball and it struck his left side. After the game he was sore but he assumed that was simply a bruise. A cricket ball is after all a hard object.

When Chris got home that night he still didn't feel well. His girlfriend Ruth commented on his colour — he looked yellow. He had pain in his left shoulder. Worse, he had shortness of breath. Chris suddenly wondered if the ball had broken a rib and punctured a lung. Ruth drove him to the hospital.

After an X-ray the A&E staff assured Chris that his lung was still intact and sent him home but when he went to bed he felt nauseated. As he lay he struggled to expand his lungs. He felt like he was asphyxiating. Something was very, very wrong and the pair dashed hurriedly to the hospital for a second time.

This time the problem was found. The ball from Danny Morrison had ruptured Chris' spleen, and it was bleeding into the cavities of his torso, pressing on his lungs and the other major organs. Only a couple of years earlier, Chris would have required major surgery and a splenectomy, but medical science had advanced and a hail of pills halted the haemorrhaging. He would stay in hospital for a week. And he'd be out for six. Rest was the only treatment.

Having a player return from injury is so often a great psychological boost for a side. This was never seen more obviously than in early January 1995. Less than a month after his spleen burst, Chris joined his Canterbury team-mates at the warm-up before a Shell Cup semi-final at Lancaster Park. In spite of his lack of match fitness, the unexpected sight of Cairns must have worried the opposing Auckland team.

Chris was determined to help his side through to their fourth final in a row. He would wear a chest guard when batting to protect the damaged area, but short deliveries were uncommon in the short form of the game. It was still a courageous decision to return so soon after a serious injury. As he walked to the wicket with the red-and-blacks 4 for 67, he wondered about the prudence of his decision. It was a nervous start — he scored just five runs from the first 28 balls he faced and built a nice picket fence of 10 singles in a row. Chris then went completely Desert Storm on the Aucklanders. He recorded his half-century in 60 balls and then 28 balls later clocked up his second Shell Cup century, the second fastest of all time. He hit sixes into the hard-hat area around the newly constructed Hadlee stand. The construction workers downed tools and watched as he sent Scuds up and over the shortened boundary. His best shot was a daisy-cutter that cleared the extra cover boundary.

It took Chris just 46 balls to move from 43 to 143, when he was caught going for his tenth six. He also hit 10 fours as the home side reached an impregnable 274. It had been one of the most destructive onslaughts in the history of New Zealand cricket. There was no need for Lance Cairns to worry about accusations of nepotism when he adjudicated that his son was Man of the Match.

John Bracewell was the first to congratulate him — he had given Chris some throw-downs and advice the day before that helped Chris a lot. But Bracewell must have had mixed feelings watching his friend fire — he was the Auckland coach.

Playing his favourite shot, Chris launches down the wicket to loft the ball for six against Wellington at the Basin Reserve in 1994.

Only one person would have grumbled about Chris' performance — his specialist. Chris hadn't even received medical clearance to play such was his desire to be back in action.

After the match Chris was asked if he was fit enough for the national side to play the West Indies. He replied that he wasn't — he had bowled just three overs competitively in the whole season. He was not only recovering from an injury that hospitalised him, but also had a tender tendon to ease into use. He had to prove that he could bowl a 10-over spell or two first. And he certainly wasn't intending to put his ruptured spleen in the way of bouncers from Courtney Walsh and Curtly Ambrose. Uncharitably, Ken Rutherford wrote that he was taken aback when Chris said that he wasn't ready for international cricket.

The tour of South Africa had turned out to be a disaster — having won the first test, Ken Rutherford's team then lost the next two to be the first team in the 20th century to lose a three-match series after taking a lead. They were outplayed by both Sri Lanka and the hosts in a triangular tournament and injuries raged through the side. But much worse were allegations and rumours of excessive drinking, widespread drug use, rape and even diamond theft. It was as if the names Kray, Capone and Jorgensen should have been on the New Zealand team sheet.

It was a terrible start for what was New Zealand cricket's centennial season. Then on the team's return, Chris heard over a gym radio that three of the young players — Stephen Fleming, Dion Nash and Matthew Hart — had admitted to smoking marijuana while on tour. Another handful of players were also suspected of being involved but denied everything. The birthday celebrations seemed like they were going up in sickly-sweet blue smoke.

Chris was to notice the effects when he returned to the team. Again the team unit had been pulled apart. There was suspicion about who had grassed about the grass. There was confusion among the trio of young scapegoats about the older players who had denied using the drug. There was also a question over the heavy-handed captain Rutherford, who had investigated vigorously. Chris could see all this in the tight faces, whispered comments and suspicious glares around the dressing room when he returned to the fold in mid-February for the Centenary tournament. The group ethos was long gone.

By the time that quadrangular tournament rolled around, Chris' bowling still wasn't quite right. He had had some long work-outs with the ball but had taken just one wicket the whole season. He could only bowl at three-quarter pace. With the bat, however, he had struck a rich vein of form. In top-grade cricket he was averaging over 45. The return of such an in-form player to the New Zealand side was a boon. Chris was back from injury, as were Crowe and Greatbatch — and one more important transition had occurred: Geoff Howarth had resigned as coach to be replaced by a caretaker, John Fulton Reid. Surfing on an optimistic wave, New Zealand won the first one-dayer against India at McLean Park.

Many years later, in hindsight, Chris has deep suspicions about the ease with which they won that game. Chris recorded fabulous figures on comeback — 8-0-17-1 — but was bowling very slowly, concentrating purely on line and length. Not fully fit, he was bowling at no more than Nathan Astle's pace, yet the batsmen were playing him very tentatively. At the time he assumed there was some unseen devil in the pitch.

When the match-fixing controversy broke in the new millennium, several games

The Eden Park pitch does bounce low and Chris gets well under this delivery against Australia during the New Zealand centenary season in 1995.

played in New Zealand were suspected of having been fixed. One had been the final one-dayer against Pakistan of the 1993–94 season, but in truth Chris had not noticed anything untoward in that match. But this Napier game was different. Chris scored a quickfire 25 to help Stephen Fleming overhaul a very modest Indian score. It was New Zealand's first one-day victory in 17 matches and 10 months.

The Kiwis lost narrowly to Australia and had to beat South Africa to get into the final of their own Centennial tournament. It appeared that the host could miss the birthday party — but the Kiwis played well, Greatbatch striking out in customary fashion and Chris scoring a brutal 33 in only 30 balls before being caught brilliantly by a diving Gary Kirsten on the cover boundary. Then Gavin Larsen and Justin Vaughan garotted the Africans with their bowling. It was a rousing victory. It was also the only highlight of New Zealand cricket's anniversary.

Apart from the suspensions of the three dope smokers, and Chris Pringle for undetailed misdemeanours, cricket had numerous crises during the festivities. Howarth quit and Su'a played for New Zealand while serving a ban from his province for abusing an umpire. There were also the performances on the field — the Kiwis suffered their worst-ever test defeat at the Basin Reserve against the West Indies.

After that victory over South Africa, the Kiwis returned to the losing habit. Australia easily won the final. Then New Zealand lost both the centenary test (against South Africa), and their first home test match (and series) to Sri Lanka. It had been a grand mal failure. Not only did they lose but the ill-discipline on the field of some of the players pushed the very limits of sportsmanship. Unfortunately the captain was one of those players.

Chris believes that Ken Rutherford's attitude to others is a hangover from the traumatic beginning of his test career in the West Indies. So damaging was that first tour in 1985 that Rutherford never seemed to achieve what he was capable of, because he clearly had talent.

Chris had missed these tests with a niggling side strain. Coming back from a major injury is not always about the repair of the affected part. Often minor injuries will occur as a player compensates for the main problem, particularly within the thousands of torques and strains of a fast-bowling action. He couldn't have maintained the quality or the quantity of bowling required for five days of international cricket. Playing as a batsman was not an option. The New Zealand middle order was fairly established and Chris averaged just 20 with the bat in test cricket.

Instead Chris continued to work on remodelling his action. He used video footage and the advice of his father and former test captain John Parker to attempt to add to his wicket-taking arsenal. It was very much like a golfer tinkering with his swing. At first it felt foreign and awkward, but Chris was determined to hone his technique. Chris would try out the action in the coda of this disastrous season — three matches against Sri Lanka. In the first he scored a run-a-ball 72 (his highest score yet in one-day internationals) to help win the game but Chris finished the match frustrated at his new bowling style and the lack of control that resulted.

In the second match of the rubber he was involved in a 79-run partnership (Chris scored 42, including four sixes) with his Canterbury team-mate Nathan Astle who, batting as an emergency opener in only his fourth match for New Zealand, scored a match-winning 95. It was an innings that cemented Astle's place in the New Zealand side for as long as he desired. This was the first of many times that these two batted together wearing the Silver Fern. Nathan and Chris were such different personalities yet they became close friends on and off the arena. Chris was a public figure, Nathan was much more private. Chris wore his heart on his sleeve, while Nathan was undemonstrative. But while these two players seemed as different as diamond and coal, in other ways they were carbon copies. They both loved the game, the reaction of the crowd. They both loved hitting the ball cleanly and hard. These two were to dominate New Zealand cricket for the next half-decade.

Two days later this horrible season finished appropriately with a loss. It was April Fool's Day. It summed up the entire summer.

14

Scorching

Three weeks later, Chris smashed his fourth first-class century, for Nottinghamshire against Combined Universities. His century came up in just 65 balls. It was to be the fastest century of the English season, although Chris quietly hoped that someone else would better the feat, as the opponents were not high echelon.

Chris was back to play the 1995 season to make up for the previous year's absence. It was great to be back, to see familiar faces — everybody from the tea-lady, to the groundskeeper, to the old members sunning themselves in the lower tiers of the main stand between gins, and of course his good friends and colleagues on the team. He flatted with David Penn and Graeme Archer in a house that had its very own bar in the lounge, complete with dartboard. At the end of the year they had to get team-mate Kevin 'DIY' Evans to come and re-plaster the wall after a few late night dart games went bad.

He loved being back at Trent Bridge. It was a mutual affection. Many of Notts' stars of the '80s had retired or moved on, and Tim Robinson was the only international among the first team regulars. Chris added a charismatic presence, a vast talent.

The season started well. In the Benson & Hedges Cup, Notts won the first three matches and qualified for the quarter-finals. Chris' bowling seemed to be reaping rewards — he took three vital wickets to beat the holders, Warwickshire, and combined with Andy Pick to help Notts take seven wickets in 13 balls against Durham. Chris bagged four of them.

However, the side strain that had dogged his New Zealand season re-emerged in a bizarre way. While fielding during the first over of the game Chris sneezed, and instantly felt the pain in his intercostal muscle. When the captain called him up to bowl he had to confess that he couldn't. Even though the injury was old, Dion Nash still claims that Chris injured himself sneezing! He was forced to perform only as a batsman for several games. He scored three half-centuries, including a 99 against Leicestershire. But when his muscles had recovered enough to allow him to bowl, any rhythm that he had developed in the early stages of the season was lost. He abandoned his new style of bowling and concentrated on line and length.

Bowlers often talk about 'rhythm'. What they actually mean by that is a combination of three things — a fluid delivery of the ball, running in to the crease with purpose, and the bowler's own self-belief. When fast bowlers 'get rhythm' they turn with confidence at the top of their run-up, they attack the crease, they bowl quickly and accurately and they end up well down the pitch in their follow-through. The body language is as easy to read as a tabloid paper, and journalists often write about bowlers 'having their tail up' and 'finding an extra yard of pace'.

'Rhythm' is a semi-conscious state. The bowler is not concentrating on the mechanics of bowling itself, on the placement of feet or the height of the delivery arm. The bowler does not 'think' but works on instinct, converting hundreds of hours of practice into perfection, or as proximate. He or she is not striving to get the ball to

CAIRNS FAMILY

Good friends. From left, Jenny and Andy Pick and Lynn and Andy Afford are dressed to kill at a '70s party at Chris' Nottingham flat. Renowned for good times, Chris' parties are always well attended.

land on a particular handkerchief-sized area. A bowler with 'rhythm' knows that the ball will land where he or she wants it to, and hence can bowl to a strategic plan. 'Rhythm' is elusive. Only the rarest and greatest bowlers have had it on a permanent basis — bowlers like Alfred Shaw, Richard Hadlee, and Michael Holding. For most bowlers, 'rhythm' comes and goes.

Chris had not found his 'rhythm' for close to two years. For most of the first half of 1995 he had been concentrating primarily on mechanics. As he bowled, a list of instructions would fill his head — feet there, arm high, head still, weight coming 'over the top'. He would also be thinking of his accuracy — 'off stump, short', 'outside off, pitched up'. His mind was cluttered, rather than the clear head that 'rhythm' requires. He often bowled quite well — accurately and incisively — but most of the time he was bowling only medium-pace, and all the time he felt he had another gear, an untapped ability hidden somewhere, waiting to be exposed and exploited.

The English season is constant. Almost every day has a cricketing component. Days off are rare — regular championship and Sunday League games and the necessary training take up the majority of time, and then there are Club and Ground matches. It is during these latter games that the professionals relax a little, try new things, improvise shots or deliveries, fugue on their talent. Playing weaker teams Chris could try out shots. One, the 'benefit sweep', which he later used in county matches, involved spinning completely around when facing a slow bowler and *driving* the ball straight past the terrified wicketkeeper. It was a good environment in which to come back from injury. There was a minimum of pressure.

In early May, Chris played in a Club and Ground match in Lancashire. The night before he had drunk liberally with his housemates and he arrived at the game with a hangover the size of Wales. It was only a university match and so most of the professional bowlers eased up on the dilettante opposition. Chris had decided to reduce his run-up, but this hot morning even a few yards seemed like a marathon for the dehydrated all-rounder. A throbbing head didn't allow for any thoughts about his action either. Chris would just run in and bowl and try to cope until lunch when he could have a rest.

Chris jogged in off only a few paces and let the ball go. It flew off the pitch and thudded hard into the gloves of the wicketkeeper. Everybody looked around surprised — the keeper had really felt the pace of the ball. The slips started to move back a step or two. The amateur batsman started to regret offering to open.

Next ball the same thing — a ball of real pace flashed past the bat of a player several strata below being good enough to defend it. Chris couldn't believe it. In the most unlikely situation, Chris had found his rhythm. His mind was incapable of considering anything other than the self-inflicted pain he was suffering — but through this fog had come his instinct, his raw ability to bowl very fast.

A few days later in the county championship, using this rediscovered rhythm, he bowled superbly against Lancashire at Liverpool, taking 5-64, his first five-wicket bag for 18 months. Chris had emptied his mind, switched to autopilot, and shortened his run-up. He was back.

In July, Chris was given the new ball at Arundel — the most sublime of all English grounds, with a grey castle at one end and oaks and broad cypresses ringing the field. It is a cricketing utopia, a paradise for those who love the game. Sussex was the opposition and the pitch promised to have a bit of bounce and carry. There was also an extra edge to the game. Franklyn Stephenson, the man Chris replaced, was their overseas pro.

The first wicket fell because of the uneven pitch, but after that the strip was blameless. Wicket after wicket fell to the rampant Kiwi through sheer speed and extra bounce. Not even internationals Bill Athey and Alan Wells could cope. By the end of the day Chris had recorded his 'CB', his career-best figures — 16-5-4,47-8.

It could have been more — Sussex's opener, Lenham, had his index finger broken by a Cairns lifter and retired hurt. The last man out was Franklyn Stephenson, who had batted bravely against his old team, after being struck a painful blow on the elbow by his former flatmate.

After Notts had built a large lead, it was Chris' turn again. Keith Newell failed to move his feet then Chris beat Wells with a slower ball. He then bowled three batsmen with fast yorkers. He had now clean-bowled seven batsmen in the two innings. Athey and Stephenson both received what the journalists called 'snorters' that pitched short then came into the body, touching their gloves.

Again Chris' figures could have been even better — Lenham did not bat at all in the second innings. He had taken 7-36. Chris' match analysis — 15 for 83 — was not only the best of the entire English season, it was the second best ever recorded by a New Zealander in first-class cricket. Notts won by 10 wickets. A week before Sussex had beaten the touring West Indians.

That month Chris attended a six-a-side tournament held at a stately home in Cambridgeshire. There were numerous celebrities, all of differing abilities — Gary

Lineker the English footballer was there, as was 'Coronation Street's' Geoffrey Hughes — and a number of enthusiastic amateurs. Sprinkled between the teams were professional cricketers. They never played too hard in these matches. Chris would play a few lavish shots and bowl one or two fast but harmless bowls just far enough away from the batsman to cause panic but no danger. The accent was on enjoyment.

Playing in the host's team Chris bowled a shorter delivery to Rory Bremner, the BBC comedian. It wasn't in truth a very quick ball but it struck the comic on the wrist and broke it. Ever the wit, when the fracture was diagnosed, Bremner announced his availability for the English side: 'After all, now I can't bat or field. I should fit right in!' In spite of the pain (unintentionally inflicted) it had been a hilarious incident and was the talk of the event.

At the end of the day, Chris was relaxing with the organiser, Charles Spencer, who owned Althorp House, where the festival had taken place, and where he and his sister Diana had grown up in the days before princes and paparazzi.

Charles is a cricket nut, a nagging off-spinner and compact batsman. He is also an extremely generous host, and when he inquired where Chris and Ruth were lodged demanded that the couple come and stay at the manor. They couldn't refuse and spent the night talking easily with Earl Spencer, before the Kiwis retired to a room of absurd plushness and centuries-old furniture.

It was an odd friendship that developed between Chris and Charles, the man from a classless society and a man from peerages and Debrett's. But these two people from polar backgrounds shared a passion for the same sport.

They were to share something else much more tragic. In 1997 Princess Diana was killed in Paris. Chris knew that beneath the public face of Charles Spencer, behind every word of his eulogy, was the simple fact of a brother who had lost a sister. Chris knew that pain and contacted Charles.

The quick bowling continued in the next matches against Surrey (a loss) and then back at Trent Bridge against Yorkshire (a win). The shortened, 15-m run-up gave Chris much more control than he'd previously enjoyed, without any loss of pace. With the amount of cricket played in England the shorter run-up would help Chris preserve his body. It was all about economy of movement, a lesson that Hadlee had taught when he had truncated his approach in the early '80s.

Chris continued his batting form too. For just under three months, from the middle of May to the start of August, Chris did not record a single-figure score in first-class cricket. He was frustrated to have had so many starts but so few big totals. In the Sunday League he could hit mightily — he smote Surrey for 69 off 39 balls — but berated himself for his lack of concentration when batting in the longer game. The press may have declared him the best all-rounder in England, but for Chris cricket has always been about constant improvement.

The game against Yorkshire in late July was notable for two announcements that came over the Trent Bridge tannoy. First the crowd were told of the death of the great Harold Larwood. Larwood had been Notts' fast-bowling genius between the wars. A short man, he nevertheless generated incredible pace — his bowling was measured at 96 mph — but his role as the spearhead of England's 'Bodyline' strategy ended his test career.

The handful of people at Trent Bridge for that game who had seen Larwood in action would have seen Chris Cairns as his inheritor. Appropriately, Chris bowled a

Operating for Notts in 1995, an injury-free Chris Cairns rediscovered his rhythm and bowled genuinely fast throughout the season.

vicious spell of short bowling to an Australian, Yorkshire's overseas pro, Michael Bevan, who never looked comfortable and holed out meekly to left-armer Jimmy Hindson at the other end. Chris took six wickets that game, but his presence infused the Yorkshire innings with panic. It was old-fashioned fast-bowling intimidation. Harold Larwood would have been proud. Trent Bridge maintained a minute of silent reverence when Larwood's passing was announced.

Another announcement was greeted with a loud cheer. Chris Lewis' contract had been cancelled and he could leave directly on a free transfer. The crowd clearly considered him overpaid and underperformed. As Lewis left he claimed that he was 'opposed because I didn't drink, and opposed for wearing certain clothes'. It was yet another mystery from this mercurial character. Vic Marks called him 'an enigma without variation'.

At times — like when he averaged 58 in 1994, when he scored 247 against Durham or when he took six wickets against Northants in 1993, Lewis had seemed worth the great sums he received every week. Perhaps that is why the Notts faithful cheered — they had seen enough to know that Lewis could have contributed so much more. But Chris Cairns was a little saddened. Lewis had immense talent, and Chris had always got on well with his namesake. Chris was now the only proven impact player in the squad. More responsibility was loaded onto Chris' shoulders.

Lord's always triggered something in Chris. Drama always occurred there. In three visits he had got a golden duck, captained the New Zealand youth team and got a five-wicket bag. This was his theatre of dreams. In August 1995 against Middlesex he walked out to polite applause from the somnolent members shaking their broadsheets and contemplating a refill of their Pimm's. Notts were in deep trouble.

When Chris returned to the pavilion at stumps, a couple of hours later, he had scored an undefeated 104. The international attack of Emburey, Fraser, Johnson and Tufnell had been plundered. Chris had also been untroubled by the fifth bowler as well — Dion Nash. After his heroics at Lord's the previous year, Nash had been signed as Middlesex's overseas player. Dion has often claimed that he had Chris LBW for 60 that day, and with the advantage of several years' hindsight Chris admits that it might indeed have been very close.

There is a rarity about appearances at Lord's that gives a special magic to scoring 100 runs there. There was something so resonant about raising his bat to the modest crowd, as if he was waving at history. Old Father Time waved back and forth in the summer breeze. The applause echoed among the empty stands. It was ghostly, haunting, as if Grace or Hobbs or McCabe or Weekes were occupying the vacant seats, discussing the merits of the innings, comparing it to knocks they had seen or played. Beyond the steep walls of the stadium the noise of evening traffic crawling away from central London could be heard, but on the pitch Chris seemed like he was living in a capsule, a different world. At the game's spiritual home, Chris had made his offering.

The next morning Chris went to his highest score — 115. It was his fifth century and his most satisfying yet. It didn't help Notts change the result unfortunately. They lost with a day to spare. That night the two opposing Kiwis, Nash and Cairns, met for a drink at a pub in Swiss Cottage. Incredibly, although they had played 23 tests and 44 one-dayers between them, the two all-rounders had never played together for New Zealand before. Usually one replaced the other when injury intervened.

They had talked casually at matches but it was over a few pints that these two rivals became friends. Dion admitted that he had spent the first few years of his career solely focused on Chris, focused on being better than him, of taking his place in the New Zealand side. It was only as he had started to carve out his own pieces of cricketing history, culminating in the remarkable performance against the English, that he realised that he didn't need to be Chris Cairns Mark II. Just like the wrestling match in a grubby flat in Riccarton many years earlier, Dion Nash had shaken the monkey off his back. He realised he didn't have to compete *with* Chris. Chris wanted him to do well and respected his immense ability and desire to win. They could compete *alongside* each other and make New Zealand a force in international cricket.

It had been a marvellous summer. Whole months passed by with little rain and most of the lush grass on the ovals of the county circuit was turned into camel-coloured hay. Water tables plummeted. The pitches were parched and dry. Wickets started to come at a premium for most bowlers and the ball sped across the arid outfields. Notts called their outfield 'the vacuum' as once the ball was past the infield it got 'sucked' to the boundary.

In the struggle for Midlands supremacy with Northamptonshire the advantage to batsmen became starkly obvious. Notts batted and scored 558. Late in the afternoon of the second day Northants replied. Chris was given the new ball in his hand and began to bowl very quickly. Some of his Nottingham team-mates swear that that evening was the quickest they ever saw him bowl. There was good bounce and carry on Northampton's hard dry pitch and Chris sent the ball fizzing through to the keeper, Wayne Noon. Tim Robinson gave Chris four slips and a couple of gullies. The ball was moving so quickly that Jimmy Hindson at fourth slip hoped that it didn't get an edge and come flying towards him. But the openers didn't falter.

Eventually the next morning the edge of the bat was hit and the ball flew sharply to Paul Pollard, who took a superb catch. Pollard was standing a full 30m behind the stumps.

Unfortunately that was just about the only joy Notts experienced. The opening partnership had been worth 188. Although Chris kept up the same pace he didn't get another wicket as Northants gathered run after run — 781 in all. Four Notts bowlers recorded centuries, Andy Afford getting 1 for 223. Chris had bowled superbly — 26-4-65-1.

In the second innings Notts were destroyed and, having scored over 500 in their first innings, lost by an innings and 95 runs. Chris was out to yet another leg-spinner, Indian Anil Kumble, who exploited conditions normally associated with the sub-continent rather than the Midlands.

Notts had a terrible end of season. They lost their last six championship games. Chris still managed the occasional defiant gesture — against the holders Warwickshire, he cracked 83 (5 sixes, 8 fours). He hit another five sixes in the Sunday League match that followed the Northants debacle. His 70 came off just 44 balls. He then hit a century against Hampshire in just 75 balls in the same competition.

Nottinghamshire finished mid-table. Chris scored over one thousand runs and averaged over 40. He was also eighth on the bowling averages, his 52 wickets coming at an average of a shade under 20. He had completed the 'modern' double.

Notts were desperate to sign him for further seasons, but Chris was reluctant to sign. He wanted to concentrate on international cricket. Finally Notts offered double what he had been on. It was an offer no one could refuse.

In August, Chris motored down to London for a meeting at Dion Nash's flat in West Hampstead. They were to meet the new coach of New Zealand cricket — Glenn Turner. Turner had signed a one-year contract, refusing longer offers, to step into the vacancy left by Geoff Howarth's sacking. Turner had vast experience and a fathomless knowledge of the game. He'd been at the top of international cricket.

Turner had very strong ideas on how to reconstruct the team after the disaster of the season before and had already actioned them. Ken Rutherford and Andrew Jones were gone from the side. The new New Zealand captain was Lee Germon, who had led Canterbury to three consecutive Shell Cups and a Shell Trophy. He certainly was a good tactician but in other respects it was a brave decision — Germon had played only a single one-day international. He had never played test cricket.

He would also take the gloves from Adam Parore. It certainly wasn't universally accepted that Germon was the best keeper in the country. The incumbent, Parore had broken the world record for not conceding byes in South Africa the year before, and in April had won the Redpath Cup for the most meritorious batting in New Zealand first-class cricket. Chris Cairns certainly considered the athletic Aucklander a sounder glove-man than his own provincial team-mate.

Nevertheless a new-broom mentality was not necessarily a bad thing. There were new players, new energy and ideas within the side, something that always brought with it a sense of optimism and positivity. During the meeting in London, Turner discussed a list of protocols concerning playing philosophy, practice, discipline and relations with sponsors and the media. Chris and Dion agreed with what Turner had sketched out. He wanted a team that would play vibrant exciting cricket. As two of the most vibrant and exciting Kiwi cricketers it sounded tailor-made for the pair.

A few weeks later Chris talked to Stephen Fleming. He was enthusiastic about Turner and said so: 'Finally we've got a coach who is respected around the world.'

15

Grand tour

A tour to India is the hardest and most arduous of all. It is constantly challenging. The simplest things in the Western world can become Herculean labours on the sub-continent. The heat and food are constant worries.

But while touring India is the most exhausting and difficult odyssey in international cricket, it is also the most rewarding. The senses are constantly assaulted — from the smells of the street-life to the heat of the food to the kaleidoscopic colours of the clothes. And even from the comfort of a bus driven from the airport to a three-star hotel, one cannot forget the shock of seeing the profound poverty of the ubiquitous beggars, untouchables and grubby street kids living in the grey area between life and death, human beings who have but one ambition — to be alive at the end of the day.

There is also the status of touring cricketers to consider. There are hundreds of millions of cricket fans in India and these 'giants' from the West are cheered and adored and followed as if they were a dozen-odd gods on a day trip from nirvana. Thousands come to greet their arrival at train stations and airports, sometimes in the middle of the night, just to get a glimpse. They are greeted with municipal receptions and brass bands, with every bugler and trombonist wearing starched white tunics and moustache wax.

Then there are the utterly surprising sights — turreted buildings that rise out of the concrete morass, cows and elephants wandering through the streets, policemen holding hands, black cabs and double-decker buses in the middle of Mumbai and always the beggars, missing any number of limbs.

There is a point where words are not enough to describe India adequately. You have to go there and experience it for yourself.

Chris joined the team in Mumbai. He was feverishly excited about returning to test cricket. Even though he had made his test debut six years earlier, Chris had played only nine tests — out of the 38 that had been played since he began. More important, the English season had restored his self-belief, the belief that he could compete with the very best. This trust in his own innate ability had taken a hammering over the previous years, first with his dropping and then with numerous injuries.

The subcontinent puts you in a strange mental state. Little things that one takes for granted in the Western world are broken, have never worked, or simply don't exist. Little things become big issues and the stress from them accumulates. Little things like drinkable water, getting laundry done, buying something in a shop, taking a taxi or simply crossing the street. It's as if tourists' emotions are heated with a blowtorch. Players sometimes explode.

Danny Morrison remembered Ian Smith belting a wall with his bat over and over again. It was pure frustration. But as hard as it all is, as annoyed and tense and tired as players get, there is the occasional palatial hotel, the odd great night out, or a stunning vista over a city that eases the pressure and makes the frustrations evaporate for a little while.

CAIRNS FAMILY

*Adam Parore, Bryan Young, Matthew Hart, Chris and Stephen Fleming enter into the spirit of the local
dress on a social committee outing in Bangalore, India.*

In between all this madness there's international cricket to be played.

After a couple of warm-up games the team moved to Bangalore for the first test.
The game became an essay on the difficulty of an Indian tour. The heat was extreme,
local umpires seemed to have different interpretations of the phrase 'benefit of the
doubt', and the pitch was desiccated. On the first day, puffs of dust rose from the
wicket when bowlers delivered the ball, and it took spin from the first hour. Even
allowing for the conditions, New Zealand batted poorly, Chris falling to yet another
spinner — Raju — who moved the ball away.

Only Lee Germon showed any stickability. Germon had a solid first game, looking
competent behind the stumps, though his captaincy manner grated. His body
language was very graphic in displaying what he was feeling and he would talk down
to team-mates. He didn't endear himself to players who had been involved with test
cricket a lot longer. Chris knew Germon's manner, having played under his captaincy
more often than anyone else, but he wondered what the older heads would think of a
skipper, yet to earn his spurs, acting in such a way.

The Kiwis seemed like they were on a hiding to nothing when they bowled. At one
stage, with Kambli and Azharuddin well set, India were 211 for 4. Then Dion Nash took
the wicket of Kambli and Chris fired up. Having earlier 'dismissed' Azha off a no-ball,
he bowled the Indian skipper, then tore through the lower order. In 22 balls he had
figures of 4 for 8. Unfortunately, the New Zealand top order collapsed in a similar way,
and Chris and Stephen Fleming were batting before stumps on the same day. The next
morning, the two set about building a defendable total, but in just the second over

Javagal Srinath, the fastest Indian bowler, and always a handful when he was fresh, took the inside edge of Chris' bat. The ball ricocheted onto the stumps. Chris had scored just 23, and India easily attained the target New Zealand set to go 1–0 up in the series.

New Zealand's performance had been inept but the ineptitude of the game's administrators affected the rest of the test series. Arriving in Madras, on the coast, New Zealand were greeted by cloudbursts of Old Testament proportions. The Indian and New Zealand Cricket Associations had agreed to a tour at the height of the monsoon season.

India batted on a shortened first day, but on the second day the team discovered most of the M.A. Chidambaram Stadium under water after overnight rain. Then, as the players began epic games of Monopoly (which Chris remembers for the under-handed deals Martin Crowe would conjure up) or started on the biggest tomes in the team library, the ground staff started mopping up — legions of women with rags and buckets coaxing water from the sodden ground.

The ground would be dry by the end of the day, then, when they returned to the hotel and night again encroached, they would hear the downpour begin, and the rigmarole would be repeated all over again the next day. It seemed an endless and futile process, but incredibly on the fourth day a few more overs were possible — Chris recorded the magnificently economical figures of 16-1-18-1.

During the wet tour of India in 1995, Monopoly became the staple pastime.

It wasn't always easy even to get to the game — one morning the team bus was bogged in the muddy streets near the stadium and was pulled out by the police.

A washout like this test is incredibly frustrating, which simply adds to the day-to-day vexations of being in India. The team start to go stir crazy. Emotions are frayed to breaking point. There were signs of this cabin fever in Madras. Nash and Greatbatch clashed at net practice one morning, while Martin Crowe was angry at ill-judged comments Glenn Turner had made about the 1992 World Cup to a magazine. Turner was certainly the initial media contact for the team, as the team protocol had established. But to have commented in a disparaging way about the captaincy of *the* senior member of the tour party seemed to suggest that while Turner was a master of tactics he certainly wasn't a master of tact.

At Hyderabad, for a tour match against a Young India XI, the New Zealanders were presented with substandard practice facilities, and a crusty pitch that made batting awkward and quite dangerous, particularly against seamers. This was another stress. The Bunsen burner had been turned up a little more. Even getting an after-match beer in Hyderabad was difficult — Andhra Pradesh is a dry state and each member of the Kiwi team had to apply for an individual liquor licence. Unfortunately, the only alcohol available was some appalling local beer that could have successfully powered small mopeds.

There was more rain at Cuttack for the final test. Drizzle shortened the first day, but there was just time for Chris to produce one of the highlights of his career, one of the two best balls he has ever bowled.

Chris considers Sachin Tendulkar as the greatest batsman of recent times. In 1995 the little master was a batsman at the peak of his powers. But when he was on 2 he received a yorker-length ball from Chris that angled in towards leg stump. Tendulkar played for the yorker but was too slow. He scraped his bat across his popping crease but the willow touched no leather. It needn't have mattered as Tendulkar had got the wrong line anyway. The ball had swung slightly, just a bat's width, away towards slips. The first piece of wood that the ball hit was the off stump. Tendulkar had been beaten for line, length and pace — any one of which would have been enough. It was a Doomsday ball, a ball surely no player could defend. Don Cameron, of the *New Zealand Herald*, called that one moment the highlight of his year. Chris had mastered the master.

After this peak there was no more cricket until late in the fourth day. It was Madras all over again. Every day would dawn brightly, but find the ground soggy and unsuitable because of overnight rain. The team would wait in vain in the concrete wasteland of the stadium to see if the drying process worked. It was like groundhog day. And all the while the chances of New Zealand levelling the test series were falling.

Roger Twose finally got to bat for the first time on his tenth day of test cricket. Later that day, Chris faced his old nemesis Narendra Hirwani on a comeback to test cricket. Hirwani had seemed a mystery to Chris eight years earlier but, now, Chris could read the leg-spinner easily. The main problem was that he bowled so slowly that timing the ball well was virtually impossible. In one of the final actions of this mockery of a test Hirwani took Chris' wicket.

The journey to Cuttack airport threw up one more of India's stresses — random violence. A riot had begun on the main road after a fatal accident and several passing buses had been upturned and burned. The only way to get the team to the airport was a convoy of taxis following a detour through tiny villages along back roads. The cabs sped along dusty tracks with New Zealand cricketers crammed in the back of each, worrying about the driver's reaction time and the quality of the brakes. Chris was even more nervous when the cars passed a gutted bus set alight by rampaging locals.

The squad eventually arrived safely in Jamshedpur for the start of a six-match limited-over series. These games were to be played early (9 a.m.), on small ovals, which were generally wide square of the wicket, but short lengthwise — Chris couldn't have designed them better for his favoured shots. The crowd seemed very close — occasionally too close, as objects were sometimes thrown at boundary riders. Huge fences of the kind that circled English football grounds for many years ringed the field. These fences, and the semi-automatics carried by the police, would hopefully stop any crowd invasion!

Crowe and Fleming batted brilliantly to win the first match, but on a dicey pitch in Amritsar New Zealand were well beaten. The third match at the resort of Goa was rained off, which at least allowed the tourists some R and R. The beach was fantastic, the seafood marvellous and several of the players hired scooters from the hotel staff and raced them through the villages. Nathan

Nathan Astle (front) and Dion Nash on hired scooters during an hilarious escapade around the streets of Goa in 1995. These two players would be Chris' first choices in any New Zealand side he played in.   CAIRNS FAMILY

Astle almost careered off into a small store when he was trying to change gear and had to switch to an automatic!

That night, after the resort had put on some entertainment, several members of the squad, including Chris, went for a naked midnight swim in the sea — that was great until someone mentioned sharks! The swim party ended abruptly.

Goa was just the kind of carefree time that made all the hardship and problems of India seem worth it.

Pune is a small 'town' of two million or so souls. There is nothing particularly remarkable about it, but it will always remain a place Chris remembers fondly. It was at Pune that he finally displayed the ability that most people suspected he had.

Whenever Chris walked to the wicket in India, the excitable crowd would chant 'sixer, sixer'. His reputation as a hitter is well known, and there is nothing the Indian throngs enjoy more than a ball being sent into orbit.

At Pune they were chanting away when Chris came to the crease with the Kiwis in crisis — over half the overs gone and just 75 runs on the board. The top order had been hamstrung by the morning dew on the pitch which was a factor throughout the series.

The Kiwis had two county professionals at the wicket — Roger Twose was at the other end — and they started to collect runs. Twose took a supporting role, giving Chris the strike consistently, allowing him to face the majority of balls. Chris began to hit cleanly and powerfully. He hit 10 fours and four sixes in an unbridled exhibition of raw power. Just as he had done for Canterbury and Notts he was now doing for his country. He was finally out in the second-to-last over for 103 scored from just 87 balls. It was New Zealand's fastest-ever one-day century. Twose and Cairns broke the partnership record for the fifth wicket against all countries. They had scored 145 runs together.

In between innings, Turner came to Chris and said simply, 'If you get four wickets then you've had a good day.' It was a classic piece of understatement, a typical prosaic comment from a man who seemed allergic to compliments. But Chris knew that the coach was not one to give out praise and, after all, as an all-rounder, it was always good to have one refocus on the other side of his game.

So Chris went out and bowled 10-0-37-3 to finish the most complete all-round performance ever in New Zealand's one-day history. Unfortunately, it was on the losing side. The Indians scored at a great clip and won with breathing space. Chris' Man of the Match award was no real consolation, as his belief has always been that great performances occur when your team wins.

Chris didn't mind that Turner was not the type of man to offer his charges any 'warm fuzzies', or as Turner called it 'massaging egos', but Chris thought his style was archaic, straight from the flat-cap, Bovril days of sport. All he was after was constructive, objective feedback. A coach should seek to get the best skill from a player. That is the skill of a great coach, and if praise is a way to achieve that then a good coach or manager should volunteer something of himself. Turner, however, believed the player should adapt to his ways and stuck to his dour manner.

Turner had been seeking to change Chris' batting stance. Chris, always seeking innovation to improve his game, was experimenting with a Jessop-like crouch. His theory was that he could see the length of the ball better if his eye-line was low. Turner argued that that was flawed — Chris' head would not be still. Yet Chris had used the 'crouch' throughout the Pune ton.

Before the next match at Nagpur, there was an informal team discussion on what had gone wrong with the top order. For the first time on tour there was a frank and open debate about tactics. Ideas were bandied about. Even the quieter members of the side had their say. It provided a blueprint for how a squad could share ideas and criticisms in a positive way. It was a cricketing brainstorm that was to have enviable results.

The result was one of the greatest batting displays produced by New Zealand. The only shame was that it occurred far away from the New Zealand public, who deserved to see such dominance. Nathan Astle scored a maiden century, Crowe and Fleming hit half-centuries, Greatbatch smashed a quick 38 to get the ball rolling.

New Zealand cruised past 300 and for a while it seemed that the world record score for a one-day match (364) could be a reality. Indeed that record should have fallen — Chris was caught by Manjrekar for 14, right on the boundary, and television replays clearly showed that he had stepped on the rope. Twose, batting at the other end, had also seen Manjrekar muff the catch and proceeded to argue with the umpire. Chris remained at the crease. Both Kiwis were eventually reported to the match referee for their actions.

The sheer fact was there was enough doubt (and no doubt at all for the home

Dion Nash (left) and Chris enjoy refreshments with some locals in Goa.

viewers) that Manjrekar had conceded six runs, instead of taking the catch, and that the umpire or even Sanjay Manjrekar himself should have reversed the initial decision. In the long term it didn't matter — New Zealand made 348 and won very easily, but it soured the relationship between the two teams. The heat was rising.

While that incident was unfortunate, the unpredictable and tragic side of India arose again. During the game, with the 30,000-strong crowd swirling and surging, a wall collapsed at the back of the stadium and several cricket fans were crushed to death. An incident like this put troubles on the cricket field into perspective.

The series was 2–2 with a game to play and the team returned to Mumbai for the last match.

By the denouement of the India tour, the management team of Turner, Mark Plummer the physio, Lee Germon and Gren Alabaster had become quite pedantic about their interpretations of the protocol that the players had agreed to back in June. Yet there had been no return to the laissez-faire attitude of South Africa. Chris felt particularly sorry for Plums, the physio. He was a good bloke, reluctantly forced to be in the management bloc. There were no senior players in the management team, only Lee Germon, a straight-out-of-the-packet captain, a person still trying to justify his own left-field selection. It is to be lamented that not one of Crowe, Greatbatch, Larsen or Morrison was included in this steering committee.

Enforcement of the code of conduct on tour had been increasingly pernickety. Earlier in the tour, Parore had been reprimanded for throwing his bat in the dressing room after being dismissed for 96. It was an expression of annoyance but it hadn't happened in public — to be fined for that seemed officious. Then there were the constant petty struggles about transport, practice facilities and appearance.

Hair was a vexed issue. As well as being contentious in India, in October, two Sunday paper columnists in New Zealand had criticised the coiffure of several players. Doull had sported a mohawk then a shaved head, while Shane Thomson and Chris had both grown their hair long over the winter. Chris wore a headband to hold his hair in place as he bowled. Other players were experimenting with facial hair. One of the critics, Bob South, launched an extraordinary attack on the lack of 'discipline' of the team demonstrated by these hairstyles. He asked, 'Why is Chris Cairns' hair so darn long? . . . Why must he look like one of the Three Stooges? And while on the subject of hair, why is Shane Thomson trying to imitate General Custer . . . ?'

South then proceeded to hold up Babe Ruth as a disciplined sporting icon who never had long hair — ignoring the fact that the Slugger was one of the most famous boors in the history of sport, consistently gluttonous, lecherous and drunk.

South also ignored the fact that some of the greatest sportsmen have had interesting follicle fashion — including Johan Cruyff, John McEnroe, and the great cricketer W.G. Grace, who wore a voluminous beard. And Chris didn't seem impeded in any way by the length of his hair — he had performed Samson-like feats on tour.

The other critic was none other than Lance Cairns himself, who suggested his son get a haircut. But what else are fathers for?

In truth, the management was not so concerned about hair length — that would have been hypocritical, as Glenn Turner had sported some pretty feral hair in the '70s, and Gren Alabaster was one of the last international sportsmen to wear the 'comb-over' style without irony. But some players felt that the experience had taken on a boot-camp mentality.

However, there was just one more match to go and then home. The team were excited being back in Mumbai. There was no more domestic travel across the country to endure. Two nights before the last one-day match, Trans World, the television company, hosted a private poolside barbecue. It was part-wake, part-celebration, as the TV people had travelled around with the team and got on well with the players. This was a 'thanks' for all the co-operation.

Later that evening the coach and captain, who had dined together elsewhere, turned up to see several of the players in high spirits. They were joking and horse-playing. Later still a group of players went out to a nightclub, but they knew the magnitude of what lay ahead in two days' time — the series decider.

At breakfast, Lee Germon ran around zealously and comically like Inspector Clouseau, trying to discover who was out late. Germon wanted to teach the players 'a lesson'. It was draconian. The players had not transgressed any rules — the code of conduct simply said that alcohol consumption was to be at 'a level appropriate to an athlete', and nobody had been absolutely hammered. There was no curfew.

Practice was at 8.30 a.m. and the team were all present and correct the next morning. Then the team were split into two — effectively those who had early nights, and those who had been out until the wee smalls. It was heavy-handed, to split a squad into two — the 'bad boys' and 'good boys', but this didn't bother Chris. What really irked him was the fact that Germon's detective work had been flawed. Dion Nash and Gavin Larsen, who had both been out, were in the 'good boys' group, who were to have a net, while a couple of innocents were in the punishment detail — who were to have extra fitness work, to 'sweat the alcohol out of their system'.

Chris was in the latter group. Perhaps Germon was trying to impose some kind of puritan morality on the squad like some overbearing head prefect, or perhaps this was a power struggle, with Turner trying to take control even of the social aspects of the tour as well.

Whatever bizarre logic they were operating by, Chris saw it as deliberate, personal and unfair — these men in their mid to late-20s were being treated like errant fourth-formers who had been caught smoking behind the bike sheds. Then, doing a set of shuttle runs, Chris felt a pain in his hamstring. Chris admits that he got petulant. During the fielding exercises he childishly tried to throw a ball to Germon with all his brute force, to make him feel his wrath through the keeper's gloves. Then he felt another twinge. That was the stone end. He was not going to risk a major injury. Seething, Chris announced that he was injured, grabbed an ice pack and a cab and went back to the hotel.

All day Chris iced his hamstring. He wanted to be involved in the last game desperately and decided to play anyway because of the importance of the match. Later that night he was called into Alabaster's room. The management team began speaking about Chris in the third person as if he wasn't in the room. It was some sort of twisted inquisition. Turner was looking directly at Germon saying things like, 'Let's review the facts, Cairns was at the party last night . . . and he left the practice without permission . . . ' It was surreal and patronising in the extreme.

When he was finally asked a direct question, about his availability, Chris snapped. He replied: 'I'm injured and not available to play for you, Turner,' and stormed from the room.

In the end, at the end of a long, stressful tour, a gruelling tour, Chris was exhausted. He had made a couple of mistakes that day — he should not have left the practice for one. By refusing to play for Turner he had forgotten who he should have played for — his team-mates.

He had played through pain before and he would play through pain again. He should have gritted his teeth and fought for the series alongside his mates. He vented his anger and made an irrational decision, which he regrets. It disappointed some of his team-mates and was to colour the media's opinion of Chris for several years.

But the Mumbai incident was still far from over. In Chris' absence, management decided to fine Chris for absenting himself from the practice. Gren Alabaster came to Chris' room and advised him of the record $2000 penalty. Chris exploded. He could not believe the trivial, inequitable nature of the whole day. Weeks of frustration and suppressed anger spewed out in an eruption of expletives and flying pillows.

The numerous stresses of everyday India, the tragedy at Nagpur, the pathetic punishments and the frustration of the test series all mixed with one overriding thing. He didn't think the New Zealand coach was a particularly nice human being.

16

First century and second cup

Chris Cairns and Glenn Turner were polar opposites. Chris was a *bon vivant*, a hedonist and an ebullient character. Turner was quite dour. Turner was an introvert, Cairns was an extrovert. Turner was puritan, Cairns cavalier. Turner hid his emotions, Chris expressed them. Turner was a batsman, Cairns a bowler. Turner was a cynic with a dark, arid sense of humour, Chris was an optimist who enjoyed scatological comedy. Chris was transparent, Turner was opaque.

They were also from very different generations. Chris had a sense that Glenn Turner never understood the young men of the New Zealand team. That showed blatantly in the team talk before the last match in India. Turner tried some 'reverse psychology' on the team, saying that the team were obviously going to lose, as that's what New Zealand teams usually did, but that they should try not to lose badly.

Glenn Turner.   PHOTOSPORT

Crowe and Cairns, both out for the match, couldn't believe their ears. Here was a coach who could not motivate positively because of some psychological block, choosing abuse and negativity as stirring words of encouragement. It was extraordinarily inept and New Zealand *did* lose badly.

There was no break from cricket on the team's return to New Zealand. Pakistan had arrived for a one-off test. There were also no selectorial repercussions for Chris and he was back in the side for the Lancaster Park test. New Zealand bowled poorly to begin with — openers Ramiz Raja and Aamer Sohail put on 135, at better than a run a minute. It was the first time in tests that Lee Germon showed some fallibility behind the stumps.

Chris returned just before lunch to take the first three wickets and begin a middle-order implosion. Pakistan were all out for just 208. Then Chris top-scored with 76 (10 fours, 1 six). New Zealand constructed a small lead but Pakistan batted very well in reply. In the last innings, Mushtaq spun Pakistan to victory, in the process picking up Chris' wicket when he miscued a drive. It was the tenth time a leg-spinner had got him out in 22 innings.

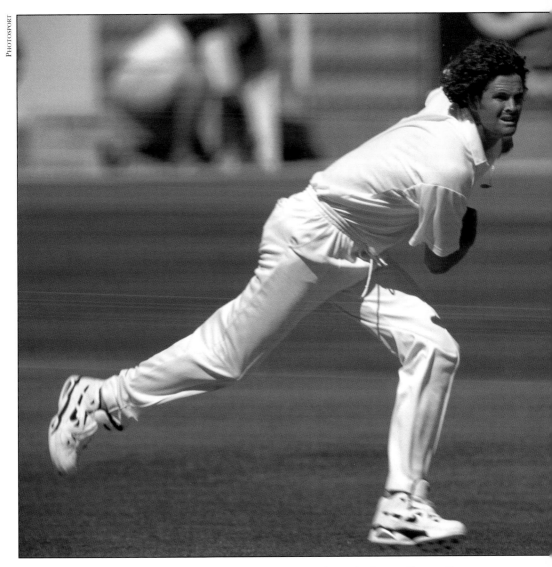

PHOTOSPORT

Chris picked up a seven-wicket haul and a half-century against Pakistan in the one-off test at Lancaster Park in 1995. New Zealand, however, finally succumbed to the wily spin-bowling of Mushtaq.

In spite of this failure, he had been one of the success stories of the match with a good half-century and seven wickets.

His form in the one-day series that followed was patchy. At Carisbrook, New Zealand batted poorly, chasing a very modest target. In the second match, Adam Parore and Chris batted together for 23 overs for a 95-run partnership that, incredibly, did not feature a single boundary. Gavin Larsen produced heroics to win the match on the second to last ball. Chris was a little anonymous in the next two matches, which were shared and, with the World Cup just two months away, the Kiwis had drawn a series 2–2 with the holders.

There is no doubt that Chris Doig is a significant reason for Chris Cairns still playing cricket for New Zealand to this day. Doig was the new head of New Zealand Cricket, an exuberant personality and opera singer. Doig and Turner had met for a debrief after the Indian tour. Turner mentioned Chris' moments of fury (Turner had also raised Chris' ire when he refused to send water out to him, when Chris was bowling in the Cuttack test, in 30-degree heat) and Doig stated his position — that Chris Cairns was to spearhead the marketing campaign for New Zealand cricket. He was the country's most exciting cricketer, a crowd-puller. He was good-looking, and even though his long tresses may have not been to everyone's taste they started earning him some lucrative work as a face for various sponsors, and he was a regular in the glossy women's magazines.

Without a supporter like Doig at the top of the New Zealand Cricket hierarchy, Chris may have been a victim because Turner wasn't simply coach, he was chairman of selectors as well. With his desire to control media aspects of the New Zealand side and his influence over a fledgling captain, it is clear that a great deal of power was centred in one individual.

Doig was enthusiastic on the team's return and extremely chipper. New Zealand cricket had turned the corner, he claimed in his rumbling bass-baritone. Chris liked Doig instantly, enjoyed his positivity, his expressions of emotion, his garrulousness. He had ideas to advance cricket throughout the country.

Unfortunately the advance stumbled when Martin Crowe made a shock announcement in January. He announced his retirement from all cricket. He was just 32 years old. His knee had been giving him pain throughout the one-day series in India and he had been unavailable for the finale and the games against Pakistan on the team's return. He had been noticeably hampered in the field as well, though his batting didn't seem to have suffered — he'd scored three centuries on the Indian tour.

Back home, Crowe and his lawyer and great friend David Howman had had a summit with Glenn Turner and Chris Doig to work out a way that he could sustain his career. He wanted to play the World Cup in February, and return to the West Indies in March. Maybe if he babied the limb he could extend his career for several years — the Commonwealth Games? An elusive century against South Africa?

He needed the knee to heal, which required six weeks. The World Cup squad was to be announced in four. He asked for dispensation. Crowe also wanted to concentrate his energies on test matches. The short form of the game, with its tight runs and spread field, put a huge strain on his knee. If he could play just test cricket and then the World Cup, if Turner could grant a little indulgence to the country's supreme batting talent, then his shelf-life could be prolonged indefinitely.

But 'indulgence' is not part of Turner's vocabulary. He said no. Crowe would have to be available for all cricket, within a month.

Faced with this inflexibility Crowe decided to retire instantly, in what Chris thinks was a reflexive decision. (Turner in *Lifting the Covers* suggests that Crowe may not even have been selected, which seems extraordinary.)

Turner's obstinacy undoubtedly cost New Zealand cricket and the entire cricket world. If Glenn Turner had cut Martin Crowe slack in late 1995 Crowe could have played in the 1999 World Cup semi-final at Old Trafford, not just the tournament three years earlier. If Andy Caddick is New Zealand cricket's great 'what might have been', Martin Crowe's later career is the great 'what should have been'.

The news affected Chris greatly. Martin Crowe was a good friend. Chris trusted Crowe's judgement and listened readily to the advice he offered. There was a bond between talents, an understanding of the mental side of international cricket. Crowe could have been a mentor to the coterie of young batsmen — Fleming, Astle, McMillan and Cairns. Chris would often simply sit and watch the master batting in the nets, studying this poem with pads, learning from Crowe's footwork, strokes, demeanour. He was a backbone for an inexperienced side. Turner was an exceptional technical coach in his own way, but Martin Crowe was the doyen of the cerebral challenges of test cricket. His brilliant batting was lost to the world, but he was to return later at the lowest point of Chris' career, to drag him from the depths.

There was another top-level meeting in December that carried something extraordinarily sinister about it. Chris Doig met with Turner and Gren Alabaster and a psychologist to discuss Chris and the management team's handling of him. Turner had earlier written to Doig, 'For Chris [Cairns] to face up to the stresses and strains of international cricket is like asking an alcoholic to work in a hotel. He needs to be successful to maintain stability, in a game which will never provide a stable environment.' The coach had clearly made his diagnosis. The principal all-rounder in his squad was mentally disturbed, unstable.

Doig approached Chris with this appraisal. Chris couldn't believe an assessment had been made about him in his absence. He was angry and deeply hurt by Turner's view of him, but his reply to Doig was prompt and direct: 'If you organise the psychologist, I'll be there as long as Turner comes as well.' The meeting never took place.

A midweek crowd of over 18,000 in festive mood, with amber refreshments stacked, and sunscreen splashed liberally, gathered at Lancaster Park in mid-January. There were Mexican waves and signs saying 'Don't focus on us, we're on sick leave'. There were a bunch of guys from Blenheim wearing overalls and floppy-haired wigs. When they turned around the letters drawn on their backs spelt CHRIS CAIRNS IS GOD.

It was the biggest crowd in the history of the Shell Cup and the best cricket crowd at Lancaster Park in a decade. The Christchurch crowd was in a celebratory mood. It was there to witness the completion of the 'perfect' season. In the 1995-96 Shell Cup competition, Canterbury won all 12 matches, including the final.

It wasn't just the fact that they won the matches — they were 'matches' in name only. The team were nicknamed the Lancaster Bombers and they carpet-bombed their opposition. There were some close calls — they tied scores with Auckland but won on a countback, and Chris took two wickets in the last over to beat Wellington by just 2 runs — but the dominance they had in the final, which they won by 116 runs, was more typical.

In the Shell Cup averages, Canterbury batsmen held four of the top five positions, in the bowling list Cantabrians had two of the top five spots. When you consider that the squad contained 10 New Zealand reps — Cairns, Astle, Owens, Priest, Germon, Fleming, Harris, Hartland, Craig McMillan and Geoff Allott — one could even suggest that this was the best provincial team ever assembled.

Chris scored 93 on Boxing Day against Otago then scored 59 against ND in front of a raucous New Year's Day crowd at Mt Maunganui. In between he was Man of the Match against Central Districts at Timaru when he smashed 69, then took 5-23, his best bowling figures yet at Cup level. In the semi-final, Chris took four wickets and, while he had a relatively quiet final, it didn't affect Canterbury, who scored a Shell Cup record 329 runs in their 50 overs.

The black Nike boots Chris wore in the 1995–96 Shell Cup final. It was a cheap day out for Nike — for all the publicity the company received they paid Chris' $200 fine. PHOTOSPORT

There was a sour note, however. Chris had worn his sponsor's footwear — Nike boots — in the match. They were comfortable, sleek and very black. Chris had no idea he was breaching Shell Cup rules, which required white shoes, until New Zealand Cricket fined him and talked about 'ambush marketing'. The media pounced, attacking Chris as if he had sold his sole. One writer, Ray Cairns (no relation) wrote: 'We had one individual placing himself outside the teamness ethic and doing the fingers to the laws of the game — with his feet. It was immature and arrogant . . .' It seemed a bizarre response to a small sartorial error, when a year later NZ Cricket also wanted the players to wear coloured shoes with their one-day uniforms.

New Zealand hadn't won a test since 1994 and were ranked second to bottom on the test rankings list. Zimbabwe were bottom and arrived for a small tour. This wasn't just a warm-up for the World Cup, but a battle for test cricket's wooden spoon.

The first test suffered because of rain. Morrison and Nash were injured so Turner selected a novice bowling attack that consisted of three debutants — Otago's Robert Kennedy, Chris' Boys High companion Geoff Allott and leg-spinner Greg Loveridge, who was destined never to bowl in test cricket when he was injured in New Zealand's first innings. Chris bowled aggressively and took three top-order wickets and the new boys chipped in with one each to have Zimbabwe at 56 for 5, but the middle order hung around tenaciously. Only an aggressive second-innings declaration by Germon breathed any life into the moribund game.

Both teams had chances to win on the last day. When Zimbabwe were on 125 for 2 chasing just 260, it seemed Germon had been overly generous considering the bowling recourses, but the captain turned to the county pros Twose and Cairns to stem the run-flow.

At the crucial moment Chris plucked the wicket of Grant Flower. The chase hesitated and the Africans stonewalled for a draw. For his six wickets in the match, Chris was given the Man of the Match award for the first time in his test career, even though Adam Parore, Andy Flower or even Lee Germon might have had a better claim to the title. Within a week he would win the award without dispute.

In spite of the accolade, Chris was disappointed at his efforts. Having been given the opportunity to bat at his favoured number-six position, he had scored just 14 runs. He had perhaps switched into 'one-day' mode too readily, bristling with aggression rather than playing time. For the second test at Auckland he was determined to build an innings and worked feverishly on his technique in the nets.

The Eden Park wicket was flat but in the first innings four Kiwi wickets were down for 117 when Chris joined Stephen Fleming. Chris started watchfully, waiting for the bad ball — his first four scoring strokes were boundaries — before Zimbabwe, who specialised in negative tactics at that stage in their test development, employed a ring field, forcing the batsmen to go over the top. The New Zealand concept had been to score fast, but even with the new ball in hand Zimbabwe had just a single slip. It was no wonder that test match crowds were disappearing. Chris and Flem enjoyed a disciplined partnership of 99. Then on 57 Chris hit a return catch to leg-spinner Paul Strang when a big score beckoned.

Chris had passed 500 runs in test cricket during that innings and passed another milestone when he had Guy Whittall caught behind in the reply — 50 test wickets. On a docile pitch, Zimbabwe registered a first innings lead, but that was knocked off by a brilliant 214-run opening partnership from Twose and Craig Spearman. A minor collapse followed and a draw seemed to be fast eventuating when Chris walked to the wicket to join Adam Parore. Few who witnessed what happened next will be able to forget it.

Chris had decried the negative tactics of the Africans in the press, so Andy Flower announced sarcastically with Chris' arrival at the wicket that the great Chris Cairns was here to show the poor Zimbabweans how to play attractive cricket.

Zimbabwe again strung a ring field around the square. Placement became irrelevant. Chris was being asked to go over the top. So he did. Chris hit aerial cuts and lofted straight drives. Some bounced before they reached the billboards ringing the field but some soared over the fence. He dropkicked a six over square leg, then stepped to leg and hit a sensational lofted drive directly over extra cover — about 30 metres over — which landed on the roof of the Number 4 Stand. Viv Richards had been the only right-hander to do that previously.

Chris had never timed the ball better. Every shot came from the middle of the bat, and his score rose exponentially. The nervous 90s lasted for just six balls. A single to square leg and he had done it, a maiden test century in just 86 balls with seven sixes and nine fours. He was ecstatic. Here was an innings like a tattoo — an indelible, permanent sign of his ability. Chris was astonished. A test century was something that he never thought

Putting one of nine sixes into the crowd at Eden Park, Chris on the way to his maiden test century against Zimbabwe, 1996. PHOTOSPORT

PHOTOSPORT

Chris acknowledges the crowd after his maiden test hundred against Zimbabwe. The innings gave Chris belief that he could achieve his goal of becoming the world's best all-rounder.

he would achieve. The crowd, on its feet, was astonished too — it had been ready to watch a grim battle of attrition.

It was the second-fastest century in New Zealand test history, behind Bruce Taylor's 83-ball blitz in 1969 at the same ground. It was the ninth-fastest ever in test cricket. And he wasn't finished. In celebration he hit another two sixes and a four before the untiring Heath Streak finally managed to sneak a yorker under his blade.

Chris had hit nine sixes in his 120. In his previous 15 test matches he had hit just three. Only one player in the history of the game, England's Walter Hammond, had hit more sixes in an innings in test cricket (ironically also at Eden Park in 1933). He had breezed past the New Zealand record — seven, by the heroic Bert Sutcliffe at Ellis Park in 1953.

His team-mates congratulated him on his return to the dressing room with whoops and high fives. He received a handshake from everybody. Everybody except the coach.

Chris had not only grabbed a test by the scruff of its neck, he had picked it up off the ground and beaten it to a bloody pulp. He was a headline item on the six o'clock news and on front pages the next day. Chris had given New Zealand a chance of victory but the pitch just seemed to get better and better, and the last day panned out into a dull draw. Chris was inevitably Man of the Match, though there was a negative note to the end of the test — Chris and Adam Parore were reported to the match referee and found guilty of over-appealing.

That night the World Cup squad were announced. Chris Harris had played his way in with his great form for Canterbury and Spearman's test century closed the door on Mark Greatbatch's hopes. No Crowe, Greatbatch or Rutherford meant three of the top five batsmen from 1992 were not in the side. In Chris' mind all three should have been there — all were still capable cricketers.

There were just five survivors from 1992 — Cairns and Harris, Patel, Larsen and Morrison. The real surprise was the inclusion of Robert Kennedy, a player who hadn't even played a Shell Cup match before that season. Turner had detected an ability to bowl accurate 'blockholers' at the end of the innings, though the two tests suggested that he struggled simply to bowl on a consistent line at all. There was no doubt Kennedy had a fair amount of pace but when he bowled 12 wides in a one-day match against Zimbabwe in Napier a few days later it seemed that some of Glenn Turner's chickens were having thoughts of heading for home and doing some serious roosting.

Chris Pringle, who certainly could bowl a 'blockholer', was missing for the second

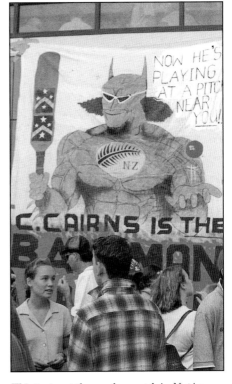

This poster at the one-day match in Napier sums up the fans' reaction to Chris' test century against Zimbabwe. CAIRNS FAMILY

World Cup in succession. Chris thought Pring's selection should have been a certainty. Guile and experience would be needed on the subcontinent, a change of pace compulsory. And Pringle was a big personality, a player who could impose himself on a one-day game. Kennedy was more vulnerable, easier to control. A few of the players were even referred to as Turner's 'puppets' by some of the senior players in the team.

Kennedy played in the Napier match because in the first one-dayer in Auckland a surge of combined pain and panic had shot through Chris' body. While he was batting, he took off for a quick single and felt pain in his calf. Then he essayed a sweep and pulled a groin muscle. Having been injury-free for the best part of a year he was suddenly out of the team and on crutches. The World Cup was mere weeks away.

Chris trained only lightly, but by the time the squad arrived on the subcontinent he knew he would be right for the first game. If the pre-Christmas tour to India had achieved anything it had been to get the squad accustomed to the difficulties of being in Asia, and the cricketing problems of early rises and dew on the grass. This prior acclimatisation certainly seemed to work for the first match — England were sluggish in the field in the morning and with Nathan Astle scoring a century of classic drives and pulls, and others contributing solid efforts (Chris — 36 from 30 balls), England had 239 to win, which always seemed a little beyond them. It was a fantastic start to the tournament.

The Netherlands were the minnow of the group and the Kiwis easily beat them in the next match, at Baroda, where the Indian crowd eagerly cheered the efforts of the

Danny Morrison forgot to bring his hair dryer to India — here Chris improvises.

Dutch amateurs. For the second game in a row, Chris raised his World Cup high score, with a 52 off 38 balls, one of the quickest half-centuries a New Zealander had ever scored in the tournament.

New Zealand were now almost sure-fire certainties for the quarter-finals. They could concentrate on getting themselves prepared for the next round. The next two matches were in Faisalabad in Pakistan. The Kiwis would be resident for 10 long days in a hotel they shared with the South Africans, their next opponents. Faisalabad is a crowded industrial centre with little to recommend it to the visitor. Again the Kiwis started to feel a sense of being imprisoned.

Pakistan also proved to be very different to India. The Pakistanis themselves seemed harder people, less obviously friendly, more suspicious of foreigners. The tournament also had the extra difficulty of being in the Islamic month of Ramadan, when the entire population fasts during the daytime. Not only was the populace less amiable than the Indians, they were also hungry.

New Zealand were taken apart by a clinical South African unit in the next match. The discipline of the South African team clearly impressed Turner. After contact with the regimented South Africans, Turner had the idea of the team rising early. On match days they would have to get up at 7 a.m. for the 9 a.m. kick-off, so it seemed like a good idea to get up very early on the other days as well, to condition and synchronise 'body clocks'. Chris thought that that was sound reasoning that could improve performance. It wasn't about discipline, it was about physiology, and had a logical basis behind it.

Having breakfast together, however, like the Africans did, seemed a little too much like boarding school. Cricket may be called a team game, but in its purest form it is a contest between a bowler and a batsman, individuals — and individuals prepare differently for the contest. These team breakfasts became a source of stress within the New Zealand camp. One morning, after breakfast, when the team were corralled for some fitness work, Gavin Larsen slipped on the dewy grass and damaged a muscle. He would miss the rest of the World Cup. He was livid.

New Zealand easily beat the United Arab Emirates side at Faisalabad, although it was almost a home clash for the Arabians — seven of their number were Pakistan-born. Then the Kiwis moved to Lahore for the final group match against joint hosts Pakistan. It turned out to be almost an exhibition match. Before the match Javed Miandad, in his last World Cup, was presented with an award for being 'the heartbeat of every cricket fan in the world' which was hyperbolic even in Pakistani terms.

The waddling Miandad was easily run out but the Pakistanis managed a grand total — 285. A number of the New Zealanders managed starts but the team fell short. Pakistan had avoided a quarter-final clash with the favourites, Australia. New Zealand would play them instead.

Australia had won the only other World Cup to have been played in the sub-continent in 1987, and had a phenomenal team without any obvious weaknesses. But that night in Madras, New Zealand fielded a team of batting talents with a tail as long as a Manx cat's. Shane Thomson, test centurion, was at 9, Dion Nash, with a test 50 at Lord's under his belt, was at number 11. New Zealand could afford to go for their shots, as they batted throughout the order. Moreover, they could alter their batting order to suit the situation in the match and even who was bowling. With three left-handers in the top order, the Kiwis could effectively 'nullify' Shane Warne, a bowler much more penetrative against right-handers. Three batsmen would be padded up at any one time. However, during the innings, Chris, Nash and Thomson would jokingly muse at the changes in Turner's batting order. They would try to pick the next order, by the alignment of the stars and how many ice creams the nearby vendor had sold.

With an Indian crowd fervently behind them — always prepared to support the underdog — Germon won the toss and New Zealand batted. When the first wicket fell the next name on the scoreboard was Germon. The rumour was that the Aussies had called for a match programme to see what he looked like, as they had never encountered the Kiwi skipper before.

Germon was a 'dispensable' batsman. If he went out early, it wouldn't really matter. He wasn't dismissed and started to middle the ball. When two wickets fell at the other end, Germon was joined by Chris Harris, who was to play the most extraordinary innings, until recent times, that Chris Cairns had ever witnessed. Harry started to hit cleanly and well. Both ends were now swinging. Warne was bullied out of the attack. Bowlers were being shuffled. Mark Taylor was looking stressed, and the Indians were cheering and dancing and letting off fireworks.

Chris, padded up and ready, couldn't believe what he was seeing. Chris Harris was playing carefree cricket, the innings of his life. There was no other cricketer that Chris had played alongside more often than Harry. He knew his game, knew his nervousness, knew his limitations. But here was a batsman playing without limitations. Looking back, this was the perfect situation for Chris Harris. Expectations were low, New Zealand were playing Australia after all, with the situation getting bleaker as each top-order wicket fell.

Chris Harris is a cricketer who puts so much pressure on himself, who winds himself so intently in his responsibilities to the team, that it can affect his play. That is why Chris believes that Harry has not yet performed with the same consistency in test cricket as he has in the abbreviated game. Harry is such a nervy, excitable character that the energy and emotions he expends cannot be sustained over the five days of a test. But put him in a back-to-the-wall struggle, a nothing-to-lose situation like Madras, or a tight run chase, and he delivers. Chris Harris is New Zealand's answer to the little Aussie battler.

Germon was out for 89. The partnership had been worth an incredible 168 runs. And then New Zealand lost a little momentum. Roger Twose was next man in, another left-hander to counter Warne, who had returned. Perhaps, at that point, a straight-hitter like Cairns would have been a better option. Twose struggled for a few balls then Chris miss-hit off Mark Waugh. The constant attack faltered slightly and, instead of passing 300, the New Zealand effort garnered 286 runs. Chris Harris had scored 130 of them.

Against any other team, 286 would have been enough on a ground with inadequate floodlights and with a sea mist slowing the outfield. But Australia had 'Junior' Waugh in top form, grinding on remorselessly to another century, and when pinch-hitter Warne was dropped on the boundary it was obvious that the day wasn't going to be New Zealand's after all. Australia had had to score the second-highest winning target in the history of the World Cup.

One can talk until one is red, white and blue in the face about honourable defeats, but for Chris defeat always stuck in his craw. For the second World Cup in a

PHOTOSPORT

Chris Harris in attacking mode for New Zealand in a one-dayer. Chris has always believed that if 'Harry' played his natural game he would have been a test certainty throughout his career.

row, New Zealand had got so very close to achieving something unprecedented. Chris churned over the events in his head, wishing that he had hit squarer and bowled straighter. He had not bowled well throughout the tournament. He wanted time to reflect on the loss, to examine his batting technique and bowling action. He wanted to go home and relax with his friends and family, and put the defeat in perspective.

Instead there was a week to wait around before exactly the same squad of exhausted men were to fly to the West Indies for a 10-match tour. That week was to be spent at a beach resort called Fisherman's Cove. Chris wanted to relax, drink a few long cool ones and eat some seafood.

17

Paradise razed

It seems incredible that New Zealand Cricket approved such a strenuous few months for their senior players as they did for 1995–96. The team were slated to play 11 tour matches, 23 one-day matches (at least) and eight tests. The squad were asked to travel greater distances than any New Zealand squad previously and had to play cricket in between. The team knew their passport numbers better than their home phone numbers. They travelled close to 70,000 km, all alongside the same essential core of players. Combine that with a pedantic management team and coach and it's not hard to see why some of the players were feeling a bit Fletcher Christian about it all.

Any West Indian tour cannot be considered rest and recreation after the World Cup, not with the bouncers at Sabina Park, the dancing mass of people in the Shell Oil Stand in Antigua, or Lara in front of his home crowd in Port of Spain. There is, however, a conviviality about the touring. The hotels are all good, several of them right on the beach. There are invitations to embassy parties in Trinidad, yacht trips to Mustique, journeys to the Blue Mountains of Jamaica, and nights at reggae clubs throughout the string of islands.

The West Indians themselves are welcoming and knowledgeable people for whom cricket is as attached to their identity as rugby is to New Zealand's and football is to Brazil's. If Brazil loses in the World Cup, or the All Blacks are defeated, there is a palpable sense of mourning throughout the country. It is the same in the West Indies, perhaps greater — the mourning is spread over six associations and 10 nations. West Indians don't expect success, they demand it. That is why every West Indies–Australia match for the last 14 years has been dubbed the unofficial 'World Championship'.

The team had a bizarre three-day journey to the Caribbean. From the 30-degree heat of Madras, the team flew to London, with temperatures in the single digits. The team went to the pubs of Covent Garden and had a relaxed night with a bunch of Antipodeans. The issues that dogged the team were forgotten at the Outback and the Springbok.

At the airport the next day, the plane was delayed several hours. The World Cup Final was being shown on Heathrow's televisions. Chris would come and go from the TV set not wanting to watch, frustrated but excited that the underdogs Sri Lanka performed so mightily to win the Cup.

When the New Zealanders eventually touched down in Jamaica they were confronted by a simple fact. A New Zealand team had not won a test or one-day international in the West Indies in either of their two previous tours.

They were to get a good indication why when they first visited Sabina Park for a practice. When they got to Sabina Park several of the players on their way to the practice nets registered the smell of marijuana, ganja, the sacred weed of the Rastafarian religion. Two groundsmen, wearing the striped tea-cosy hats and smoking a huge doobie, were driving the heavy roller in a very peculiar fashion. They were circling around and around on the block to be used the next day.

The 1996 New Zealand team to the World Cup and West Indies. These two tours did not prove the happiest of times for many of the players.

The Kiwis were in hysterics until they started to notice the method in the madness. The Rastas were 'polishing' the pitch. The strip was like glass, with a shiny veneer. The roller was working like a lino polisher.

The next day when New Zealand went out to bat in a warm-up match, the ball spat off the pitch at a tremendous pace for the first few overs before becoming, as the polish chipped off, a very flat batting strip. The crowd was evidently there to see some head-hunting bouncers and intimidation as an entrée, before settling down to watch some big full-bladed shots as a main course. They weren't to be disappointed.

Sabina Park is always electric, vibrant and often damn intimidating. Astle and Spearman must have felt like Christians heading into the Colosseum. There was soon some blood. Patterson Thompson, touted as the fastest bowler in the West Indies, a player who was so broad he was nearly topographical, hit Astle on the chin. First-drop Germon took guard with bloodstains on the crease line.

Later, as Chris came out to bat, the crowd was baying and yelling, as excitable and hostile as any crowd he'd experienced.

But Chris launched, hitting the quicks out of the attack and then beginning on Jimmy Adams and Viv Richards himself. The Master Blaster must have watched with admiration as shots sailed over the boundary and seared through the off side like tracer bullets. It was breathtaking stuff.

Chris had admired the calypso style for so long and was keen to make his mark in a fashion the locals could relate to. There were no catcalls from the Jamaicans now. It was simply applause, respect and recognition. Chris was eventually out for 107 off 73 balls, and then the Kiwis turned around and destroyed the Invitation XI and won by 207 (!) runs.

The first international, in the cauldron of Sabina, should have been a victory to

Hamish McDouall

Queen's Park Oval, Trinidad, 1996. Scene of New Zealand's first one-day victory over the West Indies in the West Indies.

New Zealand. Dipak Patel and Adam Parore batted brilliantly and pushed the score to 243. The West Indies were 221 for nine but Roger Harper hit 15 runs off the 49th over, bowled by Dion Nash. The match had been burgled. To lose by such a small margin was gutting. Patel compared it to the loss in the semi-final at Eden Park in 1992.

Port of Spain might sound like an exotic place but the truth is that it is a big multi-cultural city, geared for the oil industry. It is the home of the greatest of all cricket writers, C.L.R. James, who wrote *Beyond the Boundary*, a book that examined the politics of cricket and race. For people in Trinidad cricket is that important, part of their psyche — after Lara had passed all records standing in 1994, the main thoroughfare that cuts through the city, with the Catholic cathedral standing proudly at one end, had its name changed from Independence Square — to Brian Lara Square.

New Zealand had two games on consecutive days at Queen's Park Oval — one of the most beautiful grounds in the West Indies, with bush-covered mountains providing the backdrop and huge trees that fill up with spectators during the afternoon sessions ringing the ground. The paying crowd is always active, dancing for most of the day to the steel pan bands. Large women whoop at the big shots and yell 'Give it a lick, maaaan' when the cricket is becalmed. It is noisy, colourful and chaotic and far removed from the gentility of Lord's.

The West Indies posted a good score — 238 — then after Craig Spearman gave the innings some momentum, Stephen Fleming began to play well, pushing easy runs and occasionally showing the Trinidadians his repertoire of strokes. Chris joined him and the two Canterbury lads picked up runs steadily, with the minimum of fuss. The wicket was so slow that Chris didn't call for a helmet even when Ambrose and Walsh came back into the attack. There seemed something inexorable about the partnership but with Chris on 41, and the partnership (92) a record for the fifth wicket against the Windies, Chris was bowled by Jimmy Adams.

Stephen Fleming went on to score his first international century at the 35th attempt. With a ball to spare, New Zealand claimed their first victory in a limited-overs international in the islands. It was a historic moment for both the team and Flem himself and Chris gave the match-winner a massive hug — it had been a truly great innings.

Spirits were sky-high on the bus back to the Hilton hotel. Frivolities were kept in check as everyone knew there was another important game the day after. But then Turner announced that Nash had been dropped for the next game and a few of the senior players went to show solidarity with him to a nearby pub called the Pirate Inn. There were discussions about Turner, and what he was trying to achieve. Chris tried to cheer up Nash and show him support, but Chris soon left for the hotel. Nash and a couple of the 'dirt-trackers', not required to play the next day, stayed on.

After the previous day, the second match was always going to be anti-climactic. A modest target looked positively minuscule when Brian Lara started playing shots. He hit the ball to all points of the compass in front of his joyous home crowd. He hit three sixes, including one straight drive that was still rising when it passed over Chris' head at long on. He cruised to a century and the Scorpion Pan band started playing 'How Great Thou Art'.

Lara is a supremely talented batsman. The debate will rage for many years over who was the best batsman of the late '90s — Lara or Tendulkar — but Chris comes down firmly in the Indian's camp. Lara seemed fallible, his confidence would oscillate, whereas Chris knew he had to be at the top of his game to have any chance at dismissing Tendulkar.

Still when Brian Lara was firing on all cylinders it was compelling, his strokes majestic and clean. It was a privilege to watch.

The next match was on the South American continent — at Georgetown, Guyana. There is a flavour of India about Georgetown — there are Hindu temples dotted around, the highway from the airport to the capital is pockmarked with potholes that could swallow small lorries, and cows amble with impunity across busy roads. Many of the West Indians with Indian surnames are from Guyana — including Kallicharan, Ramadhin and Chanderpaul.

The team were joined there by Dr Justin Vaughan, who had flown in as a reinforcement. His medical skills were soon to be employed. As the team minibus was driving through the filthy pitted streets they witnessed a traffic accident where a young boy cartwheeled over

The Scorpion Pan band can make steel drums come alive and create a unique atmosphere . . . pure Caribbean. HAMISH McDOUALL

the bonnet of a speeding car. Chris heard a dense, nauseating thud and 'Jock' Vaughan leaped out of the van to see if he could help. He did as much as he could — checking the boy for broken bones and other obvious injuries until help arrived — but when he returned to the van he said that the boy was in a bad way.

Vaughan knew the boy needed a brain scan and treatment for head injuries. The kid was never going to get the necessary CAT scan in this part of the Third World and would probably be brain-damaged. Often, when touring beyond the five-star world, the team as a whole would feel powerless in the face of such hardship. No one talked for the rest of the journey.

Guyana was a place where security precautions were advised. The team were told not to leave the hotel in groups of less than four as the town is renowned for muggers. In fact, Guyana was to be the scene of a different robbery altogether. In one of the greatest one-day performances of all time, New Zealand pickpocketed the fourth match.

Bourda Oval is small and a big score is desirable, and expected. At the team meeting the night before, 300 was thought to be the minimum, and Chris was eager to use his power on the short boundaries. New Zealand's top order hit out well but after that there were very few contributions except for Chris with 29 (off 36 balls). The visitors crashed to be all out for 158 in the 36th over. They were booed off the oval by the disappointed crowd. In such a poor country, tickets are expensive for locals and they like to get value for money. To complete the humiliation, New Zealand had to bowl before the lunch break.

But then the artful dodging began. Lara was always considered the key wicket. Once he was out, the West Indians seemed vulnerable. The little master smashed Patel for three fours off consecutive balls, but then he lamely chipped the ball into midwicket's hands off Gavin Larsen and the complexion of the game changed. The New Zealanders went into lunch upbeat with the Windies keystone removed.

The Kiwis then fielded sublimely, belligerently chasing every ball, making the Windies earn every run. Harris and Larsen bowled brilliantly and, along with Germon's field placements, kept strangling the home side's scoring chances. It was, inevitably, another edge-of-the-seat affair. The second to last over saw the West Indies lose their ninth wicket for 153. A single to big Courtney Walsh and they required just four, a single boundary, to win the series. Justin Vaughan had wanted to bowl the last — he had bowled well for someone still recovering from a 40-hour trip — but Germon had turned to the man he knew could do the job. Chris was surprised to be called up from fine leg. He'd been used sparingly over the past few games, but both men had shared moments like this going way back to their schooldays. Whatever their personal history, Germon knew Chris could win the game.

'The death' is a paranormal time in a cricket match. To be a great bowler at the death requires skills different from other times in a cricket match. There is no room for the robotic accuracy of a Larsen or Chatfield — one needs flexibility. There is no scope for letting the ball do the work, with vast amounts of swing or seam — the ball is old, the field spread, the batsman unpredictable.

There is no place for bowlers with low confidence. A great bowler at the death — like Glenn McGrath, Waqar Younis or Wasim Akram — must have an innate belief in his ability to do the job, to put the ball in the right spot. Yorkers and full tosses are common weapons, but an ability to change the ball at the last split second is vital if a batsman is using his feet, stepping down the pitch or to either side. A slower ball is an absolute necessity, and a clear head is the most important thing of all.

With no margin of error, on the first ball of the very last over, Chris slipped a fast yorker under Walsh's bat to win the match. The only sounds audible on the television microphone were the whooping and yelling as the victorious 11 came together to congratulate each other in a delirious scrum surrounding Chris.

The crowd was nearly silent in disbelief. The entire New Zealand team were awarded the Man of the Match award, and that seemed fair. It was an ensemble effort. The series was still alive. It was the lowest score New Zealand had ever successfully defended — thievery at its epitome.

The West Indians are not only passionate about their cricket, they are parochial. In St Vincent, for the decider, the crowd was smaller than expected because two players, Samuels and Cuffy, both Vincentians, had not been selected. Never mind the fact that neither player was in form good enough to justify selection. It would be a bit like half of Auckland not turning up because Blair Pocock wasn't selected for the Black Caps. A boycott was announced and many Vincentians stayed at home, though most of them would have had one eye on the television.

It was one of those days where the 'rub of the green' did not go with the tourists. There were a couple of half-chances, and a pretty good shout for LBW against Lara that was turned down, but the West Indies won by eight wickets. It was a series the Kiwis could have/should have won. They had only been completely outplayed once — and Clive Lloyd stated that it had been the best one-day series ever in the Caribbean. Chris was deeply upset at the end of the match. He had been inconsistent. He blamed himself for the loss.

St Vincent was a pleasant break from the hustle and bustle of the big cities. It was a quiet backwater with friendly locals and beautiful black-sand beaches.

Several players' wives and girlfriends met the team in St Vincent, including Kim Morrison and Ruth. If, in the joy of seeing their menfolk again, the women didn't initially notice the stresses in the side they were soon made obvious. Television New Zealand did a broadcast from the team's hotel. The majority of the squad was gathered around the pool having a drink. Just before filming, Germon rushed around insisting that no glasses be filmed and the drinks were whisked away before the scene was recorded. This was typical — the pictures showed a happy veneer only. The reality was a lot different.

Day to day, the contact Chris had with Glenn Turner was fractious. There was barely a civil word exchanged between them in the hotel corridors and when they met at practice it was always some terse comments about the game. Socially, the two never mixed. Turner would dine with Germon and his fiancée, Toni, rather than the rest of the squad.

Justin Vaughan was selected as captain for the tour match against a Board XI at Kingstown, St Vincent. The venue was Arnos Vale, the home of St Vincent cricket, where a decent skywards shot from Chris could easily float into the flight path of the airport. The runway is literally just over the back fence and the planes seem to rise directly out of the main stand, drowning out appeals, snicks, calls, conversations and the crowd. For a few seconds, cricket becomes like charades in a sea of white noise.

The game was surprisingly easy. A solid batting effort was followed by a grand spell of bowling from Chris, who took 5-28 off 16 overs. He had bowled quickly, and felt that he was getting his rhythm back. He had been aggressive in attacking the crease and his follow-through was good. And when he hit the batsman's pads he would appeal vociferously. His confidence was rising. It was 10 days before the test.

At the end of the day, Turner came to Chris and told him to desist, told him that he was appealing too much, that he shouldn't pressure the umpires, that he was upsetting the local crowd. Chris was incredulous. An appeal is as much a part of the game as the stance a batsman takes, or the fields one sets. The fact that Glenn Turner never took a single wicket in test cricket was never more plain.

A good declaration in the second innings and Morrison, Cairns and Kennedy blazed through the Board XI line-up like a fire through sugar cane. Vaughan had captained positively, even going against the desire of the coach to bowl first. Justin Vaughan knew that he might never get the chance to captain his country again and wanted to give his team the best chance of winning. The records will forever show that he was captain when New Zealand recorded their first-ever first-class victory in the West Indies.

On a night of celebration that should have eased the discord, a sour note had been sounded. Shane Thomson was not bowling his off-spin, and could not throw, because of a shoulder injury. Turner evidently considered Thomson a specialist bowler rather than a batsman, as late one night, after Thomson had had a few pool-side drinks, he was ordered to undertake a fitness test.

Thomson couldn't believe the timing and almost inevitably failed the test. It was decided that he would be replaced. Thomson was allowed to stay on the tour for a few days as his girlfriend had joined him, but he was disappointed and disillusioned.

Chris was upset for Shane. He'd been badly treated and another of Chris' friends in the team had been dismissed, more baggage disposed of. Thomson never played for New Zealand again, preferring instead to live in Europe, and a talented all-rounder was lost to the game at the age of just 27.

The squad kept island-hopping. The next match was in Grenada, 60 km south. There had been only one day between the game in St Vincent and the start of the match against the President's XI. In that day the squad had to travel between the two countries, set up in the hotel and practise on a shoddy ground. Add to that the problems some of the wives and partners were having travelling between the islands and the stress level in the party was rising.

On the morning of the match the bowlers were practising on the edge of the block. The outfield was uneven and unsuitable for even casually rolling one's arm over. This routine warm-up was interrupted by the coach striding angrily towards the group. Turner told the bowlers to stop bowling on the square.

The bowlers stared at the little red-faced man, and even Gavin Larsen, the most temperate of the entire squad, couldn't understand why there was a problem. Larsen, after the calf muscle strain in the World Cup, was worried about rolling his ankle on the corrugated outfield. Chris Cairns was exasperated. Yet again the coach was taking the side of the local administration. The players evidently had no one lobbying for their point of view. Surely Turner could defend his players for once on this tour.

An hour later, Germon won the toss and chose to bowl. Two days after they had bowled New Zealand to victory, the quicks were being asked to do the hard work on a pitch that looked flatter than roadkill. The weather forecast for the day was scorching. Chris had earlier asked Turner what the captain was going to do, but the coach didn't reply at first. When he finally told Chris that they'd be bowling, Chris couldn't believe it.

Some locals told the team later that no one could remember the last time someone had chosen to bowl first. The opposing captain had a look of unbridled joy as he left the field to pad up.

Queen's Oval is in a windless gully behind the Grenadan capital, St George's. There is one grandstand but the rest of the public areas are bleachers, while the entire northern end is a corrugated iron fence that radiates warmth like a microwave. Out of the shadow of the stand there was nothing but relentless heat, which didn't stop several Grenadan fans dancing for the entirety of the two and a half days of the match.

The same heat drained the strength of the New Zealanders. The West Indian tyros had something to prove as well. Openings had started to appear in the West Indian team, players were getting older, losing form or retiring. The opening batsmen for the first test were anything but certain. The New Zealanders never knew what hit them.

In this oval-shaped fry-pan, the New Zealand bowlers were basted with coconut oil and fried with plantain and okra. The batsmen helped themselves. No one escaped the riotous punishment of Robert Samuels (134) and Floyd Reifer (154). During this hard day's work in cricket's sweatshop, Chris took four wickets. Turner still found room to criticise Chris, even after such an effort in a rippling heat.

By the end of the first day, the West Indians had scored 353 and had begun ripping into the New Zealand batting. Cameron Cuffy and Nixon McLean roared in and began uprooting stumps as if hurricane season had come early. Ambrose, Bishop and Walsh weren't getting any younger, and these guys were lining up as the inheritors. Only Roger Twose stayed fast. He was last out, for 19. New Zealand had made 113. They followed on.

There was more of the same in the second innings. This time Chris offered resistance. One memorable shot was off Nixon McLean bowling for his place in the Windies side. Chris strode forward to the pitch of the ball, realised it was shorter than he originally saw and wafted his bat in the direction of the ball. The fielder at mid-on sensed a catch, but the ball kept rising like a firmly struck pitching-wedge. He ran towards the boundary but could do nothing. The ball landed just metres over the rope. Chris was out for 94 off 71 balls. It had been the best innings of the match. The packed grandstand rose as he wandered off, to applaud the strokemaking they had witnessed. Everybody joined the ovation, except for a couple sitting almost directly above the tunnel leading into the dressing room. Gren Alabaster and Glenn Turner were still seated and Turner was not even clapping — his arms were folded and he was looking away to his right as if this moment in time never existed. Something snapped in Chris Cairns and he swung the bat hard into the metal railings below Turner's seat. The sound reverberated throughout the stand. It was the sound of a man on the edge.

The New Zealanders were staying at Grand Anse, one of the beaches that is always mentioned when West Indians are arguing about the most beautiful beach in the Caribbean. Chris went to the beach but not even the presence of Ruth could calm him. He was in a bad way. He watched young men juggling soccer balls as if they were balloons and old women braiding tourists' hair. Boats sailed into St George's harbour just to the north and waves rolled in gently, but this peaceful maritime scene couldn't soothe him. Nor could a swim or a Mt Gay rum. He chatted with Justin Vaughan for a while but then found a secluded spot. Gavin Larsen remembered seeing him looking

The pose says it all . . . Chris discussing 'issues' with Justin Vaughan on the beach at Grenada, 1996.

like the loneliest man in the world. Chris Cairns was brooding. He was thinking of his dream — to be a great cricketer, to play for New Zealand. The dream was rotting like a shroud. Something had to be done.

That night a team meeting was called. It was to be a watershed in New Zealand cricket. Before the meeting several players — Chris, Danny Morrison, Adam Parore, Dion Nash, Roger Twose and Shane Thomson — met in one of the hotel rooms. None of the players who gathered there was happy. Here was an opportunity to get to the core of the issues that were eating away at all of them. It wasn't mutiny they were discussing, but a meeting where everything could be discussed, where brutal honesty would be first on the agenda.

The 'forum' began with a statement read out by the manager. That wasn't a good sign. Then Turner stated that 'as far as he was concerned there was a small group trying to undermine management and railroad the team . . . [he] made it clear that was not going to happen'.

The floor opened and Twose and Nash were both vocal. Chris then started to defend his actions after Turner levelled accusations at him. The coach said that Chris hadn't tried in his first spell. Chris replied he'd bowled seven overs for 10 runs and had a catch dropped off his bowling. True to form, however, it descended into a slanging match. Turner wrote in his book: 'I didn't see how I and others could have been more patient or tolerant towards [Chris]. He was told that henceforth he was to cease undermining management and accept management decisions.'

Stephen Fleming, ever the diplomat, stated that the problem was communication and that it was a two-way thing — that a squad could not operate with the flow being solely from the top down. It was the type of wisdom from a young man that would see him captaining the side within a year.

With Turner's style coming under scrutiny from the team, Chris could see the coach becoming more agitated with each comment. Alabaster called an end to the evening and the caucus resolved to communicate better. The hui from hell was over.

There was optimism throughout the team, and the majority of the squad and their partners went over the road for a meal. There was a unity and camaraderie that had been suppressed for some time. The players thought they had got their point across. They could get on with the job of beating the West Indies, not each other. Germon came to the restaurant and Chris asked to speak to him in private.

They had known each other since they'd been sopranos. Chris could see that Lee had an opportunity to lead the team as a player — to make a stand at practice the next day, to tell his team-mates to forget the past and build for the future. It was an Alamo moment, a line in the sand. Germon listened intently.

The next morning the team were bubbling. Germon called a meeting in the dressing room, just as Chris had hoped. Chris bounced in and sat down eager to hear Lee take the reins. After 30 seconds he switched off. Germon stated that the team needed to back the management, not undermine them.

The mood in the room was the lowest Chris could remember. They'd taken one step forward and three back.

No one's heart was in the practice. When pointless practice occurs, injuries can smell the air. Dion Nash broke down and was not to bowl again on tour. The team had had eight days' cricket in nine.

The team flew to Barbados for the first test. The next day at a morning net practice Chris ran in and bowled furiously. He needed to vent his anger. When Fleming wants to rile Chris these days he simply says, 'Just imagine it's Barbados and I'm batting at the other end.' The nets at Kensington Oval were lively and the batsman thought it was the fastest he'd ever seen Chris bowl. Then a muscle in Chris' left ribcage pinged. He rushed to the dressing room to have it assessed. Perhaps it was psychosomatic. Perhaps his subconscious was driving his body to breaking point. Plummer looked at the internal bleeding and told him to ice it.

When he got to the hotel, Plummer assessed the muscle. Chris would miss the first test for sure. Maybe he could bat in the second match and bowl a little. But he certainly wouldn't be bowling in the first test. He was a specialist bowler. He'd been batting at seven regularly on tour. Shane Thomson had already been sent home and he was more a batsman than a bowler. Chris' tour was over. He would miss Antigua with its 365 beaches. He would miss the parties of Barbados, he would miss the wind-down of Bermuda. He would miss the chance to play the West Indies in test cricket.

Chris knew what Turner's reaction would be. Turner would probably be gleeful that this troublemaker, this disrupter, this 'individual', could not play. Chris discussed playing possibilities with the physio. Chris toyed with the idea of offering himself as a batsman only for the second test but Chris knew Turner would never go for it. With Plummer as his only point of contact with management he then made a massive error. He regrets never going to the coach personally and confirming whether Turner required him purely as a batsman for the rest of the tour. By not verifying that one thing, he gave Glenn Turner ammunition. The southerner could always state, from then on, that Chris Cairns had bailed on the team.

It frustrates Chris that many people think and Turner wrote that he abandoned the team, deserted, walked out. But the devil is in the detail — a cricketer cannot simply walk out of a tour. All the players were on contracts specific to the tour and to run off would have been a breach of contract and very probably seen a long time spent in litigation. The New Zealand team manager didn't object to him going. He arranged the tickets and handed them to Chris on the day of his departure. That was the only contact Chris had with the management before he left.

Of course his team-mates were disappointed, they had lost a quality player. But some of them admired and understood his actions. He had been the most vocal and voluble about the situation with management, when younger players felt that their positions would be compromised if they piped up and senior players were content not to rock the boat. Chris had an equal share of courage and belief on what was right.

Shane Thomson and Chris flew out on the same flight, but it was holiday season and the only seats the pair could get were on a charter flight in the smoking section. These two friends flew off into uncertainty surrounded by sunburned Brits smoking their way back across the Atlantic.

As they ordered their drinks from the overworked hostess, they both thought they were flying into the international wilderness, that their international careers were over.

18

Change for the better

People in New Zealand have little concept of the hero status Chris commands throughout the county of Nottinghamshire. Now that it is six years since he played for the side, his feats have taken on an otherworldly, mythical status. The team talk of a shot that knocked a fieldsman off his feet, such was the force, and spectators mull over the 70-m throw to run out a batsman direct.

They are still remembered vividly by players like Usman Afzaal and Jimmy Hindson, who witnessed them when they were young. Players also talk of the day in a festival match when he started a competition to see who could bowl like Wasim Akram or the '70s costume parties Chris hosted.

The stories are great. There is the tale of a benefit match in Lincolnshire when Chris kept hitting the ball over some tall trees. Behind them was a grand mansion. When asked why he kept hitting in the same direction, he simply said, 'I want one of those windows.' There are stories of him throwing a cricket ball right out of Trent Bridge, just because he wondered if he could. Then there is Andy Afford, sitting in the bath in the Trent Bridge dressing room receiving commentary on one of Chris' innings from his team-mates in the viewing room, when suddenly he heard the player say, 'He's got hold of that one. It's coming in here!' and the sound of breaking glass.

In 1996, Trent Bridge was like a sanatorium for the player. He got back frayed at the edges. He was instantly in demand from the New Zealand sporting media, who saw his exodus from the team in Barbados as a walk-out or some kind of truancy. But having left the tour, Chris was no longer muzzled by the media protocols. He decided to make a last stand. He needed to make public the unhappiness of the squad.

He arranged to do a radio interview with Murray Deaker. The phone was not connected at his house so he found a phone box and on a dark night, standing in a freezing booth in Middle England, he unleashed the pent-up frustrations. It was risky and courageous. He knew he would gain nothing from it except, no doubt, an exclusion from the next New Zealand side. He knew he wouldn't play under Turner again but he wasn't going to let the captain and coach play happy families.

In late April, before the second test beginning

Chris Doig, the man Chris credits for turning New Zealand cricket around after the dark days of the mid '90s.

in Antigua, Chris played as a batsman in a non-competitive warm-up match against low-level opposition. Twelve thousand miles away, it caused an uproar.

From the perspective of the slavering press, it was clear that Chris had a 'sham' injury. He had absconded from the tour, 'done a bunk', as Glenn Turner eagerly described it. From NZC's perspective, it was ill-timed, provocative and embarrassing. From the New Zealand team's perspective, it was just disappointing. On the eve of the second test the squad felt let down by their world-beater.

But again the detail has been obscured. Chris still couldn't bowl — his torn intercostals would not allow that. With a rib injury, he was capable of playing as a batsman only.

When this maelstrom of negativity reached Chris he regretted playing and he bitterly regretted not getting an assurance from Turner that he wouldn't be wanted for the second test as a batsman only, but as he was to explain in a letter a couple of weeks later, he left with the impression that the management felt relieved to have him depart early, which Glenn Turner admits.

Reams of fax paper were used as NZC sent complaints to Notts and Chris himself. Notts declined to select Chris for the first handful of one-day games, even just as a batsman. Chris Doig was particularly vehement in his criticism of Chris but in a strongly worded letter there was a ray of optimism in the gloom. Doig clearly understood that Chris was not the only person at fault. He wrote that the team coach's deficiency in communication had contributed 'in no small way' to the current problems.

Among the raft of castigations was also the clear statement that Chris Doig was a supporter of Chris Cairns — 'You have years of cricket ahead of you and we both know you are capable of being one of the greatest players we have produced. Don't let this issue and this current environment deflect you from that purpose.'

Chris was contrite. In his reply to Doig, he apologised for his public criticism of Glenn Turner and agreeing to play for Notts, even in a throwaway game. He gave an undertaking to commit wholeheartedly to New Zealand cricket, the New Zealand team and to whatever regulations team management would reasonably require of him in the future. He admitted he was partially to blame for ignoring his own responsibility to Turner's strict codes, but also stated for the benefit of New Zealand Cricket that his position in the side had become untenable because of the coach's ill-disguised contempt for him personally. He pressed the green 'send' button on Nottinghamshire's fax machine and got back to the thing that he took comfort from — smashing English bowling.

In the first matches of the county season he was regularly absent from the bowling crease because of his rib injury. It was the most painful 'sham' injury he'd ever had. His bowling did not recover for a couple of months, then he picked up a groin injury and was sidelined again. The rhythm that he had discovered the year before was gone and while he still picked up wickets he no longer ran through sides. The Windies impasse had affected his bowling. He didn't get a five-wicket bag until the second-to-last county game of the season, when he took 6-110 against Yorkshire.

Thank goodness he could bat — and bat he did. He could be both bludgeon or barn door. He scored 66 not out against Warwickshire with just 15 scoring strokes, and hit one not out off 39 balls when saving the game against Worcestershire.

In between these two innings, he scored his seventh first-class century, again against Gloucestershire. His 114 helped Notts win their first County Championship game of the season. Unfortunately it was also their last. If Durham hadn't been appalling, Notts would have finished last by some distance. Notts lost eight of the last 10 four-day matches they played. Chris averaged 39 with the bat (1 century, 6 fifties) and even more with the ball.

In first-class cricket it had been a very bad season. In one-day matches, Notts was a different side altogether. It beat undefeated Worcestershire, the holders, at New Road, largely thanks to Chris' 41 off 29 balls. At Taunton, Chris sent two huge hits out of the ground, towards the River Exe and the Foresters won again. They won the last eight games they played.

It seemed that the team would go off the boil for the County matches then be stung by the defeat to superhuman efforts on the Sabbath. But try as they might they couldn't overtake Surrey. They were level on points after each of the last four games, but Notts' run rate was always fractions lower than Surrey's. It is a shame that their head-to-head clash at the Oval was the only match abandoned because of the weather. Surrey simply didn't drop points in the last month.

In the last match, Chris took 5 for 41 against Yorkshire (and hit a six first ball) but it wasn't sufficient. Notts was runner-up. Still, it had been a great contest. Chris averaged 16 with the ball and, to complete the near-perfect summer, was second in the batting averages with 69.

In mid-July, Chris heard the news that Glenn Turner had been replaced as coach by Australian Steve Rixon and that Gren Alabaster's job had been given to John Graham. These two newcomers were to change Chris' career forever, on and off the field. Although Chris initially thought it odd to have a foreigner appointed to the top job in New Zealand cricket, on second thoughts it seemed prudent. Rixon had been untouched by the personality conflicts that had dogged New Zealand cricket. New appointments and new ideas are always a cause for optimism. Steve Rixon would have a plain without debris on which to begin his work.

Seeking to get to the root of the impasse Doig ordered an independent inquiry on the team's return from the Caribbean where the players could express themselves confidentially without fear of reprisals. The findings revealed aspects that helped lead to Turner not being reappointed.

Glenn Turner claimed to have been sacked but the truth is less dramatic. After interviewing four candidates, including the incumbent, New Zealand Cricket chose not to renew Turner's contract. In the end it was not his prickly personality or his stringent discipline that was the *main* reason behind his non-appointment. According to Doig, the reason he was not reappointed was because New Zealand Cricket found someone they felt was more appropriate for the job.

The atmosphere of disillusionment that pervaded Chris' time under Turner disappeared overnight. He would have a chance of playing for his country again, which meant everything to him. But in hindsight, Chris thinks that under a different manager, a less school-marmish manager than Gren Alabaster, with a captain not still struggling with the whiplash of a hasty promotion, Glenn Turner might have been a success. With, say, a man of the mana of John Graham, and a captain with the confidence of Stephen Fleming, and the influence of Gilbert Enoka, Chris believes that there would not have been the top-heavy structure that toppled over in 1996, that the stability would have been present to allow Glenn Turner's skills to function.

In 1998, Glenn Turner's account of his time as coach arrived on the shelves and in shop windows. It was a caustic work. The black-capped villains of the piece were obvious — Chris Doig, Adam Parore and Chris Cairns. Turner had clearly personalised his conflict and disappointment in *Lifting the Covers*. Chris has never read the book, but enough was quoted in newspapers on release, and in subsequent articles, for him to taste its bitterness.

A 'documentary' about the Turnergate affair also came out the same week, with Lee Germon making ill-judged comments as well. Chris was stung by the criticism that pained him and his family but restrained himself from any knee-jerk reaction. The attacks seemed designed to discredit Chris' character and to give the assertions in Turner's book some validity.

Chris stated that there would be a time and a place to respond. He has had six years to ponder the events and he realises that he made mistakes, that he should have done some things differently. He is also at peace with the knowledge that he stood up for what he believed in. Having had time to reflect, Chris is convinced that there was a facet of his personality that Turner identified in himself. He wonders what the coach feared that made him want to exclude the all-rounder. He hopes that Glenn Turner has since found a less destructive way to confront himself.

19

A new dawn fades

Chris Cairns did not instantly warm to Steve Rixon. He had created distance between himself and coaches. He was cautious to say the least, but the events of the previous summer were never brought up. Rixon, known universally as 'Stumper' (he'd been a wicketkeeper), often called Chris 'lazy' over the first few months of their acquaintance. He thought Chris was relying on his natural talent to get *good* results, rather than working hard to achieve *great* results. It was, Chris concedes, probably a fair assessment.

Steve Rixon wanted the Kiwis to play aggressive cricket, which suited Chris fine. He also demanded that they become the best fielding side in the world, and hour after hour was taken up with catching and throwing drills. Chris threw his 95-kg frame into the exercises.

The first engagement of Rixon's reign was the Singer Akai Trophy one-day tourney in Sharjah. The Sharjah CA Stadium that had risen out of the sand of the Arabian desert always provided a fairly true batting surface.

The first game was against Sri Lanka, the new world champions and high favourites. New Zealand won. Chris hit a sublime 71, then took two wickets in Sri Lanka's middle-order collapse. On his return to the New Zealand side, Chris was named Man of the Match. Three of the 'malcontents' of the season before produced great performances. Chris added to his half-century with his most economical bowling ever (10-2-18-3), against Pakistan. Parore hit 93 and 78 in two round-robin games. Then, in the most dramatic match, Sri Lanka equalled New Zealand's 169, with two wickets in hand, before Danny Morrison steamed in to get both batsmen and earn a tie. Morrison's five wickets for 34 runs were his best-ever return.

New Zealand made it to a Sharjah final for the first time, though that wasn't cut and dried. The tournament referee initially awarded the final berth to Sri Lanka (who had finished equal on points, but with a higher run rate) before Chris Doig petitioned the ICC about the rules and the New Zealanders were established as rightful finalists, having beaten the Sri Lankans head to head. Doig's efforts at securing the final place were sublime. He ploughed forward for his players for a just cause.

New Zealand had a chance to break their duck — they had never won a one-day tournament overseas. Rising to the occasion, the Kiwis fielded and bowled mightily in the desert. The talented Pakistani batting line-up, including new starlet Shahid Afridi and Wasim Akram (who had scored 257 in a test only weeks before), was restricted to just 160 all out in the 49th over.

All the bowlers performed superbly (Chris with the best figures of 2-24), and it seemed the drought would be over. New Zealand were 98 for 3, and with Larsen at number 11, batted forever. But then a monumental collapse occurred and the remaining batsmen were all out for single-figure scores. Seven wickets fell for 21 runs. Total — 119 all out. Most of the New Zealanders thought it was a little surreal.

It could only get better. They flew to Pakistan. In a restrictive society like

Pakistan it is hard for Westerners to have fun in the ways they're used to. There are no nightclubs, no bars and no casinos, so the social committee becomes as vital to team harmony as the physio and coach. On the tour to Pakistan, the social committee was Messrs Doull and Cairns. The team's first stop was a tiny nowhere called Sahiwal, where they were billeted at a biscuit factory (!), a little distance from town. The team were accommodated three to a cabin. The rooms were primitive, the beds uncomfortable.

It seemed that this part of the world had no local translation for the expression 'mod con'. No bar, no television, no pool table, no mousetraps even. For five days. In this Spartan environment the social committee stepped in. Chris had located a fireworks shop in town and armed with many thousands of the local currency had bought almost the whole shop. Cairns and Doull then staged the greatest fireworks display witnessed by a New Zealand touring team.

Chris swears he saw tears streaming from the faces of his manly team-mates as they watched the finale, a huge explosive concoction of whatever was left in the fireworks bag — though the tears may have been tears of laughter as Chris and Simon nearly had their backsides set alight as they ran from lighting the pyrotechnics.

The first test was at the Gaddafi Stadium in Lahore. The Kiwis began poorly — 155 all out. The new brand of cricket ball approved for the series was swinging wild distances in the air. Simon Doull, with his ability to swing the ball both ways, was virtually unstoppable. He took five top-order wickets and wanted to take a patent out on these fantastic balls. Justin Vaughan mopped up the tail and New Zealand were a meagre 36 runs behind.

At 101 for five, New Zealand were teetering when Chris joined Stephen Fleming. Flem had dropped anchor and was happy to push the ball around. Soon after Chris went in, the ball settled down, having lost its shine. This allowed Chris to start dominating the bowling. Chris beat Fleming to 50 then kept on hitting, sending the brilliant young spinner Saqlain Mushtaq thrice over the sight-screen.

It was a mighty innings. The dynamic between the pair was perfect, with Fleming feeding Chris the strike and preserving his wicket, which provided the stability Chris could spark off. In sight of a century in consecutive tests, Chris was undone by his old nemesis, little Mushtaq Ahmed, for 93. The Canterbury lads had added 141. Fleming ran out of partners to finish 92 not out, yet again short of a maiden test century. By stumps that day, Pakistan was punch-drunk at 42 for 5 chasing 275.

That night was almost unbearable for the New Zealand team. They were so close to winning. Chris had never experienced such excitement. His enormous appetite was suppressed, he couldn't concentrate on the book he was wading through and he decided the best thing was to simply go to sleep.

Chris admits he was so close to victory that he tried too hard the next day. Instead of concentrating on line and length he went out with the intention of finishing the game in five balls. He bowled loosely and went for 62 runs off his 16 overs. Luckily Patel and Doull broke the Pakistani resistance and the game was won. It was New Zealand's first test win in Pakistan for 26 years, the first test win against anyone for nearly two and, at the eighteenth attempt and after seven years of trying, Chris Cairns' first test win. Mark Greatbatch knew this. He pulled a stump out of the ground ran over to Chris and handed it to him. It was the most emotional moment Chris had experienced in cricket — all the struggles and all the pain were worth it.

If anyone had doubted Chris' desire to play for his country, they should have witnessed the scene in the dressing room. As he went to congratulate Simon Doull, the Man of the Match, tears of happiness and release, seven years' worth of tears, filled his eyes.

Rixon had taken one game to achieve what Chris had been trying to do for seven years. A test victory is something so pure and special that it is hard to describe. To battle against the opposition *and* yourself over five days, on and off the field, takes courage, skill and resolve. To celebrate that with those who partook in the journey binds players together like nothing else in sport.

And celebrate they did. Mark Plummer, who had been physio for the great Auckland Ranfurly Shield side of the late '80s, organised a rugby-style court session with a jockstrap and tie dress code. It was a new experience for most of the cricketers — Bryan Young was persistently punished for incorrect procedure, and lasted only an hour before being put to bed — a raucous celebration interrupted only by Steve Rixon reminding everyone of practice the next day. Everyone assumed he was joking.

The next morning, to their horror, the players found notes under their door telling them the bus was leaving at 11 for practice. The net was proceeding very tentatively when Chris noticed Stephen Fleming go down on one knee in the net. He rushed to see what was wrong only to find Flem struggling with his stomach contents. On seeing this Chris reacted in the same way. The pair rushed out of the nets to the sound of the coach barking and their team-mates in fits.

The next test was at Rawalpindi and the news got better. Waqar Younis joined Wasim Akram on the injury list. He was replaced by a youngster, Mohammad Zahid.

Before the game, the Pakistani authorities arrived with a bunch of balls and the New Zealanders leaped on the box of red cherries. But the balls were different. The magic jaffas that Simon Doull had been able to move about like a poltergeist had gone. When they asked about the other balls, the officials smiled and replied that there were no more left in the country. Perhaps the Pakistani Cricket Authority had twigged to the fact that the tourists seemed better able to exploit these balls than the locals.

The Pakistanis did a lot better with the new ones and New Zealand was all out for 249. Chris had several batteries thrown at him from the crowd after he dismissed Zahoor Elahi with his second ball, but then Saeed (149) and Ijaz (125) broke all sorts of records with a 262-run partnership. Chris was still struggling with his rhythm but he kept plugging away. He eventually dismissed both centurions and finished with 5 for 137, only his third five-wicket bag in test cricket, and his first since 1992. It had been a victory of persistence over penetration.

Unfortunately, Mohammad Zahid chose the latter method in the second innings. Helped by five LBWs, the young debutant went through the New Zealand batting order like a vindaloo. He took seven wickets and the Kiwis lost by an innings and 13 runs. Ironically, this performance encouraged Nottinghamshire to sign the speedster as their overseas professional when Chris required an ankle operation and had to pull out of the contract.

With Akram and Younis back for the one-day series, it was always going to be difficult. The games were played very early in the morning to avoid the diabolic heat of the mid-afternoon but the early hour produced two odd situations. One match was delayed because of morning dew, while the other was delayed as the rising sun was shining into the batsmen's eyes!

New Zealand chased hard in both games without success but in the third, at Karachi, Bryan Young and Nathan Astle started positively, Parore built on those foundations, and Fleming (48 not out) and Chris (25 not out) administered the coup de grâce. It was a great way to end a good, hard-working tour, a tour where there were far more positives than negatives. Chris was on form and had chalked up his first test win, though he had been dismissed four times in four test innings by the wrist-spinner Mushtaq. But the biggest positive had been the coach. Steve Rixon worked.

On their return to New Zealand the national reps went straight into the Shell Cup competition. The Canterbury contingent set about defending the silverware they'd made their own, but the team were not the steamroller they had been the season before. A loss to CD in the first game back ended the record 14-game winning streak and on the way to the final they had a couple of hiccups against Wellington as well. However, they also whipped the men from the capital in a sensational match that was over in 39 overs. Wellington was all out for 70, and during the break the Canterbury team booked an early flight back to the South Island, then batted furiously for 11 overs in order to get to the airport on time.

Chris' form was good — he scored a workmanlike century against Otago in a group match, then took a personal best and a Canterbury record 6 for 37 in the minor semi-final. The final was at the Basin Reserve, which was experimenting with playing music over the public address system. Chris didn't mind the noise and banter. It encouraged a sell-out crowd for the final, and Chris was a big fan of the 'bums on seats' policy. It reminded him of the huge dance party on The Mound at Sabina Park.

Predictably, Chris walked to the wicket to the strains of 'Get a haircut and a real job'. His hair was shoulder length and trailed behind him, but it didn't seem to affect his ability. On a very green wicket, Chris put his tousled head down and collected runs. He high-scored with a restrained 42 off 77 balls, which, incredibly, included playing out a maiden over from left-armer Mark Jefferson. In reply, Wellington was destroyed by Mark Priest, Geoff Allott and Chris himself — all out for 81. The Cup was Canterbury's for a fifth time in six seasons.

Chris was the top player of the tournament, finishing second in the bowling averages and averaging 45 with his bat. It was only during the final that his strike rate slipped below 100. But all this was only an apéritif for the big feast of cricket to come. In early January, Michael Atherton's England side arrived in the country.

While Australian dominance always raises trans-Tasman ire, Chris feels a duty to puncture the condescension towards the 'colonials' when playing England. He loves reading the bile that the Fleet Street press spews out when the Kiwis win, and he enjoys defeating his peers from the county game. To beat England at their own game is a special thrill.

England arrived in New Zealand after an unconvincing drawn series in Zimbabwe (and a 0–3 whitewash in the one-dayers). But they should never be discounted. The Kiwis found this out in the first test in Auckland.

England won the toss and, ambitiously Atherton sent New Zealand in to bat. The English steadily picked up wickets and before the close of play Chris was taking guard (two legs) with the New Zealand score on 215 for 5. Yet again Stephen Fleming was at the other end. The ease with which the pair ran singles, communicating almost telepathically, astounded the English press. They had batted together 10 times already

After viewing this photo, Chris wondered if Craig McMillan (right) was happy for him that he had just taken a wicket for Canterbury . . . or if he was just laughing at the hairdo?

that summer for both New Zealand and Canterbury and averaged 45 together — batting confidence sometimes is as much about who is at the other end, taking the pressure off with big shots, milking singles and encouraging each other.

The next morning the couple continued merrily. Chris was the senior partner, belting Tufnell over the boundary a couple of times (one a miscue) but they kept fairly in step. Suddenly Flem accelerated through the nervous nineties and raised his bat to the crowd. It was his maiden test century, in his fortieth innings. He'd been so close before, and Chris was ecstatic for him. He knew the feeling. Soon after, Chris was out for 67. The two had shared a partnership worth 118.

New Zealand managed 390 but this was overwhelmed as Stewart and Thorpe shredded the bowling attack as though it were paper-thin. On the last day, Tufnell caused a collapse in the middle order, and Alan Mullally got Chris. Suddenly New Zealand were 105 for 8, without even enough runs to force England to bat again and with over three hours still to negotiate. Simon Doull lasted a while, then last man, and possessor of the new world record for the number of test ducks, Danny 'the Don' Morrison, joined Nathan Astle.

Two of Chris' closest friends in cricket, with the weight of the nation on their shoulders, proceeded to play careful, calm cricket. There were no rash strokes, and Morrison did it in singles. On and on the pair went as Atherton shuffled his bowlers and the batsmen steadily built a lead. Danny Morrison blocked, fended and left 133 of the 206 balls bowled during the partnership. It was one of the greatest of all rearguard actions.

In the last act of the match, Astle hammered a ball to the boundary to bring up a deserved test century. The tenth-wicket partnership, an undefeated 106, was a test record for New Zealand against England. The relief was palpable in the dressing room.

The honourable draw didn't paper over the cracks, however. The New Zealand bowlers hadn't done their job, and the batting seemed susceptible to both spin and seam. New Zealand shuffled their deck, hoping to come up with trumps. In fact, they came up with two left-arm bowers. Morrison and Vaughan were replaced by Geoff Allott and an 18-year-old who looked like a cross between a maths geek and the school scruff. Daniel Vettori became the youngest player to play test cricket for New Zealand when the match began at the Basin Reserve on Waitangi Day.

Chris felt a lot of sadness when Danny Morrison was dropped. He understood why Danny was angry but felt he left the game bitter and that he lashed out at a few people in a knee-jerk way. Danny didn't get the opportunity to show his style again, so the public saw him finish not as who he was — the little bowler with the huge heart — but as who he wasn't. Chris is glad to see his mate back in the game today, paving a career for himself in broadcasting. As himself.

The first day of the second test dawned wet. Late in the day, the Kiwis batted and in the 30 overs possible they were annihilated — 56 for 6 by stumps. Expat Andy Caddick and Darren Gough had taken all six wickets between them. The New Zealand batsmen had played some prodigal shots. At a time of crisis, when defence would have been preferable, several players had sparred at balls they could have left. Their knowledge of the exact location of off stump seemed so poor that it should have been painted Day-Glo. One of the guilty parties was Chris Cairns.

The next day was even worse for Chris. During his third over he stopped a powerful drive from Alec Stewart. His index finger swelled up quickly and soon he couldn't even hold a ball let alone try and bowl the thing accurately. This was his second injury in days — he had sprained his ankle in Gavin Larsen's benefit match four days prior to the test. At first the ankle was thought to be so bad that he couldn't play but he iced it non-stop. Chris (and the team management) wanted him to play even though he could hardly run. The future was to show that he would have been better to sit this one out.

Saturday saw Chris sitting in the players area disconsolately. Chris had known the night before that he couldn't field, he couldn't bowl, and he'd bat down the order. His entire contribution to test cricket was being marginalised by bad luck and the fragility of his body. The media was confused though — Rixon the night before had said Chris would play a full part.

About the same time as Chris was carrying the drinks tray onto the ground for the first drink session, a bloke from Wellington, a taxi driver by trade, was ringing a talkback show. He thought he knew why Cairns wasn't on the field. He'd been working late the night before. He'd picked up a New Zealand cricketer from a nightclub, at 4 a.m. that morning.

Sometimes the general public looks at their sports stars as infallible people. They demand that these icons follow the strictest of moral codes as well as perform great feats on the field, court or track. *Hoi polloi* often ignore the fact that these sports stars are most often young and male, with all the attendant lusts, insecurities and braggadocio that attaches to that age. In early February 1997, Chris Cairns was struggling with his personal life.

Chris had asked Ruth Leslie to marry him in England the previous summer. Ruth was a salve for Chris, an intelligent, beautiful design student, who had known Chris since primary school. The sheer aeons of the time they had spent together since childhood meant that they understood each other well. Ruth had known Chris well before all the fame and its trappings, well before the tragedies and triumphs. She had been there for him when his sister died. She was his best friend.

The nuptials were arranged for early April 1997, a double-header with Chris Harris' wedding to Linda. But Chris was having a crisis of confidence. There was bickering within the family about the arrangements and a heated argument had occurred just before the Wellington test match that made him wonder if the wedding was going to go ahead. Suddenly the one stable thing in Chris' life, his family, was a source of stress. There was now no break from the mental battles of test cricket.

That Friday night he had gone out with Simon Doull, Adam Parore and Nathan Astle. They'd had dinner and went to a bar for a nightcap. It had been a terrible two days of test cricket. All of them were angry at themselves. Chris was devastated with this new injury to his finger. At least it wasn't his ring finger, but even that thought brought with it some bursts of worry and panic. The other three headed back to the hotel but as there was no chance of Chris playing the next day, or maybe even the rest of the test, he decided to risk it and go out.

There are no excuses he can offer. Chris admits he was wrong in every respect but his head was not allowing him the space to think in a logical or mature way. When the cabbie rang the radio station that morning, it lit a fuse. At the other end of the fuse was the manager of the New Zealand cricket team, John Graham.

John Graham (or D.J. as he's widely known) had been an All Black captain in the

Steve Rixon (right) and D.J. Graham. Rixon gave Chris his drive to perform and get the best out of himself. Graham gave Chris life lessons. Chris sees Graham as an honourable, proud man and has enormous respect for the way he lives his life.

'60s, and had been headmaster of Auckland Grammar for many years. He had been appointed by the Ministry of Education to be an emergency commissioner for the 'failing' school Nga Tapuwae College. He was a man with mana, a man who could command respect effortlessly, through a demeanour of honesty and dignity. In 1996 he was rung by an old teaching colleague of his, Chris Doig. Doig had a situation on his hands a little like Nga Tapuwae College. He had a 'failing' team.

John Graham is a lifelong cricket fan, who remembered sitting in the stands at Eden Park wincing, as New Zealand was bowled out for just 26. He had played for his school but his talent was with the oval ball. As headmaster of Grammar, he fostered the talents of players like Martin Crowe, Mark Greatbatch, Dion Nash and Matt Horne. D.J. Graham accepted the job in the time it took to hang up the receiver.

Graham remembered seeing a young boy called Cairns in the '80s, playing for Christchurch Boys High against the Grammar firsts, and causing problems for some of the Auckland batsmen. Now more than 10 years on, that same boy Cairns was causing problems for him.

When the news broke of Chris' indiscretions, the manager and chief executive, Graham and Doig, agreed that the best thing would be to downplay the story, and keep the discipline in-house, particularly while there was a test going on. After all, New Zealand was playing badly and when D.J. Graham had witnessed the collapse to 23-5 he must have wondered whether this was a repeat of that disastrous Eden Park afternoon in 1995.

But even Graham, who had experienced so many trying situations in a diverse career, was surprised at the ferocity of the journalists who had congregated for the third-day press conference. It was to be Graham's first and worst press conference as manager of the team.

He read out a statement that was breathtaking in its brevity, a carefully worded denial of essential facts and support for the players, a small puncture to deflate the story. But the clamour that greeted the statement threw Graham completely. The reporters were rabid and he reacted angrily to their response before leaving abruptly. The journalists sensed obfuscation. What had been intended to take the heat off Chris publicly achieved the opposite. The papermen went after the story, and if the Raurimu massacre had not occurred the same day, Chris, booze and early mornings would have been front-page news in the Sunday papers. On back pages and in editorials, Chris was crucified.

That Sunday, Chris didn't get to bat. Rain and his finger meant he had some breathing space, long deep calm breaths. Meditative breaths. D.J. Graham came to him and talked. They talked as equals. Graham apologised to Chris that his own ineptness in the face of the press had dumped Chris in it. Chris in turn apologised for his foolishness. They agreed to put it behind them. Chris didn't feel chastised by D.J., but he felt even worse. He knew he'd threatened his place in the side. He knew he had let his supporters down. But worse he had let this great man down. He vowed never to do that again.

D.J. suggested some standards should be set, inviolable rules. Chris nodded. They were all sensible and rational. Later these were formalised in a meeting with senior players. This code of ethics is still in place today and has never been disputed.

The next day Chris tried to save the test. He dug in and batted for an hour, but with a finger that throbbed with pain every time the ball struck his bat, he couldn't lead his side out of the quagmire. Chris was last out to a brute of a delivery from Caddick that leaped, hit his hands and flew to slips. New Zealand had been lamentably bad.

Chris suffered many professional lows in the '90s. He could well have assumed that his dropping in 1993 was the bottom of the pit, or his patellar injuries, or the whole West Indian charade. But the worst moment of his career came not a kilometre from his family home.

Chris had been selected for the third test, controversially. Sponsors, including (ironically) Dominion Breweries, stated that reports of late-night drinking were disappointing, as had been the results on the pitch. The harsh spotlight of attention would be on him in the match. Until then he had other commitments. Before the test series he had begun a campaign for the Child Cancer Foundation. He was going to shave off his locks for charity. One of the promotional events for this campaign was at the Riccarton Mall shopping centre. This was his home territory. His mother lived nearby. There were several Canterbury celebrities participating. A large crowd had gathered and cheered the famous names and faces.

When Chris Cairns' name was read out there was some polite clapping. The whole thing was so muted. He was shocked. He wanted a large trapdoor to appear so he could disappear. Realising that the public had lost faith in him was the biggest and most trenchant lesson of his career.

He had to confront more demons the next day. There is no doubt that his muddied public image was affecting the private man, and when he got to the net practice he was out of sorts. He played and missed and mistimed shots. His finger was still paining him as was an ankle and there was hesitancy in his footwork, anxiety in his body language. He felt he was spiralling. At the end of the net, he wandered out exclaiming to the new batting coach Martin Crowe, 'I can't do it. I can't bat. I don't know what I am doing.' Crowe recognised something in the desperation. Chris wasn't just talking about his injured hand. Chris had lost his self-belief.

Martin gave Chris some throw-downs then they went to get some lunch. They ended up with takeaways, sitting in Chris' apartment. If anyone else had been there, maybe the outcome would have been different, but Martin Crowe knew all about the worm of self-doubt. It had gnawed at him throughout his entire career. On a napkin, Martin got Chris to write down some affirmations. They talked over the things crowding his head, and slowly, one by one, dealt with them. Chris always needed a clear head to perform at his peak. The day before a test is usually about creating mental space for the desire, natural ability and hours of practice to find expression. Martin was creating that space for a troubled mind. Anyone else might not have understood Chris' situation, but Crowe's timing, as a friend, a batsman and a mentor was always spot on. The next day Chris scored a fine test 50.

The Lancaster Park test is a landmark for New Zealand cricket in the late 20th century. They didn't win — Michael Atherton batted devotedly to nurse his English team to victory and the Kiwis performed in fits and starts. But it was significant in two ways — first, Stephen Fleming captained his country for the first time; second, New Zealand showed a desire to win, a mental toughness, the 'mongrel' they would continue to show five years on.

Lee Germon was injured before the game and the palm fell to Fleming, even though he had never captained a first-class side before. In a parallel universe, if

PHOTOSPORT

Sweeping against the English in the third test at Lancaster Park, 1997. Before the match Chris didn't know how he would score a run . . . he ended up scoring 50 in both innings.

Wellington and the West Indies had never occurred, maybe Chris would have been considered for the role, but it was impossible in the atmosphere pervading cricket in 1997 and he of all people knew that. With Mark Greatbatch, Gavin Larsen and Justin Vaughan not commanding places in the side, Fleming was the only real choice. He had often been talked of as a potential captain but at 23 years old he was still very young. But cometh the hour. Fleming had a wise cricket head, a pleasant manner with the press and respect throughout the team.

And luck. Atherton won the toss and inserted New Zealand, which was quite daring considering Russell Wylie was the groundskeeper. Wylie possessed an 8-ton steamroller called Big Bertha that had spent most of its life crushing gravel, but was now put out to stud on the Lancaster Park block. Wylie claimed that he had never prepared a bad pitch with this mighty piece of machinery.

It was late in the day before Chris got to bat. The plan was to bounce Chris out, exploiting his finger injury, but in spite of the fact that he occasionally flinched with pain, it was a flawed strategy — on this truest of pitches a good length outside off would probably have had better results. Chris compiled a solid 57. It was his slowest test 50 so far, but was also evidence of his renewed application.

Chris' ankle injury, which had almost caused him to miss the second test, was still giving him pain. He couldn't bowl at full pace and he was reduced to the status of a fourth seamer, behind Geoff Allott, Simon Doull and Heath Davis. He still managed to contribute — he dismissed Nasser Hussain, but this was Cairns 'lite'.

The English tally was 118 shy of New Zealand's, but wickets fell regularly in the second dig to the two spinners, Welshman Robert Croft and Cockney Phil Tufnell. Chris strode onto the ground with the score 76 for 4.

Matt Horne showed backbone when he batted with a broken hand for almost half an hour. It had been this kind of hardball attitude that had been missing in Wellington. Parore had earlier had a verbal spar with Dominic Cork, which confirmed that New Zealand were there to compete with attitude.

Chris and teenager Vettori added 71 runs, expanding the lead the whole time. Chris scattered the gaggle of close fielders with some aggressive hits, but was out playing one lofted stroke too many — caught on the extra-cover boundary for 52. It was the highest score of the innings. New Zealand set a target of 307.

On any other wicket but Wylie's it would probably have been too much for the team batting last. As it was it was a near thing. New Zealand had their chances to win the game but when Daniel Vettori's arm finally went numb after an incredible 342 deliveries New Zealand had nothing left. They had fought like wildcats but lost, by four wickets.

It had been a spirited performance that restored the public faith in this side. This was demonstrated when 25,000 people turned up to the same ground to watch the first match of the one-day series. It was the first day-nighter at Lancaster Park and an excuse for licensed madness, with helicopters buzzing around like *Apocalypse Now*, music between overs and endless Mexican waves. Chris loved it. The game he loved was becoming a spectacle. To add to it all he had his long tresses shaved off for the child cancer appeal at the interval together with Paul Holmes.

Paul Holmes (right) looks on as Chris has his locks cut for Child Cancer during the break in the first ever day-night match at Lancaster Park in 1997.

England chased well and won, and won again in the next match at Eden Park when the Kiwis were defeated by antiquated rain rules. Germon, back from injury, erred in choosing to bat when dark clouds were circling above Auckland's volcanic cones. Chris scored a fine 79 off 74 balls to remind the 24,000 crowd, and the English press, of his hitting power. He was absent from the bowling line-up, however, as the ankle injury was worsening.

The game in Napier turned out to be a classic. With what seemed like the entire population of Hawke's Bay crammed into McLean Park, the New Zealanders posted 237. England chased well and with the fiftieth over to be bowled they required eight runs. Geoff Allott, making his first one-day appearance, was bowling. Third ball, Craig White tested Chris' arm at fine leg, trying to turn one leg bye into two and failing by metres as Chris' throw blew the stumps apart. Next man in, Croft, got four and out, and then requiring two runs to win off the last ball, the English sneaked a bye to Germon. The match was tied.

With that result the pendulum swung and New Zealand won the next two matches, thanks largely to the batting of Astle and the bowling of Harris and Larsen. England seemed an exhausted side at the end of a long tour, but New Zealand fought back well to square the series, their confidence on the rise.

Directly after the last one-dayer, the team for the test match against Sri Lanka was announced. Chris was in as a batsman only, but the real controversy was that Lee Germon had been dropped.

In truth it was no surprise to those in the team. There was still bitter residue from the West Indies tour. Germon, however much he denied it, had been Turner's proxy. In the new dynamics of the Rixon regime, Germon had tried to mend the wounds but he was operating in cricketing triage. The selectors decided to cauterise the wounds by removing the root cause.

In his one test behind the stumps that summer, Parore had again proved a better keeper. Germon had also made some poor decisions during the English series, whereas Fleming had seemed to the mantle born. In the end even outsiders could see the balance of the side was all wrong — Christopher Martin-Jenkins summed up the collective wisdom when he wrote 'Germon's absence makes New Zealand a stronger side'.

Bryan Young compiled an extraordinary innings at Dunedin of 267 against Sri Lanka in 1997. Young was a very compact opener who scored most of his runs square on the off side, and a lot of them off the back foot. But no one could have imagined that he had such a huge innings in him. There were also good contributions from Horne, Fleming and a 70 from Chris Cairns. Simon Doull took eight wickets and New Zealand won by an innings and 36 runs.

It had been 11 years since they had recorded an innings victory. On the evening of the fourth day, karaoke versions of Dave Dobbyn and Crowded House resonated around the concrete dressing rooms of Carisbrook's main stand. Champagne corks added percussion. It was the sound of New Zealand moving out of the basement of world cricket.

Four days later the Kiwis were scarcely less dominant. On a dodgy Hamilton pitch, New Zealand established a small lead that they inflated to over 300 in a determined second innings. The target always seemed beyond the Sri Lankans, who found Heath Davis' pace and Daniel Vettori's flight too challenging. New Zealand had won a series for the first time since 1992. It was the first time the nation had celebrated consecutive test victories since 1985. Cue more rousing choruses of 'Loyal' in one and a half part harmony.

The two teams shared the one-day series that followed — with Cairns earning the Man of the Match award in Wellington for a patient half-century, his seventh in ODIs. One-all with the world champions was a great result. After the murky times of the English tour, these were salad days indeed, but the summer wasn't over yet. Canterbury met Otago in the Shell Trophy Final, again on Russell Wylie's batsman's utopia, Lancaster Park. Chris Harris scored 198, Astle 160, five other players passed the 50 mark (Chris 57), and Canterbury finished on 'nelson' — 777 all out. It was the highest score ever in New Zealand first-class cricket. Canterbury lifted the trophy on a first-innings win, of 588 runs.

On 5 April, Chris and Ruth married at St Barnabas' Church, Fendalton. Wayne Allport was best man, Craig Rogers and Mike Smith the groomsmen. The reception was at Mona Vale and the bride looked stunning.

Messrs Morrison, Parore, Astle, Fleming and Davis were there from among Chris' workmates. Even though Chris felt his popularity was at an all-time low, there had been a bidding frenzy for the exclusive rights to the wedding among the women's magazines, and the journals that missed out reported that they'd been snubbed.

Chris' indiscretions off the field meant perhaps that these people felt they could treat Chris with contempt — after all, if he didn't respect himself why should they?

In spite of this, the wedding was a wonderful day. The summer had ended peacefully. Chris Cairns could take time to reflect on where he was heading.

CAIRNS FAMILY

Three of Chris' closest friends from school. Craig Rogers (left), Mike Smith and cousin Wayne Allport.

20

Out there
and back again

In May, Chris found himself in Asia for the fourth time in 18 months. India was hosting a quadrangular tournament to celebrate 50 years since the end of the Raj — the Independence Cup. In the dry heat of the Punjab, at Mohali, New Zealand beat a weakened Pakistan side, then were slaughtered by the home team in Bangalore. Most galling was the loss to Sri Lanka in the last match. Having held the world champs to 212, the Kiwi middle order proved brittle and fell well short of a place in the final.

The summer of '97 raises the dilemma of Chris as a specialist. Apart from a couple of adagio overs in the last game, Chris had played purely as a specialist batsman for nine ODIs, and two tests in a row. His form with the bat was good (2 fifties in one-dayers, one in tests) but by no means good enough to justify an extended time in the top order. And Chris never enjoyed just being a batsman. He also *always* wanted to bowl when he was in the field.

It was the same if he was batting down the order — he would get vexed that his opportunity to build an innings, to create the foundations from which to launch one of his ballistic assaults, would be disappearing. The fact is that when Chris Cairns isn't fully involved in every facet of the game he gets frustrated.

Chris spent his first winter in Christchurch for several years, recovering from an ankle operation. He enjoyed setting up home with Ruth, but soon cricket was to intrude on the marriage, with devastating results. The New Zealanders began another packed season of cricket that was to include tours through Africa, Australia and Sri Lanka, three triangular one-day tournaments, as well as the domestic season, with Zimbabwe and Australia visiting. For a New Zealand regular, it was another gruelling schedule. All cricket associations need games to provide the funds to exist, but there comes a point of saturation where the players can fall into physical exhaustion.

The long haul began in East Africa, in Kenya, with the hiss of a ball flying through the air, and the roar of a crowd. The Gymkhana Club in Nairobi is not a big ground. It was where Shahid Afridi had smote a one-day century off 37 balls with a record 11 sixes. In the first one-day match there against Kenya, Chris was cruising along at a good clip (he brought up his half-century at nearly a run-a-ball) before he found another gear altogether — overdrive, as it were. His next 105 runs came from just 29 deliveries. He cleared the boundary 13 times.

Chris' 157 from 87 balls should have bedecked the lists of ODI records for many years, but there was a problem — even though Kenya had full ICC membership this wasn't an official one-day international. Chris felt aggrieved when it was rumoured that New Zealand Cricket had declared the two games unofficial, so they wouldn't have to pay out almost-guaranteed win bonuses. Unfortunately, this incredible innings remains in the grey zone beyond official statistics.

After another win over Kenya, the team travelled to Zimbabwe for a month-long tour. Cricket is a family game in Zimbabwe and there were two Flowers, two Strangs, two Rennies and two Whittalls to keep the commentators confused. The coach was Heath Streak's father. The sport is played by enthusiasts and amateurs, accountants and farmers. In the warm-up matches Chris was still working on his ankle and bowled off a short run-up but the operation seemed to have been successful.

Harare Sports Club is next door to Robert Mugabe's huge palace among the avenues of North Harare. For the first test, the jacaranda trees were in beautiful blue bloom around the ground. It was another world there, far removed from the teeming pavements and steel and glass towers of downtown not a kilometre away.

New Zealand had a good first day with Chris and Shayne O'Connor, on debut, working well together. Chris took three wickets off a shortened run, as he tested his ankle, and added two more the next morning. Extending himself more than he had on the first day, he registered impressive figures of 8-5-4-2 from the morning's work. 'Zim' was all out for 298. Chris had taken 5-50, his fourth five-wicket bag. He had easily been the best of the New Zealand bowlers. His lift had squared several batsmen, who sent balls into the slips three times, twice to Stephen Fleming (who equalled the world record with five catches). Only Grant Flower had shown long-term resistance, scoring a century before Chris had dismissed him.

Chris was at the crease early on the third day. He started cautiously as the Strang brothers kept him quiet. He pushed 12 runs in an hour and a half. Eventually, Chris was run out after a moment of cricket genius from Heath Streak. New Zealand was all out 91 runs short of the Zimbabwe total.

This lead was extended to over 400 the next day. Grant Flower hit a second century and the runs had come quickly. Before the end of the fourth day, two Kiwi wickets were down. People started making plans for the next afternoon, because the cricket would be over, surely.

Martin Crowe had returned to Zimbabwe in his capacity as a broadcaster. But he was also moonlighting as the Kiwis' batting coach. After the fourth day's play, Martin came to the dressing room for a drink. Martin talked to Chris about his technique to counter leg-spin.

The conversation lasted just five minutes but that five minutes changed the rest of his career. Leg-spin had been Chris' Achilles heel. Attacking the spinner was fine but his defence against the turning ball wasn't as composed. Crowe had spotted the flaw in his willowcraft. Chris' head was not over his bat. Too often, thinking he was balanced, his body would lean over to the off, ruining the shape of his defence and exposing chinks in his armour. Crowe told Chris to get his head over his hands, knowing that he would have to face leg-breaks for most of the following day.

The task was simple. If the nine remaining batsmen could hold out for the entire last day then they would draw the test. It was a situation all too familiar to the Kiwis. Chris cast his mind back to Perth in 1989 when he and Paddy Greatbatch had willed the minute hand to move faster and the Morrison–Astle heroics only months before. This thing could be done.

By the time Chris strode to the wicket, it seemed like a case of misplaced confidence. Blair Pocock's straight bat was still there, but Fleming and Astle had both gone within four balls. It was 4 for 118. A commentator said as Chris took guard, 'This is not his kind of situation.'

Pocock was out soon after, replaced by Parore. People began drifting away. Chris blocked resolutely, carefully waiting for the ball that could be hit to the boundary, concentrating on his head position. Adam Parore was more aggressive, choosing attack as the best form of defence, batting at close to a run a ball.

The closer they got to the target, even one as unlikely as 403, the more Zimbabwe would trade attacking fields for defensive ones. The partnership was like the perfect good cop, bad cop routine. When Parore was out for 51, New Zealand was 200 for 6. There were three hours to survive.

Chris Harris became the aggressive partner. Cairns rarely strayed from his almost monastic devotion to a straight bat. Only when Adam Huckle pitched short did he scythe the ball over midwicket for six. Zimbabwe were now offering the rare spectacle of two leg-spinners working in tandem. Neither troubled the two Cantabrians.

Heath Streak finally ended Harris' innings after tea. He had scored 41 runs in a 66-run partnership. Daniel Vettori had clearly been watching Chris carefully. He blocked well until one of Huckle's leg-spinners bit and turned and an edge flew to Rennie minor at short leg. There was half an hour to play and Shayne O'Connor, making his debut, walked to the wicket. Only Heath Davis remained padded up. Alistair Campbell ringed the batsmen with close fielders waiting for a ball to flick from the bat, onto the pad and balloon up to waiting fingers. Chris kept stepping out with his long legs and smothering the spin. He did his best to shield the new batsman but occasionally it would be O'Connor facing the wiles of Huckle and Paul Strang. Chris encouraged the tail-ender, told him to fight hard, that he believed in the Otago man.

Ten fielders were now gathered around the bat, some as close as a metre away. If the ball hit pad, the flannel-clad vultures would rise as one, screaming at the umpire to raise his finger. Shadows were being cast on the pitch. Again and again a ball popped up to hands or glided past the outside edge and the Zimbabweans would go up like desperate stockbrokers five minutes from the close of market. Somewhere in the middle were the batsmen.

Suddenly it was all over. The umpires pulled up the stumps and handshakes were shared. Chris walked back to the pavilion with his arm around O'Connor. They had saved the test. His 71 runs had been scored off 236 balls. The innings had lasted over four hours. Chris had showed a maturity, a focus, an Anzac spirit.

The second test was played at Queen's Oval, Bulawayo, a venue so unpretentious and quiet that it doesn't seem like test cricket at all — more like a club match or village friendly, but Daniel Vettori will remind everybody that it is a test ground, and that he scored 90 there.

On a pitch as flat as the surrounding savannah, Zimbabwe scored nearly 460 runs. In reply, Astle, Harris and Vettori scored half-centuries, but Zimbabwe had become more ambitious in their play and an enterprising declaration from Campbell resulted in a finish almost as exciting as the previous match.

The leg-spinners bowled for the entirety of the last session and all four results were still possible going into the last over, but when Vettori was out, and with all the 'Zim' fielders on the boundary, the game reached stalemate with only a couple of balls remaining.

The test series had been annoying. Chris had now played Zimbabwe four times in a row without success, and this time the home team talked about a 'moral' victory. They had 'outplayed' New Zealand. In the basement of test cricket, New Zealand were now ranked bottom. Yet Chris knew that the Kiwis were man for man a superior side.

Between series, Chris and a few of the Kiwis were invited to Heath Streak's home in the Matapo region. Streak is a farmer, and speaks fluent Ndebele. The pair of fast bowlers went hunting and then sat on the farmhouse's stoep, had a drink and watched Africa slip into dusk. Chris and Heath got on well. These two players are not in the best teams in world cricket but share a mutual respect on the field that translates to a friendship off it.

The first match of the one-day series heightened the frustration for the Kiwis. Chasing a modest total, New Zealand steadily lost wickets and only a brilliant innings by Chris Harris dragged the Kiwi total anywhere near Zimbabwe's. Fifteen runs were needed off the last over and Gavin Larsen was running to complete the fifteenth off the last ball when he was beaten to the danger end by a throw from Craig Evans. It was a great piece of fielding as hundreds of Bulawayo's school-age children were sprinting onto the field, and Evans had to avoid the youngsters in his pick-up and throw. The game was a tie. New Zealand had now played three tied matches within a year.

New Zealand were well beaten in the second ODI in Harare, posting a small total. Chris had started watchfully then went out playing his first big shot. The defeat chastened the entire team. One correspondent had written that Zimbabwe clearly had more players of quality than their opponents. Rixon called a meeting that night. His first statement was simple — 'You looked like scared rabbits. You look like you're not enjoying it.' The word 'enjoyment' struck all the players. Chris was asked to open the batting, and he decided to enjoy himself.

The experiment, regrettably rarely repeated, was a huge success. Chris miscued several lofted drives, but with the field restrictions in the first 15 overs he did so with impunity. He also had the benefit of facing a new ball which raced off his bat. Chris hit 9 fours and a six in his 71 (78 balls), to grab the initiative in the match. Craig McMillan struck 5 sixes later on and New Zealand set an unassailable score. Chris was Man of the Match, the series was halved and at last New Zealand had revealed their ability.

The next series against Australia had special significance for Steve Rixon. He had been rejected as a replacement for Australian coach Bobby Simpson several years earlier when Geoff Marsh had been appointed without even an interview. Rixon encouraged the New Zealanders to fight fire with fire — if sledged to give it back, to irritate and disconcert.

The Aussies were famous for their lip, the constant ticking of Ian Healy behind the stumps, the sarcasm of Shane Warne or the abusive tirade that Glenn McGrath could deliver — one of the nicest men off the pitch but capable of R-rated malevolence on it.

Rixon, who played test cricket in the hard-nosed Chappelli era, implored his team to respond with the devastating one-liner, the barb, the jibe, anything to probe the mental weakness of a batsman.

In fact, it was the Kiwis who were initially softened up with two innings losses to state sides. Queensland won in the tropical humidity of Cairns, then New South Wales took their former coach's team apart at Newcastle. The second tier, the journeymen of Australian cricket, the solid Sheffield Shield players, were smashing their Kiwi cousins. The depth in Australian cricket seemed unfathomable.

Morale was low so Simon Doull organised a Melbourne Cup sweepstake. Every player drew a horse from a hat then had to draw the jockey's colours on a white T-shirt

PHOTOSPORT

Mental disintegration is Steve Waugh's fancy phrase for sledging. Here Chris politely asks Steve how the family is doing.

with crayons supplied by the social committee. The team had been invited to a Cup party and when they arrived in their hand-coloured T-shirts they discovered all the other guests wearing haute couture. It didn't matter — Geoff Allott was runner-up in the best-dressed-man competition and four days out from the start of the test the team had bonded.

The first test began in Brisbane in November and the Australians walked into a hail of insults. Parore was one of the main verbal cudgels. Behind the stumps he could chip away. Over the pitch microphones, the new-found spite could be heard. Mark Waugh came in for special attention. Waugh was in poor form and 'Mav' Parore merrily reminded him about the batting trough he was in. Often.

These two excelled at banter. Parore asked Mark Waugh, 'What's it like earning half what your twin brother earns?' Waugh replied later, deadpan. 'Adam, what's your deal with Slazenger? Wholesale — 50 per cent off?' Even the Kiwis couldn't help sniggering.

The chutzpah was matched with solid performances from the New Zealanders in the first test. Chris started the series with one of his great spells of bowling. He took the first four wickets to fall before lunch — those of Elliott, Blewett and the Waugh twins. It was Chris' slower ball to Steve Waugh that he would treasure the most. Waugh was a prize wicket and Chris ran in looking like he would bowl fast and hard, like he intended to blast the batsman out with pace. The arm came over at the same speed, but Chris had wrapped his index finger around the ball and brought his thumb off the bottom of the seam, and rolled it out the front of his hand. The ball looped and dropped at 30 km/h slower than Waugh was expecting it. His bat was long through the shot and the ball hit his back leg. Umpire Crafter pointed heavenwards, where it seemed the ball had come from.

It was cricket's version of the feint, the luff. The victory of brain over brawn. It had been learned in hundreds of hours playing on featherbed pitches across the British Isles.

Australia were listing at 4-53 but righted themselves with their lower order. Catches were grassed and the early advantage lost. In reply Fleming, Craig McMillan and Chris all had great duels with Shane Warne. It was test cricket at its most fascinating, attacking batsmen versus incisive bowler.

Chris won the first exchange — he made 64 in just under three hours before chopping a delivery from Glenn McGrath onto his stumps. New Zealand had batted well and achieved parity with the great Australians.

In the second innings, the Ockers were struggling, 163 for 5, after Chris snared another three top-order wickets, but again the resilient lower order saved Australia. On a decaying pitch a target of over 300 was always going to be unlikely and sublime bowling from McGrath and Warne finished the match. There were compliments. Mark Taylor congratulated the Kiwis for their gutsy effort, they were good competitors.

Chris Cairns captained New Zealand for the first time against Victoria at the Optus Oval in Melbourne. It was a great honour, a dream that he'd cherished since boyhood.

He had spectacular success. With the toss. After that it was fast downhill. New Zealand were all out for 82, their lowest total in Australia for the entire century. Chris had played a captain's knock, a high score of 24, but when he got back into the dressing room he was shell-shocked. The teams recorded exactly the same score in the next two innings (173) and in the end New Zealand nearly recorded an unlikely win.

The second test was a return to Perth, but it wasn't a familiar WACA belter. The chief groundskeeper had resigned just days before, unable to cultivate a good surface after a winter of Australian rules football and rugby league. Stephen Fleming won the toss and decided to use the pitch first while it was still reasonably true. It was a good ploy but required better execution — New Zealand were all out for 200 just after tea.

If Craig McMillan (54, with a cracked thumb) and Chris (52) hadn't combined for a 74-run partnership, it would have been a bona fide disaster. As it was it was merely terrible. Chris rates Australia's fielding display that day as the best he ever witnessed.

Australia batted aggressively while the pitch was still intact but declared when great canyons opened across the deck. The edges of the cracks started to crumble and the ball zipped to all points of the compass from these crevasses. A line and length specialist, Simon Cook, making his debut for Australia, became virtually unplayable. Chris was bowled by a ball that moved nearly a foot. Cook took the last five wickets and New Zealand lost by an innings.

Losing a little poise, Chris evades a Glenn McGrath bouncer at Brisbane, 1997.

In the dressing room, the New Zealand team sat in silence, eyes downcast for long moments after the match. This time they hadn't competed. It was the first loss New Zealand had ever suffered in a test at Perth. They'd lost a record, a record that Chris and his dad and Mark Greatbatch and Richard Hadlee and Martin Crowe had all contributed to.

Suddenly the two youngsters in the team, McMillan and Vettori, stood up, grabbed two golf putters and went through to the shower room. There they started practising their putting. The sound of the golf balls travelling across the floor and their laughter at missed putts was too much for Chris. These guys were meant to be in mourning. Chris stood up, went into the next room, slamming the door behind him, and unleashed his anger and disappointment at the horrified rookies.

Chris decided to walk back to the hotel. He worked hard to calm himself down, to work through his disappointment. Eventually, when his fury had long abated, he rang McMillan and Vettori and asked to meet them in the hotel bar. He explained why he had reacted like he did and that he could have handled it differently, but that it didn't take away how disappointed he was. There were apologies all round.

After three patchy days, only a stunning declaration from Stephen Fleming, 150 runs behind Australia, made anything other than monotony possible from the third test at Hobart. The Australians in turn left the Kiwis 288 to score in 61 overs. In a limited overs match, with fielding and bowling restrictions and strict parameters for wides, it would have been a gettable target. Even without those aids, New Zealand had a tilt at it. Chris, batting at three, scored 18 off 21 balls, and the other batsmen also followed the adage that one should risk a loss to get a win.

Team-mates can often play nasty tricks. Chris and Dan Vettori have toothpicks inserted in their ears while catching some sleep during a plane flight in Australia, 1997.

However, steady bowling was followed by a steady turnover of wickets and eventually Simon Doull and Shayne O'Connor, New Zealand's last pair, were at the crease. They blocked or left the ball for over an hour. Between them they faced 66 balls from the world's finest without flinching. The partnership may have only been worth just one run, but it saved a test. It could have been different. Early on Doull offered a catch to Simon Cook, the hero of Perth, but it was spilt. After this match Cook, who had come from nowhere, slunk back into obscurity.

The World Series Cup was sponsored by Carlton and United in 1997–98. New Zealand's campaign kicked off with a double-header at Adelaide. It was a great start. They beat South Africa with Craig McMillan (86) batting well. Although the Adelaide ground is a difficult shape for a straight-hitter like Chris, he scored a good 55. The usual suspects — Harris, Larsen, Astle and Cairns — bowled superbly to restrict the Africans. The sense of relief was tangible. It was the first victory of the Kiwi tour.

After such a good performance on the Saturday, the Sunday was inevitably disappointing. Two hundred and sixty was a good total but, in a repeat of the Madras quarter-final, Mark Waugh chased down and overhauled the target.

Tasmania has been the scene of some great triumphs for New Zealand but December 1997 was not one of them. Chasing just 175 to beat Hansie Cronje's team at Hobart, New Zealand started well. Chris scored 29 from 27 balls but the run surge never materialised, dammed by some great bowling from Allan Donald, and a slow low pitch. Even though those specialists in last-over chaos Harris and Vettori were still at the crease, the Kiwis had choked, one run short. Perhaps because of the narrowness of this margin, New Zealand lost badly in the last match before the Christmas break. They scored a paltry 157 and even though Chris almost made the

Chris, Lance and Cameron Cairns — Chris' brother from Lance's second marriage — pose with Lance's horse OK Boyo.

total look defendable when he took four quick wickets, they still succumbed.

The season's festivities were held at home, a rare treat for the busy cricketer — this was to be his last Christmas at home for several years. Family has always been important to Chris, even more so after Louise's death, and he loved seeing his cousins and their children, and his teenaged half-brother, Cameron — Angela and Lance's child.

After a handful of games for Canterbury, Chris was back over the Tasman. In a warm-up game against an Australian Country XI, Chris, fielding on the boundary, attempted a throw on the turn and strained his right rib muscles, a niggle that he carried for the remainder of the tour. In the first match back, at the Gabba, South Africa rattled up a breezy 300. At 6 for 124 in the thirtieth over, the obituary notices were being prepared for the Kiwis. With nearly nine an over required it was an understandable assumption but the lower order were filled with determination. They began to take to the Proteas' bowling. Chris at one end hit 64 (2 fours, 4 sixes) from 53 balls while Adam Parore caned 67 off just 46 balls.

When Chris was out, terminating a new partnership record against South Africa, Parore was joined by Dion Nash, who hit 38 off 31 balls. The target came ever closer, but in the last over with 13 needed to win the Kiwis could manage only 11. They had lost by one run. Yet another 'honourable' defeat — but a loss by the very minimum was as comforting as a split lip.

At the Sydney Cricket Ground after the next match, New Zealand batted feebly, chasing Australia's 250. They were all out for 119. It had been their last chance at finals cricket. Yet again they were also-rans. Chris was out cheaply and sat in his corner of the dressing room. His muscle strain was still affecting him — he was bowling well below full pace and just couldn't shake it. Sitting and sifting over the debris of his

PHOTOSPORT

The MCG is one of Chris' favourite cricket grounds. Here he is about to take up the attack against Australia in 1997.

expectations and dreams, he decided that he shouldn't play the last two meaningless matches. It would be best to go home and get treatment for the injury.

Chris hates the deflation that comes from defeat. He hates the doubts and the self-recriminations. After a long tour where his team had lost three state matches, two tests and now five ODIs in a row, he had picked up a nuisance injury. Chris talked to D.J. but the manager knew perception was important, and knew that the team needed Chris.

'Do you trust me?' asked D.J. Graham.

'Yes, of course,' replied Chris, as his trust and respect for Graham had never been in doubt.

'I sincerely advise you to stay on the tour.'

Chris realised that Graham was right. It was the best thing for the team, to be there with them. To help them fight through the disappointment. In the game at Perth, history was made as the opponents included Makhaya Ntini, the first black South African to play international cricket. Then on their return to Melbourne they beat Australia and the disappointment dissipated.

Nothing breeds success like success and on their return home there were more triumphs that replenished the camaraderie in the Kiwi camp. The Kiwis stormed through two ODIs against Zimbabwe.

Then swaggering over the Tasman came the all-conquering Australians, for a week-long, one-day fest. The Aussies arrived with the attitude that this tour was an end-of-year junket. They brought several younger players and rested some of their stars.

Their confidence seemed justified after matches in Christchurch and Wellington, where the Baggy Greens won at a canter.

In Napier, Chris triggered a collapse. Five of the last six wickets fell to his bowling. Australia were all out for 236. A Fleming ton brought about a victory. Chris' bowling figures, 5 for 42, were his career best in ODIs. He became one of only 11 players to take five wickets for New Zealand in that form of the game. He joined the great names of bowling — Hadlee, Morrison, Collinge and Chatfield and, errr, Rod Latham — on the list. Near the top was that other fellow Cairns as well.

The art-deco capital always seemed to inspire the Kiwis. Perhaps playing in the provincial heartland, in front of a crowd there to enjoy a rare day of big cricket, reminded the team of their support. The Kiwis went to Eden Park for the last match on a high. Having successfully chased a good score in Hawke's Bay, they now defended resolutely. Chris, Simon Doull, Chris Harris and the recalled Mark Priest all bowled excellently to stifle the Australian run-getting. Two–two, a good result, a result that steadied a wobbly season.

They next went head to head with Zimbabwe in two tests. The two teams had oscillated between bottom and second-to-bottom on the test rankings, but this series was to decide the issue of supremacy once and for all.

New Zealand took control of the first test on the very first morning when Simon Doull ran through the African line-up. Chris was run out for nought the last ball before lunch on the second day, trying to steal a third run for Craig McMillan to bring up his 50. He was so disappointed that he spent a full hour lying on the dressing-room floor in all his gear. McMillan went on to score a maiden century.

New Zealand's lead was vast and they concentrated on patience and persistence to take the 10 wickets necessary. Don Cameron wrote that 'as if savouring the prospect of tasting a rare wine, New Zealand took their time drawing the cork'. Finally the wickets were collected (Chris taking the wickets of dangermen Goodwin and Campbell), the handful of runs scored, and the victory wine supped.

The bowlers — Doull, Vettori, Nash and Chris, along with Adam Parore — hired a limousine and drove to Mt Victoria, overlooking Wellington harbour. Sitting in the stretch limo they drank champagne and smoked cigars. They had won by 10 wickets. They deserved the indulgence. New Zealand had never won three home tests in a row. By the end of the week they made it four, with an even more comprehensive victory.

In Auckland, Alistair Campbell won the toss and erred, deciding to bat on 22 yards of grassy mischief. The Kiwi seamers again rolled Zimbabwe, with Chris mopping up the tail — taking three wickets in 14 balls for no cost at all. A big total was earned through application and discipline, then Fleming's men chipped away. Chris took four wickets, Doull another four and this time the Africans didn't even make the Kiwis bat again.

The one-day series was also won, when, after a one-run hiccup at Christchurch, the last two matches went to the home team. New Zealand had beaten Zimbabwe 2–0 in tests, 4–1 in the one-dayers.

The domestic season was almost over barring the occasional shout for LBW at Dudley Park, Rangiora. Canterbury was in the Shell Trophy final for a second year running, this time against Northern Districts, who had finally managed to beat them in a Shell Cup Final back in January.

As if to make up for that defeat, Canterbury decided to bat forever. Every one of their batsmen got double figures, and Warren Wisneski at number 11 scored 89. In reply to their mammoth 524, ND collapsed, Chris taking 4-39, and the northerners lost by an innings.

Another team going for a hat-trick of titles was one of the greatest of all time, the Chicago Bulls basketball side — the team of Luke Longley, Scottie Pippen, Denis Rodman and, in his last year, Michael Jordan. Jordan, like Pele, Bradman, Sergei Bubka and Tiger Woods, transcended his sport. He was not only a great basketballer, he was one of the greatest of all athletes. Chris wanted to see this icon in action. He decided to fly east to his next cricket engagement — another Sharjah competition — rather than west. He, and Ruth, would go via the States.

The baseball season was under way and the couple went to historic Wrigley field to watch the Chicago Cubs play. After the match, Ruth and Chris and their friend Brendon Charteris were in a small bar. Suddenly Scottie Pippen and Ron Harper walked in and sat at the end of the bar. They were both massive. Chris, six foot three inches, felt small for one of the few times in his life. Ruth tried to encourage him to say hello but he remembered the times he'd been out wanting a quiet time after a game, not wanting to be disturbed.

He was also a little intimidated. Chris may have been a star, but these men were *super*stars. They were on a different level altogether. Ruth went and had a chat instead, much to the jealousy of the two men.

Tickets to the Bulls matches are paper gold so before Chris had left he arranged some seats through Richard Reid, his good friend and contact with Nike. The next night, when he and Ruth entered the United Centre, they kept descending from the vomitory, lower and lower, until they were just a few rows from the court. The seats were nearly ringside and they watched the speed and skill of these huge men, the strength and vision of Jordan.

Ruth and Chris then flew to New York, again catching some court action — at Madison Square Garden he saw the Knicks perform and saw their number one fan, Spike Lee, in the crowd as well as JFK junior and Donald Trump.

Chris was given the opportunity through Andy Haden to meet Kevin Roberts, the marketing guru, a naturalised Kiwi now running Saatchi & Saatchi. Like John Graham, Roberts had an intoxicating blend of intelligence and charisma. Chris was in awe meeting a man who had made it to the top of his field — in the world. As they walked the streets of SoHo they chatted easily about rugby, cricket and America.

Chris liked America. He had never spent much time in the States and he enjoyed the American service-minded attitude, and the ability to get what you pay for. He loved the fact that success was respected.

However, the concrete canyon of Seventh Avenue was soon replaced by the mosques and minarets of the Emirates. The Coca Cola Cup, yet another trinket paid for by oil money, was to be competed for between India, Australia and New Zealand. The Kiwis had never beaten either of those teams in Sharjah and the first two matches went with form. The opening match, against India, looked evenly poised but the Kiwi batting collapsed to the movement of Agarkar and the spin of Kumble when victory was in sight. Australia cruised like ships of the desert to win the second.

Some of the commentators complained about the quality of the side — Sunil Gavaskar suggested that New Zealand shouldn't be invited back. Such hubris was inevitably rewarded. New Zealand beat Gavaskar's beloved India in the third match thanks to a great bowling effort (Chris, 10-1-26-3) and an unhurried run chase. The Kiwis also played themselves into a winning position against their nearest neighbours — they set up a target of 259 with Chris contributing 56 from 50 balls — but the Australians chiselled their way to a victory by four wickets.

The tour to Sri Lanka in 1998 was one of Chris' unhappiest yet. Without a sage like John Graham advising him, Chris might have unravelled emotionally in the way he had in the past. This time he wasn't just dealing with the daily hassles of touring. There were also problems at home.

The tour started positively. Chris was again given the captaincy for the opening match against a Board XI. He won the toss and led aggressively. The New Zealanders took a first-innings lead, then an aggressive declaration set up a win for the tourists, particularly on a turning wicket. Dan Vettori opened the bowling, and Chris maintained attacking fields, but the crucial breakthroughs never came and the game was drawn.

The New Zealanders faced a team that had not lost on home soil for 12 matches. In the previous test at the R. Premadasa Stadium in Colombo, Sanath Jayasuriya had scored 340. The first test was to make a mockery of those statistics. New Zealand batted first and made 295, then Chris steamed in to take the first two wickets, caught behind, one of them Jayasuriya, and later returned to bowl Arjuna Ranatunga with a beautiful slower ball. The Sri Lankans were routed, Chris getting 3-59.

The pitch then developed into a great batting strip and both Fleming and McMillan brought up centuries. The lead was an intimidating 465 and in the last innings the Kiwi spinners Vettori and Paul Wiseman spun a web and the victory was

'Adamanda' Parore, 'Simone' Doull and 'Mattie' Horne in Sharjah, 1998.

Paul Wiseman (centre) with the victor's trophy — a lifebuoy — for finishing first in the Dubai swimming races. Runners-up Simon Doull (left), Nathan Astle and physio Mark Harrison.

snared. New Zealand had now won three tests in a row, another record.

It was during this game that Dion Nash and Chris fell out. Nash was smarting from the fact that he was to miss out on the next two test matches. All the pitches on the island seemed spin-friendly and two or even three spinners had to be accommodated. Chris, who would be playing, was fielding and wanted to preserve his fitness. He asked Nash to swap from midwicket to boundary duty. Nash refused. The pair did not speak to each other for most of the rest of the tour until the two friends patched things up over a beer or two at the end of the tour and laughed at their pre-school petulance.

The winning streak was broken at Galle, a new test venue. When the Kiwis arrived at the ground, they found an impossible pitch, a strip so friable that they were able to jiggle whole clods of hardened earth, such were the cracks. The two seamers New Zealand took into the match were simply a gesture towards convention. Chris bowled just five overs in the whole test, enough to knock the shine off the ball, before the spinners took over for the rest of the day.

Rain delayed the result, but in an alien situation the New Zealand batsmen struggled and the Kiwis lost by an innings and 16 runs. Bowlers took 27 wickets in that match. All the wickets fell to spinners. The pitch had crumbled to dust on the first morning.

Chris' one-year-old marriage was also crumbling. The constant absence was straining the relationship. Chris was spending hours every night on the phone to New Zealand. In the small shared hotel rooms he would shuffle through to the all-tiled bathroom so as not to wake his team-mates, and sitting on the floor, or the toilet, would talk to Ruth, trying to reassure her of his commitment.

What is incredible is that with all the stresses, living in a world of sleep deprivation and anxiety, Chris was still able to play great cricket. When the third test started at the Sinhalese Sports Club, Chris dismissed Jayasuriya again in the first session of the match, then in his first over after lunch took the wicket of match-winner Mahela Jayawardene caught behind, then Aravinda de Silva caught at long leg, hooking. It was his 100th test wicket. He had joined the greats of New Zealand bowling — Motz, Bracewell, Chatfield, Collinge, Taylor, Morrison and B.L. Cairns. While he was still 300-odd wickets behind Richard Hadlee, the 100-wicket barrier was a huge milestone. He also became just the third Kiwi, after Bracewell and Hadlee, to reach the 100-wicket, 1000-run double.

In another situation he might have celebrated the achievement, but he was in a private hell. He felt every inch of the distance between him and Ruth. One of his good friends, Dion Nash, was blanking him and Asia was still playing its constant mind games. A thing as petty as the fact that the rest of the team had finished the chicken soup in the dressing room while he was batting became a catalyst for an outburst.

Added to all this was his team's performance. Having taken a lead in the series, the Kiwis now looked likely to lose the rubber — particularly when a small first-innings lead was puffed out by a nuisance last-wicket partnership between Kaluwitharana and Muralitharan. Suddenly New Zealand had 296 to get to win on a pitch that was providing the awkward mixture of balls popping or dropping. An ordinary bowler like Bandaratilake became a world-beater, and combined with the freakish Murali to bowl New Zealand out within two sessions. Chris provided a little resistance, using his feet to belt two sixes off Bandaratilake, and top-score with 25, but it was never enough. The series was lost and Muralitharan was named Man of the Series.

The triangular one-day tournament that followed the tour was an outright disaster. The Kiwis were well beaten by Sri Lanka in the first match, then the next four matches were ruined by rain. The facilities at Galle proved inadequate and two games there were abandoned without even a ball being bowled. In the last match of a nine-month season, New Zealand were set 293 by Sri Lanka. To make the final of the grandly-titled Singer Akai Nidahas Trophy, they had to get the runs in a fraction under 42 overs. The Kiwis were never close and the team limped to the end of an arduous season that had seemed without end. The lessons of 1995–96 about over-utilising their player resources were still being learned by New Zealand Cricket.

At the very end of the Sri Lankan tour, Chris was invited to play in the Princess Diana Benefit match at Lord's. He naturally accepted and flew to London with Ruth.

It was a glittering occasion, with the stands full and Earl Spencer numbered among the crowd. Chris bowled very well for the 'Rest of the World', recording easily the best figures of 10-1-34-1. His opponents, the MCC team, included Atherton, Azharuddin and Shivnarine Chanderpaul, who scored a century. This was seen and raised by Sachin Tendulkar. In what Chris considers the greatest innings he has seen, the little Indian scored 125 off 114 balls to win the match. The opposing bowlers included Glenn McGrath, Allan Donald, Anil Kumble and Javagal Srinath. Even accounting for the festival atmosphere (one correspondent wrote: 'Even Mushtaq appealed for LBW no more than every other ball'), it was a phenomenal performance on a pitch that was doing a little bit.

Afterwards Chris relaxed with some of his contemporaries, particularly the Pakistanis Saeed Anwar and Wasim Akram, players he normally never had a chance to socialise with. Chris learnt of the great respect the Pakistanis had for Martin Crowe — that they considered some of his innings the greatest of recent times. It was an enjoyable and unique time of cricketing camaraderie.

21

Without whom

Leanne McGoldrick became a part of Chris' life in 1998. She had been introduced to Chris the year before through a mutual friend. Having owned the Budget Rental Car franchise for the South Island for 10 years alongside her husband, Bryn, she was looking for new challenges. She was drawn towards sports management at the suggestion of her friend Brent Todd. Chris had been a client of Andy Haden, and enjoyed the association with the former All Black. He appreciated the contribution Andy had made to his career, but in 1998, Chris was looking for a manager who lived in Christchurch. Logistically it had become difficult having his agent in Auckland, where Haden was based. The two parted company on friendly terms.

Chris wanted to find someone who would give him the time and space to do what he was good at — play cricket. He wanted someone who could handle the monetary side of things, but who also never lost sight of the fact that the commodity being purveyed was also a person, with fragility and frailties. The job description fitted Leanne perfectly.

When the two met to discuss a partnership, they agreed on two things — first, Leanne would handle everything professional off the field, from contracts to appointments to daily banalities. Chris would concentrate on one thing — consistency on the field. With consistency, Chris knew he could become what he always craved — the world's premier all-rounder. Secondly, Leanne and Chris agreed that the relationship would be based on one ingredient — trust. It was to be open and honest.

Leanne is a formidable business person. She is fiercely defensive of Chris, yet amiable and approachable. She can hold conversations with someone on her red-hot cellphone, with a passenger, and each of her three kids, all at the same time, and all while easing a vehicle through Christchurch's hellish 'school run' traffic. Her multi-tasking is a marvel. Astle and Nash may be Chris' preferred partners on the cricket field, but he would choose Leanne to go in to bat for him in all other professional situations.

The pairing has given Chris the opportunity to befriend a wonderful family over the last four years. He attributes some of his cricketing rebirth to Bryn, Leanne's husband, through his passionate and wise advice and views on innumerable topics (topics over which the two have shared many a wine into the late evening).

Chris has also got to know Bryn and Leanne's children — teenage Laura (13), a talented young actress, Christopher (11) and Timothy (8), both aspiring cricketers. Chris spends many hours at the McGoldrick residence but claims that he could have spent less time but for Leanne's ability to tell the longest stories he has ever heard!

Chris and Leanne's relationship has given the cricketer a sounding board, an opportunity to discuss issues and come to conclusions that may not have been so clear to him in previous years. He trusts her guidance in these matters and together the two will arrive at a decision. She has become a friend and confidante, a manager and mentor.

Chris and Ruth separated in August 1998. There were numerous reasons why the

Leanne and the kids. Christopher (left), Timothy and Laura. Chris spends many hours at the McGoldrick residence and has formed a special bond with this wonderful family.

marriage didn't work — the lifestyle in which husband and wife were apart for so much of the year was one. Many of the reasons, however, are private and personal and have no place in the public domain.

It should be enough to say that the parting was amicable, and that Ruth and Chris remain friends, and that Chris was devastated at the failure of his marriage and the mutual pain that resulted. They had both come from broken families, and had both been determined not to become yet another 'statistic', but had lost. Chris was inconsolable. He stayed with Leanne and Bryn for several weeks, trying to come to grips with the sadness.

Leanne was also with Chris when the Turner book came out and the documentary shown. It was Leanne who gave him an unforgettable quote that influenced his decision not to speak out. She'd heard it once and remembered it vividly — 'Life affords us many opportunities to say nothing. Seize them all.' His decision was to bide his time and to let his performances on the cricket field speak for him.

Public opinion is a fickle thing, however, and soon after the book launch Leanne remembers going to a packed bar on Christchurch's 'strip'. Chris, who with his height and presence was always readily recognisable, was being abused loudly by several patrons. He didn't rise to the bait. Again, maturity and restraint came to the fore. Leanne's presence calmed his rage. He would win the public over — on the pitch.

In fact, that kind of incident wasn't unusual in those days. In December that year, Chris and Leanne were walking along Courtenay Place in Wellington during the Boxing Day test, after an early meal. Several people commented loudly about Chris being out drinking again — it wasn't even 8 o'clock.

To compound his stresses, the injury jinx reoccurred, and Chris missed the ICC trophy in Dhaka, Bangladesh, and the Commonwealth Games in Kuala Lumpur, because of his tendonitis.

New Zealand's pool of cricketing talent is small. Rugby skims off much of the cream and other sports such as golf, triathlons and yachting gain adherents with international successes. Players of rare quality like Chris or Adam Parore or Martin Crowe or Dan Vettori are selected young because there is no other option. New Zealand Cricket is forced to allow its best players to grow up within the side, in public, in a fishbowl. In a situation with few older heads providing guidance to the tyros, players also mature in a vacuum.

Chris Cairns had grown from the raw youth with the famous name. In late 1998 he was close to the finished product. He was thoughtful, he was determined, he was relaxed. He still had a wild heart — all fast bowlers should — but the tension had dissipated, focus and desire were now his companions.

Chris Doig, Steve Rixon and John Graham had helped. So had Gilbert Enoka, sports psychologist and former New Zealand volleyball captain, who had joined New Zealand Cricket's management team that year. Like the famous comment about Mike Brearley, it seemed that Enoka had 'a degree in people'. Enoka thought from their very first meeting, when Chris was a teenager, that behind the laddish exterior, behind the youthful bravado, was both a deep thinker and a sensitive individual, a jewel that needed polishing. He sensed that criticism and barbs penetrated Chris' tough exterior and pricked him.

In 1998, when Enoka became player co-ordinator for New Zealand Cricket, he saw a personality in trauma, a player who was working his way through a painful awakening. Both he and Leanne had found it difficult relating to how Chris was perceived — aloof, arrogant, precious — with the humble and generous person they met daily.

In his public life, Chris' desire to preserve areas of his life for himself was often misconstrued. In his cricketing life there was a perception that he was trying to be the 'hero' of the team to the detriment of the team effort.

Leanne's aim was to create some space for Chris, to be both a filter and firewall for him. Even at the lowest points of his career, Chris has been in demand worldwide, everything from appearances to gear to autographs. Leanne took the burden of processing these demands. Enoka's aim was to make Chris into a 'hero-maker' rather than just the 'hero' of the team, to have his actions on the field being just one part of the role he had in the team.

Finally, it was a process that Chris had undertaken himself. A soul-search that began in the grim days after the West Indies tour, through the Wellington hell, to the chore of Sri Lanka. Chris had voyaged from chaos to calm. He had been out there and back again.

Finally, in November, he returned to the cricket field, in the short-lived Shell Conference competition. Chris appeared for the Southern team, who made it to the final against the imaginatively named Northern team. Chris scored his seventh first-class hundred (101 not out) in the second innings to set up a victory. While the matches themselves were little more than warm-ups, with very little at stake except personal form, Chris' success with the bat laid the platform for some of the greatest innings he would ever play.

22

Renaissance

Dion Nash thinks of the last few years of Chris' career as a 'boy's own' story. It is a time when Chris has performed great feats on the pitches of the world, where nearly every match has contained a remarkable piece of skill. Only Chris' long-time companion, injury, has blighted these years. And it all began at the Basin Reserve on Boxing Day 1998.

The first test of India's tour had been a damp squib, a complete washout, so the series effectively began in Wellington straight after Christmas. Chris Doig decided to copy the Australian example, and have test cricket played on 26 December, at New Zealand's premier cricket venue. It proved hugely successful.

A good crowd cheered on Simon Doull as he roared in to take seven wickets and the early advantage. Chris, however, looked out of sorts. Nash scored a vital 89 not out, but Chris was out softly, chipping Prasad to mid-off, for 3.

The fourth day was India's as Tendulkar scored a century and then their bowlers took four New Zealand wickets before the close. For the first time ever Chris had failed to take a wicket in both innings of a test.

That night he was nervous. He hadn't contributed at all. A win was possible, but a collapse equally likely — and Astle had a broken hand and would bat only if required.

Fourth ball of the day, and 74 for 4 became 74 for 5 when night-watchman Paul Wiseman was out. Chris joined Craig McMillan. New Zealand required 139 runs to win. Then a sliver of luck changed the momentum of the game. Chris pushed a single and Jadeja attempted to run him out. The throw was astray, there was no back-up and the ball screamed to the boundary. Chris was off the mark with a five.

Srinath and Kumble couldn't settle and Chris and Macca took toll of the loose balls. Boundaries started to come and Azharuddin was forced to spread the field. It wasn't a tentative partnership of pushes and glides, it was more like the fortieth over of a one-dayer. Chris hit a six out of the ground and McMillan registered a 50. Chris brought up his thirteenth half-century, his first in seven tests, and suddenly the Kiwis stood on the threshold of victory. Chris swung to score the winning runs, but the ball spooned directly up, and he was out for 61, with only two runs needed.

As he walked back towards the Vance stand, the crowd rose to applaud him. It had been a sixth-wicket record against India, a match-winning partnership. Nash scored the winning runs next ball. New Zealand had recorded its fifth home win in a row. Again the limo ride, again the Havanas, again the champagne.

At Trustbank Park in Hamilton, New Zealand recovered from 0 for 2 to post more than 300 on a hard seamer's wicket. Chris, however, shouldered arms to Robin Singh and was bowled for just 2.

Chris took four expensive wickets, including centurion Rahul Dravid who had batted sublimely, but dropped catches prevented New Zealand from working their way into a winning position. A couple of mini-collapses put India in the box seat, then Chris and Dion Nash came together. The New Zealand lead was just 175 with 4 wickets remaining, but Parore and McMillan had batted aggressively, and the two all-rounders decided to follow the example of their colleagues. In a rousing last hour of the fourth day, Chris struck several boundaries. When the new ball was taken, shots raced away from the Indian fielders as rapidly as their hopes of squaring the series. Chris fetched a ball from Srinath from well outside off stump, and sent it over square leg for six, to bring up an exhilarating 50.

Stephen Fleming had no thoughts of an early declaration and stated that the Kiwis would bat out for a draw. As three of his bowlers had ailments, it seemed a prudent decision to ensure the series, but if people thought the last day would be for dullards they were wrong. Chris started where he left off, hitting boldly. Dion Nash was run out but soon Chris registered his second test century. His maiden ton might have been magical, but his second was confirmation of his status. The first 100 was no one-off. He could repeat the feat.

He should have been out a few balls later when he defied the laws of physics. A ball from Prasad hit his stumps but didn't dislodge a bail. The game was safe and he carried on, enjoying himself immensely. A straight six off Kumble, a few more boundaries and he had his highest test score. When he popped a catch to Dravid off Kumble a few balls later, he had scored 126 off 202 deliveries with 16 fours and 3 sixes. Fleming declared immediately and Chris defied tiredness to get the token wickets of both openers. The game petered out to a draw, and the series was won.

Chris started the one-day series in the best possible way, inaugurating Owen Delany Park, Taupo, into international cricket by having Tendulkar caught at second slip in the third over. New Zealand were well on their way to victory when a fuse blew at the new ground and the floodlights failed. The holiday crowd sang '60s classics while the electricians worked on the overload, and the labyrinthine Duckworth–Lewis system handed the Kiwis an easy stroll when light was again shed on the situation.

Napier yet again produced a cracker, with India prising victory in the very last over, bowled by new skipper Dion Nash, who had replaced the injured Fleming at the helm. After an abandoned match at Wellington, Chris' bowling almost swung the doomed Auckland game towards the home side. Chris took three wickets, including Tendulkar's, when defending a small total, but India notched the required runs.

Chris had now scored 23, 44 and 44. Each time he had set himself a launching pad, but had not blasted off. He had been stuck in the ignition phase. India led 2–1, and the sides were clearly evenly matched, but a couple of factors turned the advantage to New Zealand. First, Tendulkar was injured. Second, Chris' next match was his 100th. He wanted to celebrate this achievement with a big score. And it was at home, Lancaster Park — the newly baptised Jade Stadium.

The night before, Stephen Fleming called a players-only meeting. He wouldn't be on the pitch but he asked his players to dig deep, to find something extra and extraordinary. Chris called for focus, for each player to focus on their role.

Inspired, New Zealand batted first and Twose and Young scored positively. Chris joined Roger Twose at 101 for 3, and like the previous innings in the series he began sedately taking the singles the spread field offered. After 30 overs, the Kiwis had scored 123 for 3. Chris went to his half-century without fuss, then a good ball from Robin Singh beat him and carried through to the keeper. The Indians went up but the appeal was turned down.

The appeal was the trigger he needed to launch and he began to flog the Indian

Cricket doesn't get any better than this. Chris strides off to the applause of fans and team-mates at Jade Stadium after his magnificent 115 against India. At the time, it was the thirteenth-fastest century in one-day history . . .

attack. Singh was hit for a six, Kumble for two sixes, and Prasad for three. One shot cannoned high to Kanitkar at deep cover. The unfortunate fielder managed to clasp the ball five times but each time it slipped from his hands. And just to heap the misery, the ball bounced from his hands over the rope — another six. Suddenly Chris was on 97. He decided to work the singles, then once the scoreboard read three figures he started hitting thunderously again.

The crowd was in a frenzy. There was a competition — a jackpot was won if a member of the public caught a six. There was joy and expectation every time the ball carved a parabola from wicket to stand. Chris was finally out for 115 hit from 80 balls. He had hit 7 fours and 7 sixes. His century, off 75 balls, was the fastest ever by a New Zealander (beating his own record) and thirteenth fastest ever. As he came off, the Canterbury faithful rose to cheer him. Fifteen thousand beaming faces, 30,000 clapping hands, a swarm of kids seeking autographs.

New Zealand set India 300 to chase but they never seemed likely to get them. The series finished 2–2, a fair result. These were two evenly matched teams.

Two weeks later, Chris played his seventh Shell Cup Final against Wellington. Chris gained a record sixth winner's medal when he, Allott, Astle and Harris tore through the opponents' batting. This was close to the New Zealand bowling attack. Chris was on form with both bat and ball. The World Cup was mere months away. The signs were all good.

South Africa arrived. Klusener, Kallis, Pollock and Cairns. All these men were vying for the laurel of the game's best all-rounder. Chris was relishing the battles. Hansie Cronje's side were many people's pick for the World Cup. The series would be a good assessment of just how well the Kiwis were progressing.

PHOTOSPORT

The first match was in Dunedin and the terraces were packed with students. New Zealand was chasing a tricky target when Chris joined Nathan Astle in the middle. The scarfies gave Chris a huge welcome. He loved playing at Carisbrook during the university term — the response of the crowd was always so vocal, so immediate, and there was always the odd couch-burning. Chris and Nath discussed tactics. They'd push the ball around, establish a rhythm and then one or both would start playing the big shots.

On the fifth ball he faced, Chris pushed a tight single into the off-side and burst out of the blocks, but halfway down the pitch he felt the ball hit his calf muscle, a large bruising impact. It was surreal though — he turned and could see Dale Benkenstein just picking up the ball — at point! He hadn't thrown it yet. Chris took another step, faltered, then collapsed like Goliath, mid-pitch. It hadn't been a ball he'd felt. It had been his calf muscle tearing apart.

As Chris was stretchered off his muscles relaxed and the pain hit him. His whole leg throbbed. The Carisbrook crowd gave the wounded warrior generous applause, but Chris didn't notice it. Beneath eyes screwed up in pain he was contemplating the unthinkable. His appearance in the World Cup was in doubt.

PHOTOSPORT

. . . And cricket doesn't get any worse than this. Chris is assisted from the ground by Lance Klusener and Allan Donald during the first match of the one-day series between New Zealand and South Africa at Dunedin, 1999. Chris had ruptured his calf muscle.

23

The quest

While he was recovering, Chris participated in a blackjack competition at the invitation of Christchurch Casino CEO and avid cricket follower Arthur Pitcher. He had never played before — gambling is not one of his passions — so he watched a video the night before and learned the rules and vocabulary.

The next day he played conservatively. The professional gamers around him were much more daring, lost more money and incredibly Chris won the initial stage. He was through to the semis. Beginner's luck helped him again. He qualified for the last place in the final, by finishing highest loser. Sitting next to professionals, for whom the words 'sit', 'hit' and 'double up' are daily vocabulary, was Chris, a novice. The play continued until the last hand. Chris was in third position and decided to bet the maximum. He was only there for fun anyway, and he'd got further than he'd ever thought.

The other players bet conservatively, then Chris was dealt an 8 and a 3. He doubled up. The card-shark in the lead went bust, the second-place man sat on 18, while Chris got a picture card. The croupier sat on 19 and Chris, incredibly, had won a professional gambling tournament! He had won more money in an afternoon than he would have earned in several months of cricket! The professionals couldn't believe it

A casino golf day hosted by Arthur Pitcher (left), CEO of the Christchurch Casino. Others in the frame are, from left: Chris, Bryn McGoldrick (golfing burglar) and Chris Doig.

and congratulated him warmly. It had been a display of both luck and good management, the two elements you need for a World Cup.

Gilbert Enoka thinks that Chris never worked so hard as he did to come back from that calf injury. The World Cup seemed like his destiny and he trained to get fit. By the end of the recovery programme that New Zealand Cricket had set, Chris was in the best shape of his life. Enoka witnessed the extraordinary focus of the man at close range.

But it wasn't just his physical fitness. Chris was preparing in other ways — developing strategies. With Stephen Fleming and Steve Rixon and the senior players, plans were developed, knowledge pooled, tactics mulled over. Gilbert Enoka and John Graham, meanwhile, developed maxims and protocols, and goals for each individual to meet. Centred at Lincoln, New Zealand's High Performance Centre, the planning for the World Cup campaign was like a war room. It was intense, exciting and, most importantly, thorough. The tour party that assembled was one of the most extensively prepared and professionally organised New Zealand sides, from any sport, to travel to the Northern Hemisphere for a world event.

To celebrate this unity of purpose, the New Zealand team were christened the Black Caps. It may have been the creation of a PR crew, but the sobriquet seemed appropriate. The Kiwis were going to execute a plan.

Gilbert Enoka had developed an idea about a year before, a collective vision for the team. It was 'Better Than Before', BTB as it was known within the squad, a goal to cover both the World Cup and the England tour afterwards. It wasn't just to improve constantly on personal results — it was also to improve on the achievements of previous New Zealand teams — to better the results of 1983, to win more than the team of '86, to be the most successful Kiwi tourists to England, ever. Not everybody thought it possible. The team were 16 to 1 outsiders for the World Cup according to betting agencies.

The World Cup carnival was opened with a reception at Buckingham Palace, with all the players introduced to Queen Elizabeth II. It was a great moment for Chris to be inside the royal residence, to be told the protocol, to look over the private gardens and to shake the majestic hand — a photo of Chris and Her Majesty taken that day hangs in his mother's lounge.

Warm-up games were vital that month as England experienced a near-Arctic May. Chris hated the cold, and could feel his injury keenly in the low temperatures. The Black Caps won all three prelims, but Chris played tentatively. He was lucky to come up against the none-too-taxing Bangladesh side in their opening World Cup match, held at the County Ground at Chelmsford. It was the perfect lead-in. Cobwebs could be shaken out, nerves could be played through and a damaged calf could be eased into service.

On a chilly morning, Geoff Allott, beginning an extraordinary month, took two wickets. Chris removed the captain's middle stump, and Gavin Larsen set about the middle order. Then Chris took two wickets in two balls, and was on the verge of the first ever World Cup hat-trick. The moment got to him. He tried too hard and sprayed the ball wide.

New Zealand taxied to the target of 117 in 33 overs. There was some criticism that they hadn't achieved the tally quick enough, that they hadn't batted first and hadn't tried to spike their run rate. Stephen Fleming simply explained that they had wanted

Matt Horne (centre) provides his own Polaroid eclipse glasses as the rest of the Black Caps use the approved issue during the 1999 England tour.

to practise chasing a target. It was as though they'd sleep-walked it. Not so the second match. That was a waking dream.

New Zealand caught Australia cold at Sophia Gardens in Cardiff. Geoff Allott began swinging the ball around under the leaden sky. The curve balls accounted for four top-order wickets, and this, coupled with an exemplary fielding display, saw Australia restricted to just 213 in their 50 overs. This seemed plenty enough when four New Zealand wickets had fallen for 49 runs.

Roger Twose and Chris Cairns, both on nought, were charged with consolidating. They concentrated on survival, taking singles when possible then, having scored just four runs off 16 balls, Chris stepped down the pitch to Shane Warne and connected. It was a mammoth shot. The ball left the tiny ground and disappeared into the Welsh wilderness. Chris knew this would create doubt in the mind of the great spin-bowler. It was a superb opening gambit.

Twose meanwhile was picking up the occasional boundary to prevent the run rate from expanding to unlikely levels. The score ticked over while Chris bided his time, waiting for the moment to aim for the boundaries that seemed so achingly close. Chris had scored just 13 from 34 balls when he struck a four off Damien Fleming. Then when Warne was returned to the attack, to bowl in tandem with Michael Bevan's 'chinamen', Chris clubbed two more sixes, one off each spinner, in consecutive overs.

A second ball was lost after the straight drive off Warne disappeared into the nearby Taff River. Warne had been hit off his line, and the control and belligerence of Twose and Chris had emasculated one of the world's best attacks. Chris was eventually caught off Damien Fleming, attempting a fourth six. He had scored 60 off 77 balls. The match-winning partnership had been worth 148 runs. Twose carried on to register 80 not out and finished the match with an agricultural pull over midwicket.

PHOTOSPORT

Chris gets airborne trying to save a run during this World Cup contest against the Australians at Cardiff, 1999.

It had been a most remarkable victory. This time they had beaten the Australians. They were BTB. Twose, broad and compact, Chris tall and expansive, had an odd mélange of styles that seemed to work. The left-hand, right-hand combination was only one difficulty bowlers had to overcome. Chris was better straight, and Twose's strength was square. Twose and Cairns were the toast of the tournament.

The bad weather continued. Umpires risked getting frostbite if they waved their fingers about too much. Allott kept bending balls vast distances beneath the solid cloud cover. And sap rose in the turf — the pitch in Southampton for the next match, against the West Indies, was a bowler's strip.

New Zealand batted and were rolled easily. It was 31-4 early on, then 75-6. The first boundary didn't come until the 21st over. Curtly Ambrose bowled 10 overs without a break and was nearly unplayable with his lift. It was a day for the nudge, nurdle and grind, but the Kiwis went for their shots, and paid the penalty. Their tally, 156, was New Zealand's

Roger Twose and Chris are the toast of the World Cup tournament after their match-winning partnership against Australia at Cardiff. PHOTOSPORT

lowest-ever World Cup score. Brian Lara later made short work of the run chase.

The situation got worse in Derby. They played Pakistan, who posted a good score (269) in spite of the comic running between wickets of one Inzamam-ul-Haq. The big fellow scored 73 from 61 balls, but managed to run out Ijaz Ahmed and labour over any single he couldn't stroll. One correspondent suggested that he should have been allowed to take a skateboard with him when he went to bat.

Again the New Zealand top order wilted, this time in the face of the most compelling bowler in the competition — Shoaib Akhtar. The Black Caps slumped to 7-61. When Chris and Adam Parore were dismissed in the same over, only the exact size of Pakistan's victory was in doubt. Suddenly, after all the optimism of the Cardiff win, New Zealand were in danger of missing the next stage.

The next day the Kiwi squad travelled north of the border to the ancient and royal city of Edinburgh, Auld Reekie, the greystone jewel of the British Isles.

The World Cup 1999 was played under a strange system that was intended to reward consistency. The group matches distilled down to a 'Super Six' from which the four semi-finalists would be selected. However, points gained in the Group Stage from victories over other Super Six qualifiers would be carried over. The organisers could not have envisaged a situation like the one that evolved at Old Trafford. The game between Australia and the West Indies had everything except a grassy knoll to entertain the conspiracy theorist.

The West Indies batted poorly. Their 119 was a losing score, and Australia began aggressively. But once the game was virtually sealed, Australia stalled. Nineteen runs were scored off 13 overs, and most of them were sundries. At one point, 32 balls in a row were bowled without a run off the bat. It is an extraordinary match in which the batting side curses the no-balls and wides of their opponents. The crowd roundly booed the gamesmanship.

The theory was simple. Australia needed to win, but also wanted to help the West Indies progress in New Zealand's stead, because they would then carry over more points to the second round. So Australia sought to bolster the West Indian run rate. New Zealand had to score at breathtaking speed to subvert the plan. It is ironic, considering the farce in Manchester, that when New Zealand batted with a similar slothfulness to gift South Africa a bonus point in the 2002 VB Series, the loudest voices of criticism had Australian vowels.

The Kiwis were amazed at the tactics of the Australians. They had to win at a sprint. A team meeting was hurriedly called. Fleming announced that Carl Bulfin would be in the team at the expense of the ultra-experienced Larsen, much to the dismay of Gav and the rest of the squad. Bulfin was picked on a whim from training that morning, where he had bowled fast. The feeling was that his pace would unsettle the Scots. Chris felt that the selectors panicked, that their thinking was not clear. It was almost a costly mistake.

The most important moment of the Scotland game was the very first act. Fleming won the toss and asked Scotland to bat. Chris was ecstatic, the dream was still on. The easiest way to surpass the West Indians' 'manipulated' run rate was to bowl Scotland out cheaply. Any other strategy was fraught.

Allott, yet again, and Chris Harris took the majority of the wickets, while Bulfin was very nervous and consequently dangerously expensive. Kiwi batsmen had the task of scoring 122 in less than 20.2 overs, to stay in contention. Against the Scots part-timers

A super six to qualify for 'Super Six'. Chris runs off the field at Edinburgh after hitting the winning runs — a massive six — against Scotland in the 1999 World Cup. The victory assured the Black Caps their place in the second phase of the tournament.

this wasn't onerous, and when Chris hoisted a huge six over deep square leg the game was won and the Kiwis had qualified for the 'Super Six'.

That night, in the bars of the Royal Mile, the New Zealand team celebrated. They were joined by two expat rugby players, Martin Leslie and Gordon Simpson, Kiwis both playing for Scotland, and scores of New Zealanders who had crawled out of the masonry. Players and supporters shared a great night, a triumphant march between establishments, a short twilit night remembered for the quality of the single malts.

The atrocious weather that had dogged the entire tournament continued. This time Headingley attracted rain just when New Zealand looked in a comfortable position against Zimbabwe. The points were shared. South Africa then did justice to their 'favourite' tag. At Edgbaston, the Africans qualified for the semis after Herschelle Gibbs and Gary Kirsten scored 176 for the first wicket. New Zealand were seven down for the same score. Geoff Allott broke the World Cup record for most wickets taken in a tournament, but that was the only Kiwi effort of note. Again it all came down to the last match. It was sudden death. If New Zealand beat India, they would progress. If they lost, Zimbabwe would qualify for the semi-final. India, already eliminated, were playing to save face.

There was one huge thing going for Chris — the venue was Trent Bridge. The ground had changed a little — a huge new stand curled round from the pavilion — but it was familiar and comforting, and the Black Caps even got the upstairs dressing room after a quiet word from Chris. The portents were good.

India lost their stars Tendulkar (bowled Nash) and Dravid (caught Harris, bowled Cairns) early but Jadeja and Azharuddin posted a reasonable total — 250 was certainly more than New Zealand had managed previously in the World Cup.

Twose, proving to be a star on familiar pitches, nursed New Zealand along with help from Matt Horne. Chris pottered around for a slow 11 and went out trying for his first big shot, leaving the Black Caps needing 34 off 28 balls. In fact, Adam Parore needed only 10 to finish the job and put the Kiwis in the last four. It had been a nail-biting match. When Parore hit the winning runs, Chris leaped around like the schoolboy who had visited the ground 20 years earlier. Then amid the pandemonium, Chris had a realisation — he was going to play in a World Cup semi-final.

Twenty years after walking in to Old Trafford as a spectator to watch his father play a World Cup semi-final, Chris returned as a competitor in the same fixture. History was folding in on itself, a wormhole between two generations. It was the biggest game of his career so far. The ugly ducklings of the World Cup had fought and struggled into the last four.

Chris believes that if current politics prevents Pakistan from playing tests on home soil, they should play 'home' tests at Old Trafford. The oval was a sea of green. Greater Manchester's Asian community was out in force. It is hard to imagine even Lahore having such a parochial crowd. The wicket was also subcontinental, a flat, low-bouncing pitch.

New Zealand won the toss and batted, which upset the usual Pakistani formula of scoring runs and defending whatever total was set. As Shoaib Akhtar ran in, the klaxons and whistles and airhorns reached a crescendo, and when he blew Fleming's poles apart there was a near-riot in the stands.

Chris was to face Shoaib for the first time ever. He took guard then looked up. The Rawalpindi Express was at the head of a huge run-up, almost invisible against the fevered green of the crowd. In his 11-year career, Chris had never faced someone standing that far back.

Then Shoaib started to run in, building up pace until it seemed like he was sprinting, not bowling, and then the ball was onto the batsman, colliding with wood or glove or body. Shoaib was very fast. Chris worked the other bowlers, but when Shoaib returned he stepped to leg and smoked a ball over covers for four.

That shot changed the bowler's tactics. Shoaib started bowling slower balls — which was great for Chris. He would guide the ball down to third man, then as he passed Shoaib would compliment the bowler, 'Well bowled.' 'Good ball.' Chris was happy facing balls at 100 km/h rather than 100 mph!

Chris made 44 not out, Fleming 46, and the top score was 47 by Messrs bye, leg-bye, no-ball and wide. Shoaib Akhtar was fast but he was also loose. New Zealand had made a competitive total — 241. Something to defend. The 'scoreboard pressure' was on Pakistan.

Geoff Allott was from Christchurch Boys High School, a good *altiora peto* boy, like Chris. His claim to fame is that he kept Andrew Mehrtens out of the school First XV. After breaking his legs several times, he had converted to cricket and bowled slow left-arm at school. He was now fast and awkward, and had a three-fingered grip, known by his team-mates as the Devil Grip, which produced the most satanic of all balls — the Devil Ball — fast, full, big in-swingers.

Allott is a man Chris has a lot of time for. He worked extremely hard at his game but was untouched by the fame that accrued. Allott was ultra-competitive but the ultimate team man. Chris thinks it is appropriate that the name Allott sits alongside Warne as joint holders of the most wickets taken in a World Cup tournament.

But on that beautiful Mancunian day there was no deviation from the pitch and no

Hitting out at Edgbaston in New Zealand's match against South Africa at the '99 World Cup.

swing in the air. Allott's swerve was neutralised. He was still bowling full, but the ball was going straight and Saeed Anwar and Wajahatullah Wasti drove down the ground. For the first time, Allott was lost and the Black Caps' most potent weapon disarmed.

The rest of the Kiwi attack were also seamers and the Pakistanis played them easily. The team probably needed Daniel Vettori that day. The conditions had gazumped the New Zealanders.

Anwar, a wonderful timer of the ball, scored a century. As he pushed the winning runs, vast hordes of Pakistanis ran onto the pitch. The ball was never fielded as all 13 players and both umpires sprinted from the ground before the onrushing crowd. The invasion was scarier than facing Shoaib.

The Black Caps had been outplayed. Just like 1975, 1979 and 1992, they had made the semi-final. They weren't BTB. They were equal but not better. It was frustrating, particularly as Lord's presented a seam-friendly pitch and an overcast day for the final.

The team returned, disappointed, to London. They had had a great run. They all watched the other semi-final on television, the best game of cricket Chris has ever seen. Australia won a remarkable match but Chris felt for the Africans, who had been the best team — especially Lance Klusener, who had been the player of the tournament, without doubt. It was a shame that the Proteas had fallen so close to their goal. The Black Caps went to Lord's for the final and, keeping the Anzac spirit, cheered the Australians as they carved up the Pakistan side and lifted the Cup.

Phase 2 of the BTB tour began. There were personnel changes — the one-day specialists were farewelled and the first-class challenges began. The team travelled to Taunton in Somerset for a match and bowled badly. The attack of Nash, Doull, Allott and Cairns was picked apart by a very ordinary county side, featuring no internationals. Somerset scored 554.

On the Sunday, the slavering English press wrote of smorgasbord-bowling and batting with a stick of rhubarb. In New Zealand, the *Sunday News* wrote off the bowling attack completely, ignoring the fact that it was a four-day game — a perilous activity.

Chris gets frustrated that scribes do not allow the game to flow. The predictable thing about cricket is its unpredictability and reporters do not seem to keep this in mind when reporting three, four or five-day games. Too often a team can be reported to be losing a game from the first day. The contest and the players are not given the chance to unfold. Chris feels that the sensationalism and hastiness of the dot.com era exploits people's frailties.

New Zealand responded powerfully to the criticism by smashing the county bowling, then a clinical destruction of the West Country batting followed. Chasing just 224, Chris and Nathan combined with an unbeaten partnership of 141, at close to six an over. Chris remembers the match as beautifully unpredictable and pure cricket.

Stephen Fleming must have thought twice about batting when he won the toss for the first test at Edgbaston. The pitched looked like a minefield. His rationale was that the pitch conditions weren't going to get better, so the Kiwis should make the best of a bad situation and watch the pitch deteriorate. The ball was sheering laterally and wickets fell steadily. Chris was dropped twice, edged through gully, played and missed, and was finally caught and bowled in a compelling half-hour. But Parore played brilliantly for 73 and the Kiwis had reached an undeserved 226.

Twenty-one wickets fell on the second day. England, then New Zealand, were bowled out, and the day finished with a night-watchman, Alex Tudor, batting for England's survival. England needed 208 to win. The lead should have been bigger. Fleming had dropped Andy Caddick in the first innings, and the expat had narrowed the gap between the sides. Nine wickets were needed to win the match. New Zealand had dominated for six sessions in a row. It was only right that that dominance should be rewarded with a victory.

Two things beat New Zealand the next day. One was beyond their control — the weather. The temperature had dropped, the wind had shifted, the conditions had changed. Peter Willey, the umpire, had turned to Chris early on and said, 'You poor buggers. Conditions are different, it's five degrees cooler. The ball's not going to swing.'

The other thing *was* their control — the seamers bowled poorly. Trying too hard to defy the meteorology, panicking, they bowled short, then fuller, trying to compensate for the fact that the ball was no longer swinging. The quartet didn't bowl line-and-length and Tudor played freely, reducing the target in blocks of four. This tail-ender reached 99 not out with the boundary that won the match.

No one spoke in the Kiwi dressing room for some time. This wasn't BTB. They sat in silence for half an hour. The test was marked by elementary errors, dropped catches, loose bowling, muddled batting. Scyld Berry, of the *Sunday Telegraph*, wrote that 'It wasn't vintage cricket, it was corked.'

That night, needing to get out of their depression, Parore, Doull, Twose, Nash and Cairns went out to dinner. At a Thai restaurant, they conducted a post-mortem. Suddenly everybody started telling home truths about their colleagues. Someone said to Chris, 'You want to be the greatest all-rounder in the world, but you're just not doing it. You've got to play harder and better.' Chris was hurt. He was trying his hardest but in the honesty of the moment he questioned himself, 'Do I have more in me? Maybe the guys are right?'

The confessions continued around the table as each player was addressed. By the end of this self-flagellation, this group — the core of the team — vowed to get more from themselves, vowed to make this tour BTB.

According to the papers, England were back as World Champion. Pundits predicted a 4–0 sweep, and the reports were infused with condescension. England were offered 'another helping of Kiwi fruit'. Little did the Fleet Street journos know what motivation they gave to Chris and his team-mates.

The Black Caps played Hampshire at Southampton. Chris had the game off but it was to be a revelatory match for him. Steve Rixon described that match as 'Nash v Hampshire', so dominant was the all-rounder.

While Chris admired Dion's feats from the balcony of the County Ground, he sat next to a small man, short of stature and rake-thin. It was Malcolm Marshall, one of the greatest fast bowlers ever. Chris remembered facing Marshall at the tail-end of the Bajan's career. Marshall was playing for Scotland, Chris for Notts in a B&H Cup match. Chris spent most of the innings staring at the legend as he ran into bowl. A couple of times he had to break himself from a trance as the ball came towards him. Then he proceeded to try to smack the stocky fast bowler for six, just so he could tell his grandkids that he had pummelled Malcolm Marshall! But the man next to him that day in Hampshire was very different in appearance. Marshall had terminal cancer. Chris talked to the great man about the art of fast bowling, players he'd bowled to, players he'd played with, strategies for batsmen. He treasured the time. Then Chris asked him, 'What do you think of my bowling?'

'Yeah, I've seen you on TV. I just don't think you run in. I think you're lazy. You don't attack the crease enough — you just cruise in. You have it all there but, remember, bowling is hard. If you want to bowl fast, you have to hit the crease hard.'

From anybody else, Chris might have thanked him politely then just as quickly forgotten the conversation, but this feedback had come from an artist. You didn't ignore Malcolm Marshall. He'd done it, taken 300 wickets, been the best in the world. That hour-long conversation with a dying man was like a year's coaching with anybody else. Chris digested the criticism, and began thinking about aggression and intent. It was to be the catalyst for the rest of the tour.

In the nets before the next game, against Kent, Chris put more energy into his bowling action, hitting the crease and following through more. He then extended his run-up to increase momentum at the point of delivery.

Chris had been in a comfort zone for the past year. He was bowling first change and bowling adequately. But that Thai dinner and the conversation with Marshall had changed Chris. He left his comfort zone. Adequate wasn't good enough. He pushed himself. He wanted more responsibility. He had been first change in the Birmingham test but Doull was injured. Chris asked Fleming if he could take the new ball in this match.

At Canterbury, Chris tried this remodelling. It was strange at first, he lacked rhythm initially but after lunch it all clicked. Suddenly Chris was bowling genuinely fast. It was pace he had been missing for years.

On a flat batter's paradise, he took 7 for 46. In the second innings he reefed his bowling a bit, easing back. He still took three to finish with 10 wickets in the match, but he was so conscious of his body. It was a handful of days before the second test, and he wanted to be in top condition. The test was at Lord's and Chris Cairns had a new toy.

24

BTB

A wicket falls and you turn and grab gloves, bat, helmet. You descend some narrow stairs, where each step is curved from the hundreds of feet that have marched down and up. As you step down, you pass the board, made of mahogany, that lists every century and every five-wicket bag a visitor has achieved at the ground. In stark black lettering, you see some of the greatest names in cricket — V.T. Trumper, C.V. Grimmett, D.G. Bradman, G.S. Sobers, K.R. Miller, B.S. Bedi, M.D. Marshall and R.J. Hadlee. Near the end of the lists are M.D. Crowe and D.J. Nash.

At the foot of the stairs you turn and pass through some double doors. You enter the Long Room. You are tentative with your steps. The floor is wooden and you don't want to damage the boards with your spikes, but there is a strange rubbery give in the floor, and there is no damage in your wake. You can't shake the feeling that you are standing in a museum.

The stud is high, to the left there are huge oils of past cricketers — Douglas Jardine, the Don, and there is a bust of W.G. Grace. On their stools, sitting at high tables are the members, with their red-and-gold striped ties. They look, but respect your focus as you pass behind them. A steward opens the final door and says 'Good luck' and you trot down the steps towards the ground. You pass your colleague who is walking the other way, being applauded politely.

You notice the slope of the ground. It angles down to your right, as you roll your shoulders the announcer tells the crowd your name. A tight group of Kiwis cheer in the second tier but otherwise it sounds as if everybody is clapping wearing gloves. The media centre looms over you as you approach the crease. You are batting at Lord's.

In 1999, New Zealand had never won a test match at the home of cricket, but Lord's acts as a stimulant. Visitors rise to the occasion, boosted by the history, the reputation. Because of the rarity of playing there, touring players often raise their game to a new level. Ordinary players sometimes perform extraordinary feats.

The days before a test are busy times — there are practices, media engagements, functions. In London, the team had had a busy day two days out from the match. They were all tired but the MCC was hosting a dinner at Lord's and D.J. Graham insisted that it was compulsory. The night was initially slow. The reluctant diners milled around one of the committee rooms while Colin Ingleby-Mackenzie and M.C. Cowdrey introduced members to players. But as the evening progressed interesting conversations sparked up, as leg-spinners talked to spin doctors, stock bowlers to stock-brokers. Simon Doull, a Kiwi boy from Pukekohe, talked for a long time to one of the principal bankers from the Square Mile. What had begun as a chore converted into a great night.

The morning before the test match, Chris was practising on the Nursery ground when his mother, Wayne and his uncle Barry Roberts arrived at the ground. The trio had travelled around the globe to watch their boy play at Lord's. It was another source of inspiration for Chris. He walked with the three to the pavilion, back across the Lord's outfield. Normally members of the public are forbidden to enter the playing area but alongside Chris it was all right. For Wayne and Barry, both cricket lovers, it was the thrill of a lifetime.

The night before the second test, Steve Rixon held a team meeting at their hotel. He didn't know what to say, how to push his charges to the next level, how to put Edgbaston behind them. So 'Stumper' asked each of them to make a statement about what they felt they could contribute to the next test, what they could do to improve their game.

The first three to speak talked in general terms — 'tighten up my defence', 'bowl a better line', 'work on my footwork' — obvious answers, answers about technique and application. Then it came to Chris Cairns, who stood bolt upright and stated, 'I am going to be on that fucking honours board at the end of this test match.' Rixon remembers hairs standing up on the back of his neck. It was a battle-cry. Chris was amped and the feeling was contagious.

When the coin spun for the toss, it glinted in the morning sun. Almost as soon as Nasser Hussain declared that England would bat, the clouds started building.

The first ball of a Lord's test has a ritual. As the team came out there was muffled applause around the ground. While Geoff Allott measured his run-up there was a buzz, a murmur. It was the sound of England expecting.

Then as Allott stood at the top of his mark, it was as if the mute button had been pushed. There was no sound and at fine leg Chris could even hear Allott pounding in. When the bowl went through to the keeper, there was polite clapping, and the sense that now they could get on with the game. With new ball in hand, Chris measured his elongated run-up and was shocked as he passed the signs painted for the benefit of television. It had been years since his run-up was so long. Chris was nervous but ran in hard, concentrating on hitting the crease. The first ball came out short and wide and Alec Stewart hit it for four through point. But at this stage Chris had built a huge block of confidence, and a single glorious blow was not enough to dent it.

He turned and ran in harder. In the eleventh over, he persuaded Butcher to edge to the keeper. After lunch, Nash and Cairns bowled superbly. Both took two wickets. It was during this session that Chris recorded the fastest ball of the entire series from either side — 146 km/h.

Chris beat Graham Thorpe a couple of times, and as is customary advised the left-hander that the ball was doing a bit. He then bounced Thorpe, who responded by pulling Chris for four. Thorpe looked down the pitch and said, 'This is big boys' cricket.'

A riposte like that will always pump up any fast bowler and he ran in harder. A personal duel ensued, which ended when Thorpe nicked out to slips three overs later. Chris ran around the retreating batsman and asked him who was still playing 'big boys' cricket' and suggested where he could put the concept. Fleming and the slips tried to turn Chris away from the cameras so he would avoid a fine for sledging.

Poor Chris Read was out for a duck in every sense. He will have to perform remarkable feats if the image of his dismissal is to be wiped from people's memories. Running in hard as Chris Cairns was, his slower ball actually got even better, the loop even bigger. It rolled out of his hand 20 km/h slower than his faster ball, and in a completely different trajectory.

Read saw the height of the ball, ducked, assuming it was a head-high full toss, while the ball dropped to his feet, between his legs and knocked the bails off. As he walked off, the delivery was replayed on the big screen. The team couldn't help but laugh at the Keystone Cops dismissal and a giggle ran around the

ALLSPORT

Young English keeper Chris Read ducks under Chris' slow ball at Lord's in 1999. Read ducked thinking the ball would go over his head . . . but it ended up going under his feet.

amphitheatre. Chris felt sorry for the young wicketkeeper.

The Kiwis were on a roll and directly after tea in increasingly gloomy conditions Chris got Headley and Mullally in quick succession. He had his five wickets. His name was on the board. As he walked back to fine-leg, the crowd stood to applaud the feat. Chris knew where Sue, Wayne and Barry were sitting in the stand above. He looked for them, doffed his cap and waved. To have them there was perfect.

Next morning, Chris was practising on the Nursery ground when Thorpe again passed by him and said, 'You're a big man when you get someone out aren't you?'

Chris couldn't believe that it was continuing, particularly during warm-ups.

'Yeah, you're real mouthy when you get someone out.'

Chris and the other bowlers told him where to go.

Chris finished with six wickets. When he got to the dressing room, he saw that someone had put a plaster on the board and on it, in marker pen, was written the name C.L. Cairns. He was chuffed.

Matt Horne added his name to the list later with a disciplined century that was an essay on leaving the ball. He was hit in the head by Andrew Caddick and battled on for a Man of the Match performance. Vettori, Twose and Chris (31) all helped extend the lead, but the breakthrough in England's second innings was long in coming.

Suddenly, in the last over before tea, Butcher butchered a sweep off Daniel Vettori and Astle took a brilliant catch at slip. It was typical of England's looseness. Instead of going into tea 60 for none, the Kiwis were buoyant. They surged out after the break, the ball began 'reversing' and two wickets fell. Thorpe, who was now the acting captain after Hussain was injured, came to the crease and hit Vettori for seven off three balls.

With all the verbiage that had passed between the two, Thorpe might have been expecting a bouncer first ball from Chris. What he got was another 'Franklyn Stephenson' special, a slow ball, which again looped up, down and under the bat. Chris was ecstatic but wanted to keep out of trouble. As much as he wanted to give England's best batsman the serve, Chris ran in the opposite direction — straight to Matthew Bell at square leg and lifted the young opener off the ground.

The later England batsmen hung around until the second new ball was taken, and the Black Caps' top order knocked off the 80 runs required. Fleming's men had won in four days, by nine wickets. There had been hundreds of Kiwis in the crowd, and it seemed like every pub in London was without some of their staff that day as the crowd gathered below the balcony for the presentations. There were New Zealand flags, and All Black jerseys everywhere.

Having just achieved the first New Zealand victory at Lord's in 70 years' worth of attempts, the team's dressing room was chaotic. Not everybody was celebrating in the usual way — Chris Harris, Craig McMillan and Daniel Vettori hadn't quite finished their game of euchre — what better time than with champagne glasses and cigars in hand.

The team sat in the dressing room for several hours bathing in the atmosphere. They had been BTB. Everybody had left and the stadium had become a sepulchre when someone suggested that the 'dirt-trackers', the guys who hadn't played, should do something to commemorate the historic event. So the 'dirties' and Ashley Ross, Gilbert Enoka and Mark Harrison from the management team went down onto the ground, and put together a back-line move, stringing passes from one side of Lord's to the other. They then finished with probably the first haka ever performed beneath Old Father Time.

A first for Lord's. After the famous victory against England, the 'dirties' performed a haka on the hallowed turf.

The team went to the East Midlands to play a couple of matches, while Chris took valuable time out and visited his friends, the Affords, in Nottingham. With the length of the tour, the management had decided that a rotational system would operate and allow players a break, to clear their minds of cricket for a little while, to come back refreshed. It was another great managerial innovation. Chris rejoined the team before the third test at Old Trafford. What followed was one of the most boring tests in the history of cricket.

The wicket at Manchester was diabolical and the new England captain, Mark Butcher, who had replaced Hussain, probably assumed that the wicket would only get worse. He chose to bat, little suspecting that the pitch was going to dry out and play better. Wickets fell regularly while England ground out runs. Thankfully, rain arrived to spare the spectators their agony.

The second day saw Peter Such score a 72-ball duck and receive the only standing ovation of the entire match. Rain shortened the third and fourth days in which New Zealand built an impressive lead. Chris got off the mark with a six off Such, and one correspondent wrote that that one shot had more audacity than England had shown in their entire innings. Just when the Black Caps looked likely to press home the advantage, rain arrived again.

Coach Steve Rixon is amused as Chris models Bruce Edgar's classic 1980s beige uniform during a rain break in the test at Old Trafford.

CAIRNS FAMILY

The most exciting and memorable event of the entire test was the arrival of a man who wanted to sell Bruce Edgar's classic beige uniform from the early '80s. The team decided to have silent tenders for the shirt. Chris was gutted when Craig McMillan won the prized possession with an £80 bid.

With the test series sitting at 1–1, things started to go wrong for the team. Simon Doull was still out injured and he was followed by Geoff Allott. Then in the next game, against Essex at Chelmsford, Chris tried too hard on a green wicket, and strained his patellar tendon. Suddenly he was in doubt for the decider. The Kiwis also lost the Essex match by an innings. They'd been away from home for more than a hundred days.

Andrew 'Gadget' Penn, one of a long list of great Wanganui cricketers, had been drafted into the squad. He would play if Chris couldn't fulfil his duty. In the lead-up to the test, Penn asked Chris hourly about his fitness and could barely sleep. Penn had an interesting tour. He was fined for turning up to the Manchester test 10 hours late after he'd been given leave to play club cricket, and another morning he missed a wake-up call and got onto the team bus still wearing his whites. As he staggered down the aisle bumping into every seat he looked drunk but had, in fact, mislaid both his contact lenses and his glasses. He was fined again and almost ended up losing money on the tour.

New Zealand to that point had dominated all but

one of the 12 days of test cricket in the series, but the first day of the Oval test was all England's. The pitch offered a little help and New Zealand relied on their tail-enders to bolster a low score.

On a dodgy knee, Chris gave an exhibition of quality fast bowling. He maintained a consistent line and length, using both the pitch and the technical flaws of the batsmen. All the while the jolts and bangs of his action sent pain around his body, and he would come off the field after each spell and work on the kneecap. Thorpe, Hussain and Irani fell to this display of skill and fervour. Vettori also displayed his all-round ability with a 50 and three wickets.

On the third day, a small lead looked likely for New Zealand — a couple of wickets were required but Mark Ramprakash was still at the crease. Chris walked out onto the ground before play and tried to size up which end to bowl from. Ian Botham was doing the pitch report and came over to Chris later to ask him what he was doing. When Chris told him the great all-rounder looked at him strangely and said, 'Just bowl'.

He was right. Chris grabbed the ball enthusiastically, took two more quick wickets, and finished with five-for. Chris then had a huge lunch thinking that he wouldn't be required for some time. But just after lunch, New Zealand was reeling. The English seamers again exploited the conditions and had the Black Caps at 37-6. The series was no longer even in the balance. It had tipped solidly in England's favour. Something special was now required.

Chris had not had a score of any substance in the entire series. His batting confidence was low. Beneath the gasometers of Kennington, someone needed to step up to another level. There is a Maori word 'ihi'. It translates loosely as 'spirit' or 'presence'. Gilbert Enoka thought of that word as Chris walked to the wicket. He had presence.

Chris loves situations like that. He was inspired by the venue itself, he knew the lower order was in fine form, which eased the pressure somewhat, and when, fourth ball, he got his feet moving and punched Caddick through the covers for four, his confidence lifted.

What followed was Bothamesque. Like 'Beefy' at Headingley in 1981, Chris did not swing the bat from the outset. On a pitch that was stopping a little that would have been suicidal. Instead he pushed some singles, sizing up the pitch, and when the ball was loose he wasn't tentative but went through with his shot. Sixteen runs came off one over from Ed Giddins. Hussain then brought Tufnell on at the Pavilion End.

Phil Tufnell was one spinner that Chris had never really dominated in test cricket — he had good flight control and had dismissed Chris four times. But Hussain erred with his field and mid-on and mid-off were kept up. There was no one on the boundary straight. To one of the biggest hitters in world cricket this was an invitation to wind up. Even a miscue would clear the field.

Chris played out a couple of maidens then he took two steps towards greatness, down the pitch and swung his bat in a full arc. The ball took off high, and fell into the seats of the Pavilion. It was a huge hit.

When he took up his stance again, Alec Stewart, the England keeper, asked him, 'You didn't really get hold of that one, did you?' Chris smiled and shook his head. He had actually got under the ball.

Two deliveries later, Chris again advanced down the pitch and struck the ball.

This time it went many tiers up the grand old brick building, one of the biggest hits ever seen at the Oval. Over the stump microphone one could just hear Stewart saying to himself, 'That's better'.

Two more sixes followed, both off Tufnell, one an extraordinary shot. Tufnell had moved into defensive mode, bowling over the wicket into the bowler's footmarks. Chris moved to leg and drilled another shot over the extra-cover boundary. Chris also hit eight boundaries and the New Zealand lead suddenly seemed almost to be enough. He had batted initially with Craig McMillan then later with Dion Nash. The Nash–Cairns partnership was the decisive pairing in the rubber, 80 runs of bravado and brilliance. Chris was eventually dismissed by Mullally for 80 off 94 balls. The innings didn't just rescue New Zealand, it injected hope and competitiveness into a team that were mentally exhausted.

Ten English wickets stood between the Kiwis and victory. Before stumps, two were down. That night there was a team meeting. It was a remarkably similar situation to Edgbaston, where they had panicked. They knew they were going to be nervous, and talked about being prepared to use the emotion, the anxiety to their advantage. Patience was needed. With patience would come the laurels.

That last day was effectively the last day of Steve Rixon's and D.J. Graham's professional involvement with the team. That was another spur to the players who took the field that morning. Rixon, through 'bloody-mindedness' and a work ethic that would make a Puritan look like a sloth, had moulded this team into a unit of many parts — a team of individuals pulling in the same direction. That mixed with Graham's unbridled Kiwi passion and strength of character to form a potent combination. The players had already given a public tribute to Rixon — they mimicked his '70s garb and wore fake moustaches when they warmed up against Essex. But the players now wanted to win the test not only for themselves, for every New Zealand cricket fan, for the future, but most of all for these two men.

It seemed an unlikely task when Atherton and Thorpe stayed at the crease for an hour. The bowlers kept their tight line. The English were adhesive, but more importantly they weren't scoring runs. Dion Nash then took two wickets in two balls. Nash's confidence was infectious and the English fell apart. Fittingly, Chris had Mullally caught by Twose, and the 11 cricketers leaped into a congratulatory maul, joined by one or two rapturous Kiwi fans. It was done.

In the dressing room, the congratulations and bubbly flowed. Chris sat with a tired grin on his face. D.J. Graham came over and the two men hugged. It was a moment for emotions rather than words. The tears in each other's eyes said everything.

Later every member of the tour party stood up in turn to say what the last four months had meant. Stephen Fleming spoke last. With tears of joy, he stated that this was his greatest moment. 'We are,' he said, 'Better Than Before.'

They had won 2–1. No New Zealand team had ever won two tests in England. No New Zealand team had ever won a series after being behind. No New Zealand team had ever won a test at the Oval, or Lord's. They had quarried their own place in history. Their results were even better than the '49ers, Walter Hadlee's great team. In a tribute to that mighty side, they called themselves the '99ers.

And Chris had performed magnificently. He was awarded Man of the Match, and New Zealand Man of the Series. This was the player who had always shown glimpses of his class but for so many reasons could never hang on to that success. He had never

The '99ers pay tribute to the coach. The whole team became Steve Rixon lookalikes — false moustaches, zinc and head bands — during warm-ups for the last county match on the tour of England, against Essex at Chelmsford.

The New Zealand dressing room at the end of the 1999 tour, and Chris delivers the poem he wrote about the side. They had just won the fourth and final test at the Oval to clinch the series for New Zealand 2–1.

found that thing that distinguishes the best from the rest — consistency. Until now. Chris had consistently shone, done and won. He had run on a gammy knee and batted at the toughest. His supporters cheered, his detractors slunk away silently.

Before the '99ers disbanded, they were entertained in great Anzac style at the Walkabout Tavern in Shepherd's Bush. The place was packed on a Monday night when the team walked in. Chris' memory went straight back to 1992, to the Cook in Dunedin. There was a huge flock of Kiwis there to celebrate with the players.

Later that evening, Chris' inhibitions had been lowered by a few celebratory drinks. There was something he had to say to someone. Chris saw his target — Steve Rixon — and walked over to him. 'I thank you for pushing me beyond my limits. I will never forget that.'

Rixon was wearing a New Zealand cap that was ever so slightly askew. He smiled under his moustache. 'No worries, mate.'

It was a no-nonsense answer from a no-nonsense man whom Chris regards as a no-nonsense friend for life.

The two turned with arms over each others' shoulders and rejoined the party.

25

Big hits green grass

One afternoon at the High Performance Centre at Lincoln, David Trist, the new New Zealand coach, brought in a bag of soil, and started to sprinkle the earth around the nets. It was one way of simulating the conditions of the Indian pitches, where spinners extract a lot of turn. It was a typical Trist idea.

David Trist had coached Chris previously and the two shared a mutual respect and close friendship. Trist had overseen the beginning of Canterbury's reign in the early '90s. He was an instinctive coach, a person always interested in the welfare of his squad. Whereas Rixon was interested in fitness, form and technique, Trist's philosophy was completely different — he would ask how a player was feeling, he would suggest taking a break, relaxing. Rixon coached cricket, Trist coached life.

Trist was willing to try novel things to get the best out of the team but, like most imaginative people, he was not always the most organised man. He needed an efficient manager like Jeff Crowe, who was willing to do anything for the squad. The Black Caps had developed an independence and self-policing through John Graham's principles and ideals, and they had acquired the discipline to implement those from within. John Graham had been the best personnel manager Chris had experienced, while Jeff Crowe is the best cricket manager he's ever had. The changing of the guard was not traumatic and the appointments by New Zealand Cricket were very astute.

It was tough for Trist to come in at that time. The team had only three weeks between tours, and in those three weeks not many of the cricketers had their minds on the job. There was general euphoria at the achievements in England, and celebrations to attend, including Simon Doull's thirtieth birthday. As much as they had the adjective 'professional' in front of their occupation, this was a time that these cricketers wanted to spend winding down.

The squad hadn't done much training by the time they left for the subcontinent, but at least there were a couple of weeks, and two games, before the first test. The preparations, however, went awry. The first game in Pune was rained out — again the situation occurred with overnight rain ruining the chances of play the next day.

The next match was at Jodhpur, but

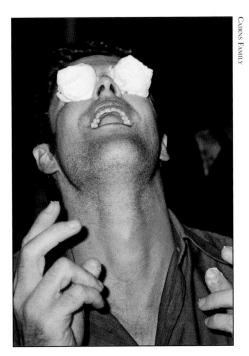

CAIRNS FAMILY

Simon Doull's 30th birthday party in 1999.
Chris says these meringues should have been
placed in his ears instead of his eyes after Doully
began singing.

Chris picked up a cold and missed the match with illness. With the first test approaching, Chris hadn't bowled a single ball in anger all tour.

Jodhpur at least provided some distraction — one night the hotel organised a cultural evening with wonderful local food, dancing and music. It was an enjoyable evening and to reply the team encouraged Shayne O'Connor to deliver a long, monumental haka.

In the middle of the haka, the man on the sitar started to keep O'Connor's beat, and searched for the war dance's melody. Shayne kept on going, pounding his chest and chanting at the top of his lungs. It is the only recorded haka–sitar duet.

In Mohali, for the first test, Stephen Fleming discovered one of the world's rare things — a green top in India. He won the toss and chose to bowl in the first-ever instance of a visiting captain doing so in a test in India. Although Chris had hardly touched a ball, he picked up two wickets while Dion Nash was up for the fray and bowled superbly. His 6-27 was his best-ever haul in tests and a beautiful display of seam-bowling on a wet wicket.

India was all out for 86. New Zealand ground out a lead of over 100 but in searing temperatures the wicket baked and in India's second innings everybody racked up good scores. The Kiwis batted out the remainder to record a good draw. Winning in India is rare, and this was one of those occasions where a draw was a great effort.

The team moved to Kanpur, where they discovered one of the most surreal things they had seen. Their hotel, a touch under two-star quality, had a world-class 10-pin bowling alley on the fifth floor, a rink that would have graced any American teen movie.

The groundskeeper at Kanpur's Green Park made sure that the ground did not live up to its name. The wicket was fragile and runs had to be chipped out like granite. The Kiwis struggled in both innings, facing a quartet of spin-bowlers. Chris top-scored in the first with a 120-ball innings for 53 with three sixes and four fours.

In the second, runs were at a higher premium. He was almost dismissed getting both his runs before Joshi lured him down the wicket and bowled him. Sandwiched between these two hands of misère was a solid Indian innings in which Wiseman and Vettori bowled tirelessly. India needed just 83 to win.

Sadagoppan Ramesh has had a short cricket career but he will always be remembered by Chris Cairns. He went back to a short ball from Chris, got an inside edge and played on to his off stump. It was Chris' 131st test wicket. Very few players would celebrate their only wicket in a match that was as good as lost, but this was special. Lance Cairns had taken 130 test wickets. Chris had overtaken his father.

In the huddle that followed the dismissal, Chris told his team-mates what he wanted to do to celebrate. They couldn't believe it. He wouldn't do that, surely. Not in a test match. But he did. Running in to Dravid with the ball clasped in front of him in both hands, he gave the delivery the full wrong-footed windmill technique. He mimicked his Dad's action. The ball slid down leg, which also, he claims, mimicked his Dad!

Andrew 'Gadget' Penn is the best tourist Chris has travelled with. He is hard-working, committed and bloody funny. It was Gadget who ordered room service in India from a rather annoying waiter, 'Nan bread, murgh tikka lababda, two hand grenades and a very long stick'.

It was Gadget, along with Chris, who gate-crashed a celebration (maybe a wedding,

Chris couldn't think of a better way to celebrate overhauling his father's test wicket tally in the test against India than bowling his next ball using Lance's famous action.

anniversary or possibly even a funeral) in Kanpur. They were invited on stage and 'sang' together, without accompaniment, Neil Diamond's 'Sweet Caroline' while Daniel Vettori got the 100-strong crowd to wave their arms in time.

Players like Andrew Penn provide the anarchy an Indian tour needs. Chris believes that Penn has not yet showcased his skills in New Zealand colours. He proved what he could do when he was Man of the Match against Leicestershire the previous tour.

At Ahmedebad, Nathan Astle dropped a top edge from Sachin Tendulkar off Chris' bowling. Tendulkar then went on to score his maiden double-century (it was the first leg of Nathan's '200' double). New Zealand made a grand effort to get to the follow-on target, with Chris top-scoring with 72 in just under four hours, and while the pitch was not a vicious beast like Kanpur, India were well on top.

During that innings Chris was hit in the head by Venkatesh Prasad, not one of the first names mentioned in conversations about intimidatory bowling, and scarcely able to get the ball to rise the necessary six feet three inches. Daniel Vettori is always quick to ask a congregation of cricketers if any of them have been hit by Prasad.

New Zealand failed to pass the follow-on target but strangely Tendulkar went very defensive, chose not to enforce the follow-on and batted with no real haste. His thoughts, revealed later, were that he wanted to keep his bowlers fresh for the one-day series following and that a 1–0 series win was as good as a 2–0 win. Chris was surprised as he has always thought that you should never give the opposition any opportunity to re-enter the game.

Opportunity knocked and the top order answered, batting the entire last day to save the match. It was especially good considering the entire squad were in mourning after they had watched the All Blacks, the evening before, being torn apart in 20 minutes of furious Gallic attack, in the fateful World Cup semi-final at La Stade de France. The devastating loss made the Black Caps determined not to lose their match.

New Zealand set records in the first one-dayer at Rajkot — 349 was their highest-ever total. India pummelled the bowling but couldn't meet the target that Astle (yet another century), Spearman, and Twose had set. They could *only* make 302!

In the second match at Hyderabad, India reciprocated. Tendulkar and Dravid both scored big hundreds and New Zealand were set 377 to win, at 7.5 an over. It was a phenomenal partnership and Tendulkar once again showed why Chris considers him the greatest batsman of recent times. When he gets going, no bowler is immune to his onslaught. The crowd responds to his presence with a symphony of frenzy — they bang plastic water bottles together, the sound making it impossible to hear in the outfield.

Tendulkar feeds off the passion and lifts his game to another level.

The next match it was Ganguly's turn to score a century. New Zealand had a reasonable total to chase — just 264 — and seemed likely to make it until some of the middle order committed the willow version of hari-kari. Chris was one of the culpable.

He was up for the next match played somewhere in the Bengali back country — a place called Guwahati, where thousands of people turned up at the airport to welcome the two teams. A wall collapsed because of a crowd surge and several people were injured. The Black Caps stepped into an insane scene of whistles, chaos, rubble and yelling. At least 400 people stayed outside the hotel the whole night just to get a glimpse of either set of cricketers.

Chris, again combining with Roger Twose, hit a patient and well-compiled 80 before he was run out for the third time in the series. He hit three sixes to keep the crowd happy. The Kiwis bowled well, Chris picking up Dravid and the Man of the Match award. It was 2–2.

The finale in Delhi was disappointing. New Zealand found batting difficult. There were some dodgy shouts for LBW upheld, and the Kiwis lost momentum. Chris scored a 41, but 179 was never going to be enough. Because of a hamstring injury, Chris bowled seven overs straight for remarkable figures (7-4-10-0), but the Indians took the game.

It was disappointing to be so close to winning a difficult series yet again, but Sourav Ganguly stated that it was the most challenging series the Indians had had since he'd been involved, which was a great compliment.

On the team's return to New Zealand, Chris made his first foray into show business — a TV game show called 'Can You Hackett', filmed in Queenstown. The star of the show was A.J. Hackett, all-round nice guy and inventor of the bungy jump. Chris was referee, responsible for keeping contestants in line as they attempted to master challenges set by Hackett. Lana Cockcroft hosted the show and Chris enjoyed his time alongside producers Julie Christie and Darryl McKewan but he struggled with the long days and the constant sitting around.

Canterbury had awarded Chris a benefit season for 1999–2000. One of the events was a match at Jade Stadium between the Young Guns of 1992 and the Black Caps of 1999. Chrises Cairns and Harris played for the Young Guns to bolster the side but the youngsters came away victors.

That December, the West Indies arrived in New Zealand. Viv Richards was coach. Chris was geared up for the series. Even though their stocks had fallen somewhat from the glory days of the '80s, the Windies still had their stars — Lara, Adams, Walsh and Chanderpaul — and they played with the calypso style that Chris had taken as a modus operandi.

The series began with a Cricket Max game. Chris hadn't played a lot of Super Max cricket previously, but the rules were plain — two innings each of 10 overs, and extra runs if the ball was hit straight. The Windies, however, were tardy in the field, and were docked one over because of their slow over rate.

Suddenly, in the labyrinth under the stands of Jade Stadium, there was an argument. The Windies refused to come out to field in the second innings. It was just a fun game they said. They shouldn't be docked an over in a hit and giggle game. But Twose, the Kiwi captain, was unyielding. The Black Caps could earn win bonuses for the match — it was a legitimate match and the rules would be adhered to.

Martin Crowe, the inventor of Max Cricket, came down to try to mediate between the parties but Twose was adamant — 'If you wanted this to be a fun game then don't pay us. But there's a win bonus here for us, and we want to win.' Chris sympathised with Crowe but fully backed Roger. Twose won the argument.

The Windies were revved up and peppered the Kiwis with bouncers in the second innings. New Zealand won but it started the tour on an aggro note. It evoked memories of the fractious tour of 1980 when Clive Lloyd's side refused to take the field because of umpiring decisions. But it also showed the Windies that the Kiwis would not roll over for them.

After the first day of the first test, in Hamilton, the Caribbeans might have thought otherwise. Both Windies openers, Sherwin Campbell and Adrian Griffith, scored centuries and Lara's side was 282 for 1 overnight.

That night Chris went out to dinner with Leanne and Bryn McGoldrick, who had been watching the match. Chris was depressed after such an abortive day. Leanne spotted a girl she had been talking to at the match and invited her to join them. She brought her boyfriend — West Indian quick Franklyn Rose.

Chris sat quietly combusting. The last person he wanted to share his disappointment with was one of the opposition. He remained very pleasant to the tourists, and after they had left all shared a laugh at Leanne's expense as she confessed she was only trying to be nice. It certainly gave him some fuel for the next day and gave Leanne ammunition for the future when next he might have a bad day on the field.

Chris and Leanne McGoldrick. The relationship has given Chris the platform to achieve what he really wants — be the best cricketer he can.

Having dismissed Jimmy Adams, Chris raises his arms in delight at his test best figures of 7-27 in the 1999 Hamilton test against the West Indies.

The Kiwis all thought that they hadn't bowled *that* badly, and they had a statistic to back that up. The bowlers consistently try to maintain a percentage of maidens in any test innings. If they bowl 27 per cent (or higher), then New Zealand usually wins that test — denial is a potent weapon. That first day in Hamilton the maiden percentage was over 30 per cent. The batsmen had scored in block areas, and the Black Caps hung strong to the stats. They would stick to their plan of attack.

Next morning, wickets fell quickly. Lara tried a few cavalier shots off Vettori and hit one straight up in the air, and the rest surrendered meekly (including Rose, caught Wiseman, bowled Cairns). The Windies lost 9 wickets for 76 runs and let the Black Caps back into the game, a game they shouldn't have been allowed anywhere near.

The Black Caps batsmen took advantage of such profligacy and all the top order scored some runs, though nobody kicked on to three figures. Chris, meanwhile, shouldn't have even got out of the starting blocks. First ball he pushed out to cover and took off for a single, but the ball ran quickly to Chanderpaul, who threw the stumps down. The third umpire was called for but only two camera angles were possible as the TV crew was preparing to show replays of Nathan Astle's dismissal the ball before.

The side-on shot was inconclusive — Jimmy Adams moved between the stumps and the camera, and although it was easy to infer that Chris was a foot or so out of his ground in both shots, the umpire could not confirm, without doubt, that the bails had come off before Chris reached safety. Viv Richards was yelling in his dressing room for the red light, but after a long, excruciating delay it was green and the Master Blaster went ballistic.

Chris didn't feel particularly comfortable. It was dark, the wicket had freshened up, Lara had taken the second new ball and the Windies' plan of attack for Chris was clearly based around the short ball. Chris nervously speared a ball from Reon King into second slip's hands, but King had overstepped. It was all the largesse he needed.

Chris had to wrest the advantage his way, he needed to dominate the bowlers, so he began to hit out. Three boundaries off an over from Franklyn Rose were followed by two in Rose's next. He pulled strongly as the Caribbeans pitched short. His 50 came up at a run-a-ball, then he hit the spinner Ramnarine for a six over long-on before he was caught going for another off the same bowler. He had scored 72 and dominated the 116-run partnership with Craig McMillan and the Black Caps had a slim lead. He had been a particular thorn in Rose's side. Chris hit his dinner 'guest' for six fours and one six.

That night Chris watched the highlights on television at the team's hotel, and was disappointed to hear some negative comments about the innings from commentator Jeremy Coney, a man who knew Chris and Chris' game very well. Coney criticised the innings as 'rash'. Coney certainly knew how difficult it was to face the West Indies quicks — he was one of the best players of quick bowling New Zealand had ever had, until Joel Garner broke his arm in 1985 and then he seemed ball-shy when he next played the Windies in 1987.

Chris enjoys Coney's company socially and thinks of Coney as articulate and intelligent. But Chris also thinks of Coney as someone reluctant to praise.

The Windies were batting the next morning but must have wished they hadn't left their hotel. Chris took the first two wickets without a run on the board. Campbell almost edged behind before having his stumps scattered the next ball. Chanderpaul had a huge LBW appeal turned down then nicked the next to Parore. Lara was then greeted with a pearler of a bouncer that raised cheers from the Waikato crowd. The next over, Nash got him.

Chris then bowled superbly to Griffith, who consistently played inside the line of the ball but never looked comfortable. After bowling three consecutive maidens to him, Chris had figures of 7-5-3-2 when rain delayed play.

On the last day the Windies began with a small lead and four wickets down. Finally Chris ended Griffith's vigil when the Bajan feathered an edge to Parore. Jacobs was then run out, and suddenly just four wickets were left. Chris got them all. He took Rose and Ramnarine in consecutive balls to be on a hat-trick for the third time in his test career. Although there was a loud appeal from the four slips and two gullies, King didn't even get close to the next ball. Nor did he get close to the slower ball that trapped him in front a bit later. Adams was caught at fine leg and Chris had figures of 5-16 that morning.

Chris had entered the record books all over the place. His second innings figures (7-27) were the third best recorded by a New Zealander in tests. Only Richard Hadlee had better figures. Adams was his tenth victim of the match — he joined eight other Kiwis on the list of those who had achieved that in test cricket, including his Dad. Lance and Chris became the first father-son combination to achieve that. Ten wickets and a half-century in the same match had been achieved only four times for New Zealand before, thrice by Hadlee and once by Dion Nash.

It was Chris' greatest all-round performance, but more importantly it came in a victory. The Black Caps achieved the target for the loss of a single wicket. Chris had talked to Ashley Ross, the team's technical adviser, before the series and said that he had never really won any test with the ball, that none of his five-wicket bags had come in the second innings apart from the first. He'd never really taken a lot of second innings wickets in his career but he wanted to sometime over that summer. Now he had in the first match — against the West Indies.

The Boxing Day test saw the remarkable debut of Mathew Sinclair. His team-mates sat in the viewing room incredulous as Sinclair displayed all the natural skills he possesses in scoring 214 in his first innings in test cricket. Chris had never met 'Skippy' before but had heard that he was a different character. Chris liked it when someone was themselves, was who they wanted to be, unique. And to see a young talent blast the West Indies all over the Basin was great. Chris thinks that Sinclair has been hard done by since but hopes that he stays strong and sticks at it, because Wellington proved that he is a very fine player.

Chris replaced Sinclair at the crease and hit his first ball, from Nehemiah Perry, for six. It was something his hero Ian Botham had done and Chris was determined to have it on his CV also. Chris then took the first three wickets but was forced into a containing role by pain in his back. His accuracy earned him two tail-end wickets to end with another five-wicket bag. The tourists followed on. Chris' injury would restrict his ability to strike in the second West Indian innings. Someone would have to fill the breach and Dion Nash was that someone, bowling incisively to get four wickets.

When Chris was called back to bowl at the last pair a bizarre spat ensued. Chris wanted Nash to get a five-wicket bag, a just reward for some hard toil. As a bowler he understood the satisfaction of getting 'five for'. It equated to a century for a batsman. The Windies were not going to come back from this situation — they needed over 100 runs just to make New Zealand bat again! So Chris bowled wide of off stump for the first few balls — hoping that Nash would get his fifth wicket the next over.

Suddenly the keeper and slip cordon — Fleming, Astle and Parore — started to object to Cairns, demanding that he put the ball on the stumps. At the end of the over, Parore came up to Chris and asked what was going on. When Chris explained that he was doing it for Dion, the keeper said, 'Just get him out. Bowl him out. Let's get off the field. Come on!'

Nash didn't get the vital wicket the next over either, and when Chris bowled the first ball of the next well wide of off stump the slips glared at Chris, Chris glared back. On the threshold of a test victory everyone was suddenly in high dudgeon! Chris bowled a slower ball and dismissed Rose to finish the match but as everybody trailed off the field to loud applause there were arguments raging within the New Zealand team about the principles involved.

A couple of hours later over some champagne they all laughed about it. That night Shayne O'Connor joined the limousine ride for the first time.

They had beaten the West Indies 2–0, the second match by an innings. But it didn't finish there. The one-day series was equally triumphant. In Auckland, in front of a huge crowd, Chris and Nathan Astle combined in a record 136-run partnership for the fourth wicket to win the match. Chris hit Reon King for two fours then went for full points after that. Six times he lifted the ball over the boundary before he was caught for 75.

Chris started the second match in Taupo in the most dramatic way — Campbell was caught at slip off the first ball of the match. With Chris finding it difficult to come back for a second spell, he bowled his overs straight through and also took the wicket of Lara.

Chris puts his whole body behind this unorthodox 'swipe' against the West Indies at Jade Stadium in 1999.

Then he joined Fleming in a solid partnership to overhaul the Windies target — 2–0.

Across the Kaimanawas to Napier and the start of the match was similar. Chris started with a wide, but got Campbell again with the first legitimate ball of the match to complete an unusual 'king pair'. Chris recorded great figures — 8-0-25-3 — but they would have been even better had he not bowled eight wides, including five in one over! His back was clearly giving him some grief. The Windies failed to set a big enough target and the Black Caps won comfortably — 3–0.

The next match was the inauguration of the WestpacTrust Stadium in Wellington into the world of cricket. There was a christening of sorts — the game was abandoned on the first day when rain fell and resumed the following day. The atmosphere at the 'Cake Tin' was not affected and the crowd witnessed a victory of ease and panache — 4–0.

The thought of a 'whitewash' inspired the Black Caps in the last match, at Jade Stadium. Twose and Astle batted vibrantly, and the home-town boys Harris, Cairns (helped by a cortisone injection in his right knee) and McMillan played impressive cameos as New Zealand recorded their highest-ever total against the West Indies in an ODI — 302. It proved too much for the sorry Caribbeans — 5–0.

It had been a mighty series, a series that brought comparisons from Colin Croft with Geoff Howarth's team of 1980 — the team of Coney, Hadlee and Cairns. Everybody was calling for the next internationals — the Aussies were due.

Before that though, Chris played a few games in the Shell Cup, one of which, inevitably, was the final. Canterbury beat Auckland to record their seventh victory in nine years. Canterbury, and Chris Cairns, had now beaten every one of the other associations in the Shell Cup Final in that period.

Canterbury were to domestic cricket what Australia were to international cricket, and Steve Waugh's team came over the Tasman determined to break records in both forms of the game for undefeated sequences.

Chris was up for the series — he got the wicket of Adam Gilchrist in the very first over but Wellington was again jinxed by the weather and the game rained off. Before the match notes were found at the Australians' hotel, 'forgotten' by manager John Buchanan, about each of the New Zealand players. The media loved it. Chris was described as a 'front-runner' but 'lacks confidence if you get on top of him'. Chris was mentally frail in Ocker eyes. The leak was a brilliant bit of gamesmanship — the focus went right off the Australians.

The next match in front of a packed Eden Park was an embarrassing loss. The Black Caps were even forced to bowl before the lunch break, so poorly did they bat. In Dunedin for the third match, they were chasing over 300 and were in the hunt at 223 for 6. Then Brett Lee struck Adam Parore's helmet and it fell onto the stumps. The delivery should have been called a no-ball but wasn't and the crowd began hurling things onto the field in anger when the dismissal was replayed on the big screen. There was a stand-off as the Australians gathered mid-pitch waiting for the anger to be quelled. Eventually the game resumed but it drifted away from the Kiwis.

At Christchurch, the Kiwis scored a record total against Australia — 301. Unfortunately Australia had also set a record against any team — 349! At Napier Chris took the wickets of both openers, defending 243, but Michael Bevan nursed Australia home. Australia had been unbeaten in a record 14 games in a row.

The two teams returned to Eden Park with the Kiwis battered but Chris was keen to make an impression before the test series and bowled superbly for 3-33. The Aussies tinkered with their batting order and only managed 191 which Chris Nevin and Stephen Fleming knocked off. The Black Caps had been well beaten by a great side but the last match was a great fillip.

On the first morning of the first test at Eden Park, Chris remembers standing with several players at the entrance of the tunnel watching the two Stephens heading out to toss. The pitch looked like it would turn early and often. Neither team wanted to bat last. The coin was tossed and Chris could see the cameras point to Steve Waugh first. It was obvious that Australia had won the toss and Glenn McGrath and Shane Warne started to dance around like schoolkids. They wouldn't have to bowl.

Chris got Slater early and the spinners, Wiseman and Vettori, started to pick up Australian wickets. After tea they were all out for 214. Australia opened with an off-spinner, Colin Miller, and wickets fell consistently to McGrath and Warne.

Australia took a small but vital lead of 51 into the second innings. Daniel Vettori bowled beautifully to get seven second-innings wickets, including his hundredth test wicket and New Zealand had a target of 281 to win. At the end of the third day Chris was batting with Craig McMillan with the score 151 for 5. New Zealand were in with a real chance, the target tantalisingly close.

The entire fourth day was rained out, but Chris spent that day in the indoor nets, trying to get some rhythm. Even though he had top-scored with 35 in the first innings he had batted poorly, his feet were leaden, his timing off. He worked hard to find some fluency in his game. The last day dawned fine and Chris came out with the intention of taking the game to the Australians — but he chipped Miller meekly to midwicket fourth ball. After all the talk about how Chris could be bullied he had wanted to prove them wrong. It was immensely disappointing.

There was some time off before the second match so Chris went back to Christchurch and travelled out to the High Performance Centre at Lincoln. He felt he had to readdress his batting. He spent hour after hour facing the bowling machine, readjusting his technique. His initial movements when the ball was being delivered had always been 'back and across' but Chris found that he was being caught on the crease regularly, and simply not batting well. Chris decided to simplify, not to move his back foot at all, to press forward slightly and trust himself, trust his ability to play anything delivered. He faced thousands of balls that week to get the movements ingrained, then the day before the Basin Reserve test he had a net and it felt great.

Chris could have chosen a better time to try new footwork. When he arrived at the crease it was just before lunch on the first day. New Zealand was five down for 66. Chris was anxious. He had never tried this technique in a test before and he was facing Brett Lee bowling close on 100 mph.

First ball, Chris stepped forward as he'd practised. He didn't really see the bouncer Lee hurled but instinctively swayed and the ball went straight past the grille of his helmet. Suddenly there was doubt in Chris' mind. Could he actually do this? Should he revert to the security and safety of his old technique?

The length of Brett Lee's run-up allows the batsman a lot of time to gather his thoughts, so as Chris strolled towards square leg he encouraged himself to stay strong with it — keep pressing forward. Just as Lee bowled, Chris pressed forward then rocked back to a short ball and drove it through covers for three runs. As Chris ran up and

PHOTOSPORT

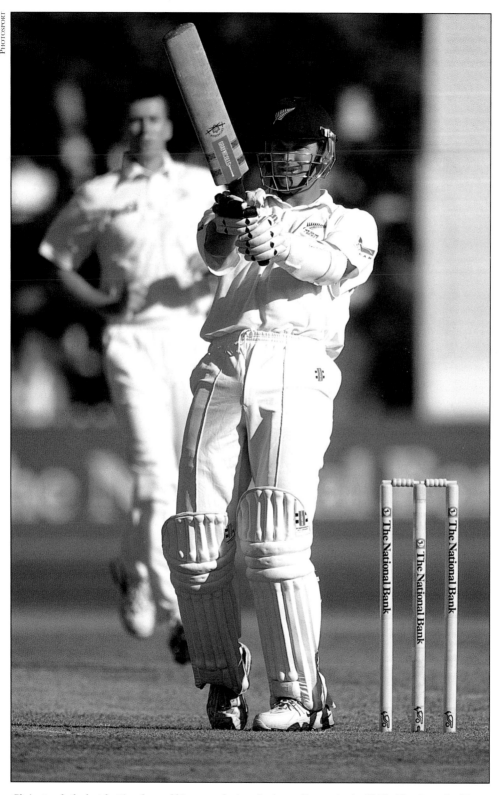

Chris struck the best batting form of his career during the Australian series in 2000. Here he pulls Glenn McGrath to the fence on his way to a century at the Basin Reserve.

down the wicket he was hoping it didn't go for four so he didn't have to face Lee again!

It was just one little shot but it had felt great. Chris went into lunch with a huge sense of achievement. His confidence was high and when he returned for the middle session his feet began to move freely and his timing was superb. Two boundaries came off McGrath then two sixes off Warne. For the first time Chris had opened his stance to Warne to counter the drift that the leg-spinner produced. It was his drift that would see batsmen overbalancing or playing around their front leg. Now with a new stance Warne's stock ball offered a free hit over midwicket, or a sweep. A great battle ensued with Warne and Cairns, good friends off the field, attempting to foil each other's most dangerous weapons.

With Astle, Chris combined for a 72-run partnership in under an hour. Coming out after tea, Chris was in the 70s, and trying to restrain his nerves. He wanted a century badly, particularly against this team. He pushed and hit more cautiously until Blewett pitched one outside off and Chris hit it through the infield. Chris had his third test century, and one of the finest.

It was Blewett who ended the innings when he took a great off-balance catch right on the boundary. Chris was out for 109. He had shown the Aussies categorically that he could play. Steve Waugh lauded the innings and drew parallels with Chris' idol Ian Botham, while Chris was asked if it was his best innings yet. All Chris would say was that he'd wait to see if they won the match.

The Black Caps started well towards that end. Chris took two wickets, Doull and Vettori one each, and Australia was 51-4, but Steve Waugh and Michael Slater consolidated, both scoring hundreds. In a see-saw series in which fortunes seemed to swing every session, the pendulum moved back towards the Baggy Greens. New Zealand's top order failed for a second time and late on the third day, as the evening darkened, Warne picked up the wickets of Astle and McMillan in consecutive deliveries. It was 88-5. Chris survived the hat-trick ball but Warne was bowling beautifully. Chris prodded around, determined to play himself in. Often the temptation after a good first innings is to start from where you left off. Chris wanted to avoid that trap.

Chris was mesmerised by Warne. He knew if he continued to allow him to bowl as he was, the leg-spinner would get him out. He had to attack, as the only way to defend. Chris advanced down the wicket and hit him for four through midwicket, then a few balls later lofted Warne straight, then over cover. Suddenly Chris had some momentum. The field started to spread, and the feeling spread as well — Stephen Fleming hit a couple of boundaries and the partnership was out of its shackles.

Brett Lee came on to bowl. His first couple of balls are generally looseners, as his body is still getting used to running that distance and going through the stresses of bowling fast. A whippet like Lee doesn't give a batsman the time to choose his shots — the fractions of a second only allow for the subconscious to function. The second ball was a bouncer, but not at the terminal velocity Lee can reach. It was a little slower and Chris hooked the ball instinctively, out of the ground into the evening traffic.

The next ball was fast. Lee was bowling with the southerly at his back. The effect of the hook was clearly to warm Brett Lee's joints up fully. It was a storming bouncer. Lee followed through and asked, 'Why didn't you hook that one, champ?' Chris could only reply, 'I can't even see it so how am I going to hook it?'

A couple of overs later, Chris spotted a ball on a length. Again it was an instinctive moment. Chris drove it on the up over Lee's head, over the boundary and over the sight-screen at the Adelaide Road end. Chris thinks of it as one of the two best shots he has made in cricket, and Mark Waugh standing at slip commented that it was the best shot he'd seen.

As the umpire raised his arms Chris' captain strolled down the pitch. It was late in the day, the atmosphere great. Stephen Fleming looked at Chris and simply asked, 'What are you doing?'

'I don't know.'

Fleming nodded his head sagely. 'That was a moment of clarity.'

Chris survived a close call for a run out moments later. The footage showed that Chris had survived by mere millimetres of shoe leather. As the Aussies watched the replay on the big screen they were in uproar at the decision. Lee walked past the batsman, glared and said, 'I'm going to stove your ribs in, champ.'

But as quick as Lee was, he was bowling two lengths — either trying to hit Chris or bowl him — the lethal good-length ball never came. Chris would duck the bouncers and drive the full-pitches past the bowler, which infuriated the Sydneysider even more.

Bad light halted play. Chris had scored his 18th test half-century. He had hit six sixes. Fleming and Cairns had pieced together a century partnership, and the Kiwis had a small lead. It was the most exhilarating passage of play Chris has ever been involved in.

The next morning, however, was disappointing. Chris was given out for 69 to a poor leg-before decision and the momentum went back to Australia. The Kiwis set Australia 174 to win, which they reached for the loss of four wickets. Australia had beaten their national record for consecutive test wins.

It was during this tour that the real genius of 'sledging' became obvious to Chris. 'Sledging' is not always a torrent of blue language and personal insults. Often the idea is just to 'mess with someone's head'. It might be as simple as a comment about the pitch or a bowler. It might be something to remind the batsman of off-field pressure, form or fitness — to have him thinking of something other than the job in hand.

One afternoon during the one-day series Steve Waugh, one of the most 'verbal' of all players, walked to the wicket with Australia needing a captain's knock. Chris called loudly that here was a big wicket and reminded everybody that Waugh had been hitting the ball regularly in the air.

'Tugga' Waugh turned to Chris and simply said, 'If I do hit it towards you, mate, you better make sure you don't drop it.' It was a brilliant line, a psychological ploy that had turned and bitten Chris right back. Now the pressure was back on Chris. Waugh was right. He was such a big wicket that to drop him would be critical.

Chris and Steve Waugh have been commenting to each other since their first encounter at Eden Park in 1992. Chris admires the Australian skipper and thinks he is a great competitor and custodian of test cricket. To sledge him in a personal way only provides him with fuel so Chris' theory has been to go a little left-field and upset him. The night before the Hamilton test Chris watched the Matt Damon, Robin Williams movie *Good Will Hunting*. Something took Chris' interest. When Chris was bowling early on the second day, he followed through after one ball seamed away and beat Waugh and recited a line from the movie.

'Do you like apples?'

Waugh frowned and replied, 'Don't be stupid, Chris. This is a test match.'

Next ball Waugh nicked the ball to slip and Chris leaped down the pitch yelling, 'How about them apples then!'

It was outré, odd and a really silly thing to say in a test match, but it worked. It had annoyed Steve Waugh, and he had got himself out. When Chris came out to bat, Waugh even put himself on, and bowled a couple of bouncers.

The Hamilton test was played on a green wicket. New Zealand scored 232 but when Waugh was dismissed the Kiwis sensationally had Australia reeling at 29 for 5. Again that constant pendulum had gone the Kiwis' way. But Simon Doull had been dropped for debutant Daryl Tuffey, which Chris thought was a mistake. The selectors had succumbed to pressure after the two losses. Although Doullie had taken only one wicket in the series, he always did well on his home ground. He'd lost some pace but Doull's movement could have been ideal in that situation. Instead of having Australia all out for a hundred-odd, the final blow wasn't delivered and Gilchrist and Martyn recovered.

In the second innings, Chris again recorded a half-century, as he tried to set Australia a challenging target. His 71 was less pyrotechnic than his other innings that summer but it still contained one of his most memorable shots. Standing with his open stance to Warne, who was bowling around the wicket into the bowlers' footmarks, Chris picked a full ball early, swivelled his feet so he was at right angles to his normal stance and 'straight' drove Warne over square leg for six.

Australia required 210 to win the test. Chris wanted to make an impact but he couldn't. He could feel pain in his knee, he could feel the strain of months of constant cricket. In the end he was thoroughly exhausted. Australia won the series 3–0, but New Zealand had had chances to win all three matches. They had given Australia the best series for some time. They had demanded and earned respect.

The loss was softened slightly for Chris when he was awarded International Cricketer of the Year. A couple of days after the test ended, Coopers & Lybrand released their updated list. Leanne rang Chris to tell him — he had risen to number 1 all-rounder in the world. It capped off an amazing three-week period since changing his batting technique. No New Zealander, not even Richard Hadlee, had been number '1'. The dream he had harboured since he was a scrawny teenager had been realised. He had joined a long list of greats — Giffen, Rhodes, Miller, Sobers, Botham and Akram.

The NZC awards dinner was a triumph for Chris. He won both the Redpath and Winsor Cups, the first player to do so since John Reid in the '50s. There was a disappointment however. In a 'Living Legends' side selected to celebrate the new millennium Bruce Taylor and Dick Motz were preferred to Chris Cairns. Though he was disappointed, he didn't take the snub to heart. The night proved to be a glittering black-tie affair, a celebration of an incredible season.

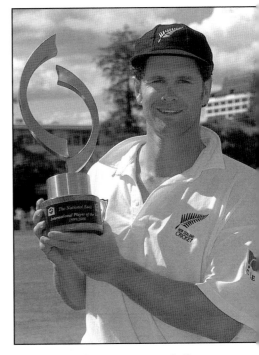

The 1999–2000 season was capped off when Chris was named New Zealand player of the year. Things got even better two days later when he was named world's best all-rounder. PHOTOSPORT

26

All's fair (or, love in a hot climate)

As part of his testimonial year, Chris held a couple of functions in England in 2000. There was a golf day and a cricket match — the Lance Cairns XI versus the Chris Cairns XI, which was well supported. And there was a dinner for many of his close friends — at Althorp. A bunch of them, including Lance and his wife, Bryn and Leanne McGoldrick, Mike Clements and All Black John Drake crammed into a Daff van, hired by Mark 'Geen' McGoldrick, that hared from London into the luxurious Northamptonshire countryside. The vehicle turned through the gates of the estate and along the pebbled drive to the mansion. The juxtaposition of a rusting beige mini van and the beautiful lines of a Reformation castle said everything about the strange bond between Charles Spencer and Chris.

The guests were apportioned among the 50-odd rooms available — grand rooms with canopied beds, and names like the Oak Room, and the George IV Room. A banquet had been prepared, and Chris joined his friends — Kiwis and Brits — in the grandeur of the dining room, with the Spencer ancestors looking down with concern from the walls. Charles arrived and the seven-course feast began, with the Kiwi boys eating off plates older than their country, and passing around a wine decanter that Napoleon had surrendered at Waterloo.

Lance Cairns XI v Chris Cairns XI, testimonial match, England, 2000. CAIRNS FAMILY

The atmosphere was far from stuffy, however, and the food incredible. When a sorbet arrived, it was presented in dishes of ice, with petals frozen within. Lance Cairns picked up his spoon and attempted to dig his way into the ice-dish thinking it was an elaborate ice cream. Even in a dinner jacket surrounded by landscapes and sterling silver, Lance was a country boy.

The night proceeded and some nice wines were enjoyed. Then Chris and his Kiwi mates felt the need to celebrate in a very unique way. A haka was decreed. In an anteroom Chris, the Kiwis, and Charles Spencer rehearsed the war dance. Then, bare-chested, the boys returned to the dining hall, and surrounded by décor from another time and another place, they performed the haka of Te Rauparaha — 'Ka Mate Ka Mate . . .'

A week later, a gala dinner was held in London at the Café Royal. Three hundred

Althorp House where a few of Chris's friends enjoyed a very special and privileged evening during his testimonial year.

Chris, Caroline Freud and Charles Spencer. Chris describes the Earl as a gentleman, scholar . . . and a dodgy off-spin bowler.

Michael Campbell (third from left) leads a haka at Chris' testimonial dinner in London. Charles Spencer, on Michael's left, follows gallantly, while Mark McGoldrick, next to the Earl, gives it his all.

guests arrived including Michael Slater, Shane and Brett Lee, John Gallagher, Martin and Jeff Crowe and Allan Lamb. This great night, with Geoff Miller as after-dinner speaker, was completed when golfer Michael Campbell led the Althorp group in another haka. Charles Spencer performed too, an honorary New Zealander, enjoying his time away from the prying press and probing cameras.

Chris returned to cricket in August for a competition in Singapore. It was the seventeenth different country he had played cricket in. New Zealand was rusty after a six-month lay-off and lost both games in the Godrej Challenge. The Black Caps were on their way to tour Southern Africa. In the tour matches in Zimbabwe, Chris really started to feel his knee and prior to the first test he sat down with the entire management team and talked about this constant injury. He'd had pain for a couple of years. He was simply sick of the constant discomfort, his diet of anti-inflammatory pills, the extra training.

Chris didn't know how much longer he could keep going. He asked if he could have a cortisone injection directly into the tendon itself as he had had in 1993 but the medical panel in New Zealand had prohibited that as too risky. A strategy had to be worked out.

The wicket for the first test against Zimbabwe at Bulawayo was benign. Zimbabwe batted at a glacial pace and for four days nothing much happened. The most exciting thing that occurred was that a tailor came and gave the Kiwis colour options for some safari suits they were purchasing — blue, pale blue and brown.

Chris had been bowling off a short run because of his knee. On the fifth morning, before play, he was bowling at warm-ups musing about his action, when all of a sudden something clicked. The great indefinable of cricket — rhythm — had returned. Zimbabwe had a small lead and were five down, but the expectation was that they could bat all day. This was a drawn test from the moment of the toss, but suddenly Chris felt good and in his second over snared Alistair Campbell, who had batted for two hours.

Three balls later, Nkala was out and suddenly the unlikely was occurring. Paul Wiseman dismissed Streak and Chris took the last two wickets to finish with 5 for 31. The last five wickets had fallen for 19 runs on a lifeless pitch. Something had been conjured out of nothing and the safari suits were debuted in triumph that night.

The second test in Harare saw New Zealand record their biggest total against Zimbabwe. Mark Richardson was given out for 99 to the last ball of the first day, a poor decision by the local umpire. The next morning Chris started to build an innings. It was not a dominating knock. He was content to wait patiently for the loose ball, as it inevitably came, from Streak or Olonga. His momentum increased when Nash joined him. Chris seemed stuck for some time in the 80s then he pulled Mpulele Mbangwa for six and pushed a single. It was his fourth test century, his first overseas. He was out eventually for 124 (3 sixes, 13 fours). Dion and Chris put on a record 144 for the eighth wicket.

Chris picked up the first two wickets, then Shayne O'Connor began to bowl beautifully. Three Zimbabweans succumbed to his pace and the home team were asked to follow on with more than two days remaining in the contest.

But the bowling attack that had worked so efficiently in the first innings just started to fail. Dion Nash broke down, while Chris could only bowl the first few overs of each session. He had strained his back during his long innings, to add to his knee ailment. The only way he could get his body 'loose' enough to bowl was to use ice-baths in the breaks, in which he would hop into a wheelie bin full of ice for a minute, then through a hot shower for two, then repeat. After this treatment his body felt relaxed but the muscles tightened up over the session. Zimbabwe batted in their second innings for nearly two days and developed a small lead. The fielders, like ancient mariners, started to go loopy.

Finally, after tea on the last day, the Kiwis were walking out for their tenth straight session in the field. They needed one last wicket, but that didn't even seem likely to eventuate. Nathan Astle was going to bowl, but suddenly Dion Nash came up to Fleming and demanded to bowl. He gave his hat to the umpire but Mark Harrison, the physio, knowing the extent of Nash's injury, ran out onto the sideline and yelled for him to stop.

Nash would not be deterred. He was on a mission. He hobbled in, bowling not much faster than Daniel Vettori, but all of a sudden there was a mix-up when Guy Whittall turned a single to leg. Nash retrieved the ball and hurled it at the stumps. Zimbabwe were all out. Again from nothing something had eventuated. The Black Caps easily knocked off the runs. Zimbabwe are hard to beat at home and no team had ever achieved a clean sweep over them before. It was the most draining test Chris had played in.

Chris wasn't selected for the one-day series to follow. It was decided to get his knee right. He flew instead to Jo'burg for a day trip to have a cortisone injection administered. In Kenya, for the ICC Knockout to follow, they had been drawn to face Zimbabwe first, so Chris watched frustrated on the sidelines as Zim won the one-day series 2–1. After the second loss, in Bulawayo, he decided that the team needed a lift.

Chris had followed his childhood dream to become a cricketer. His cousin Wayne Allport had followed *his* dream to become a flyboy and was working as a commercial pilot in Zambia. Wayne came down to spend time with his cousin and offered him a lift in his plane to Victoria Falls the next day. It would save a six-hour bus journey. But Chris had an idea to raise morale. There were a few more seats on the aircraft. Chris decided to host a 'Survivor' series to decide which of the Black Caps would join the cousins and travel in luxury. What ensued was one of the best nights any of the team can remember — as pacts were made and broken, votes lobbied for and one by one team-mates were excluded.

Finally the seats were filled and the next morning the plane swept over the Zimbabwean landscape, made a sensational pass over the great cataract and landed two hours before the team bus arrived.

With the 'Survivor' contest and a sunset cruise on the Zambesi River the following night, some atmosphere was restored within the squad. The Black Caps arrived in Nairobi on an upswing and when they got there they were further boosted by the prize money up for grabs in the knockout tournament. Although all the other test-playing nations were there, the Kiwis felt they had an even chance of making to the semis and beyond.

The practice facilities were poor so Chris hadn't really managed to test out his knee, but it seemed OK. So he was selected for the opening match. New Zealand batted first against Zimbabwe and with the pain numbed Chris was running singles harder than he had for many years when he got to bat. Then just as he was settling into his work, he turned to run a couple and, as he pushed off, one of the cords of his kneecap tweaked a little. Bothered by this distraction, Chris played a poor stroke and was out for 13. He tried to bowl but couldn't do himself justice and hobbled off with the knowledge that even if New Zealand won, he'd miss the next match.

The Black Caps did win, thanks to intelligent bowling from Wiseman, and they played Pakistan, yet again, in the semi-finals. Chris watched from the commentary box, where he broadcast for some of the networks. Talking about the game released some of the frustration of not playing. Chris watched a great run chase from his colleagues — Astle, McMillan and particularly Twose. On the tiny Gymkhana ground, the Kiwis ran down the Pakistan total. They were in the ICC Knockout final.

There were four days before the final and Chris was not about to miss the game. New Zealand had never been in the final of a major international tournament before. He was going to be there, savouring the experience. He iced his knee near-constantly, overdosed on anti-inflammatories and in the end he gritted his teeth through the pain as he passed the fitness test.

Chris often senses how the game is going to go before the match. He had some throw-downs and felt good — he was timing his strokes well. He was up for the match.

His optimism was bruised early on. Geoff Allott, in the dry conditions, got no swing at all and lost his line in his first two overs. It was Old Trafford all over again. Ganguly and Tendulkar smashed the wayward deliveries. Stephen Fleming had no option. He turned to Chris and asked him to bowl. Chris had been hoping to come on later, when a few wickets were down and the field was spread, but he was needed urgently.

Running in to bowl was a short journey into mystery — he had no idea at what capacity he could perform. His first over, however, was a maiden. He fielded aggressively off his own bowling in a bid to shake the team out of their shell-shocked start. He only went for 4 an over and bowled his 10 overs consecutively. India eventually scored 259, but should have scored more. On a small ground with a good pitch that seemed more like 220. At the change of innings Chris was quietly confident.

Chris was batting in the thirteenth over. When he went in the score was 82 for 3. The pressure to score fast was off. Chris could pace himself. Wicket preservation was the key. He took 12 from a loose Agarkar over, and lofted Tendulkar into the crowd but he and Chris Harris mainly just gathered singles, with the occasional expressive shot to keep the bowlers honest. They scored just 31 in 10 overs at one stage and the run rate expanded out to nearly nine an over, but Chris was not worried. He was calculating the risks, waiting for the averages to fall his side. The boundaries were short if push came to hit.

With 45 needed off five overs, Chris decided it was time — he advanced down to Kumble and hit him for six, then four. Harry chimed in and it was back to a run a ball. Suddenly Chris got goosebumps. He realised that they were going to win. Chris pushed three singles then raised his bat to celebrate his third one-day century. It had been a paean to control. Tim Robinson had once said that Chris batted with his heart rather than his head. Here was a 'head' innings.

With two balls to go Chris pushed the winning run to square leg and hurtled down the pitch with his arms splayed wide — 102 not out, and they had won the match, and the trophy. It was New Zealand's first one-day trophy won overseas and the zenith of Chris' career.

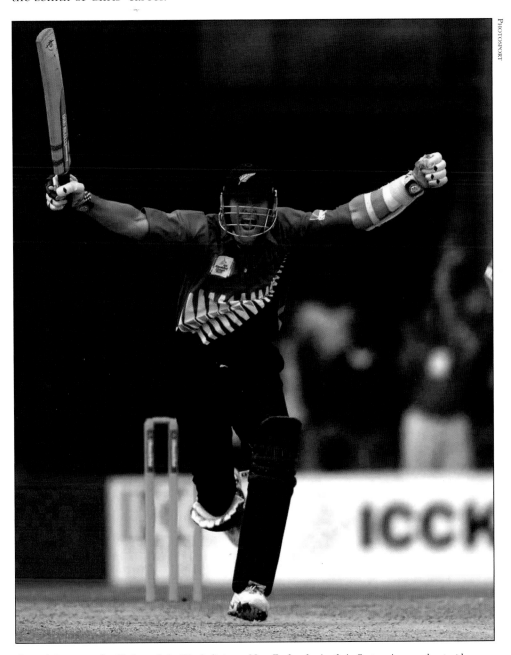

PHOTOSPORT

A special moment for Chris and the Black Caps as New Zealand win their first major one-day trophy. Chris scored an unbeaten century against the Indians to win the Man of the Match award in the ICC Knockout final.

As Fleming went out to collect the silverware, Chris told him to give it the full FA Cup treatment, the big brandish. A year earlier, on the balcony at the Oval, Chris had stood next to his captain and watched him sheepishly raise a trophy to eye level. This was a massive win and needed an appropriate celebration!

Later still, in the dressing room, the players were joined by ecstatic New Zealand Cricket Chairman, Sir John Anderson and Chris Doig. Doig, who had never sung with the team, belted out the national anthem in full opera voice.

Chris regrets the fact that the team didn't go home after that triumph, to share it with friends, family, supporters. Instead, the next day the squad flew to South Africa. There were six more one-dayers to play. Chris shouldn't have played on. His knee was constantly sore, but he was fuelled by the incredible atmosphere in the squad. He probably should have returned home to recuperate, but he stayed and would never regret that decision. It was in South Africa, not a week later, that he met his partner, Carin.

The first one-day match was at Potchefstroom, an hour and a half from Jo'burg, but just when South Africa looked likely to break batting records, the sky went dark and great black sheets of rain arrived to ruin the game. The team were keen to stay in the satellite town, get a meal and go out, but Jeff Crowe, the manager, insisted that they return to Jo'burg that night. It seemed like an unnecessary hassle but Crowe was adamant and later they all arrived back at the big Sandton complex in the city. Some of the single lads wanted to go out so Daryl Tuffey, Zach Hitchcock, the team's IT guru, and Chris asked a local to recommend a club. All Bar None in Turtle Creek was suggested.

Daryl Tuffey is responsible for Chris Cairns meeting Carin van den Berg. Tuffey asked Carin and a friend to join the boys at their table. She accepted. Later when Tuffey went to buy a round of drinks, Chris started chatting with Carin and within minutes they had connected. The conversation topics ranged from tennis to the mind and finally when the players couldn't get a taxi, Carin agreed to drive the lads back to their hotel. After dropping the men off, Carin was about to leave when Chris realised he didn't have her number. She gave it to him.

The Kiwis were based in Jo'burg for their games in Benoni and Pretoria, (which were both lost) so Chris arranged to meet up with Carin again. They grew to realise that they had shared a lot of trauma in their lives. Both had lost a sibling — Carin's brother Robin had died of cancer when he was 20. Both had parents who had separated.

Carin learned that this great conversationalist was actually a famous cricketer. She had had no idea — indeed had never even watched the sport. Chris discovered that this woman had brains to complement her charm and beauty — she was finishing a university degree in economics. She also had drive and determination. Her father and mother had started a lily farm thirty years earlier. When Carin's father passed away, her mother Liesbeth continued to run the farm in the sexist rural Afrikaner environment. Carin meanwhile had grown capsicums commercially as a sideline. She loved the flower farm and her experiences there gave her the goal to one day take over the family farm. She had gone to university to further the dream.

They talked and talked, and each night would finish with the pair sitting on a couch in the hotel with their faces illuminated by the great electrical storms of the high veldt. Carin had high morals. Her father, an immigrant from the Netherlands, had founded a school for blacks on the farm. While apartheid divided the races all over the country, on the van den Berg farm, Carin grew up at a mixed school believing in equality. She had also been brought up not to fall for strangers at bars, so when

Chris invited her to come to Durban, she initially refused, then agreed on one condition, that she found her own accommodation.

After the fourth match, in Kimberley, when Chris' injury restricted his ability to bowl at the pace he normally could, the team management decided to send Chris home to recover. He was disappointed with his performance there — Boje and Boucher both hit crucial sixes off his bowling. Chris went to David Trist to apologise for letting the team down but the coach understood the anatomy of the situation — he told Chris to play the last two games and then to head home.

The Black Caps could have won a low-scoring match at Durban, and should've won a high-scoring match at Cape Town. Under Table Mountain, Chris played one of his best innings. He batted with Roger Twose and hit powerfully. He struck Kallis for three fours in the first over he faced. Later he lofted two sixes in an over off his rival all-rounder, and then did the same thing at the other end to Shaun Pollock. He scored 50 off 38 balls, and finished with 84 off 76 and a record partnership (150) for any wicket against South Africa. Lance Klusener batted at a similar pace to win the match off the last ball. It was the end of the tour for Chris.

Earl Spencer has a home in Cape Town and while in town Chris was invited to a barbecue at Charles' place. Chris asked the New Zealand squad if any of them would like to follow him to the barbecue, without mentioning the host, but most of the team were tired and declined. Chris then went to two of the new boys, Daryl Tuffey and Brooke Walker, and suggested they join him for the evening. Not wanting to upset their senior player, they reluctantly obliged.

When they arrived at Charles' home, Tuffey thought he recognised the Earl but couldn't for the life of him remember where from. As the evening progressed, Tuffey asked Chris who the host was, how he knew his face. Chris told them that it was Princess Diana's younger brother and a veil was lifted. Brooke Walker sat stunned and could only say, 'If my mother could see me now, she'd be so proud.' A great night ensued.

On the way out of the country, Chris had a two-hour stopover in Johannesburg. He rushed out of the airport, grabbed a taxi, rang Carin, and arranged to meet her 'now now'. They had less than an hour together, but in that rushed time over coffee Chris convinced her to come to New Zealand for a holiday. The one-day series was lost, but he wasn't going to lose this woman.

Carin and Chris. A special relationship that started courtesy of Daryl Tuffey. CAIRNS FAMILY

27

Joyful and triumphant

Chris attempted a comeback in early January. He played a game for Canterbury then was selected for the first ODI of the year, against Zimbabwe at Taupo. He was still in some discomfort but his knee was much better than it had been. Then 20 minutes into the game, in just his third over, he felt something burst in his knee, and the joint swelled up with fluid. His bursa had blown. To be injured is bad, but to be injured during a game is shattering.

Chris fooled himself that he could return, but in Wellington before the next match Sir Richard Hadlee, chairman of selectors, came to Chris and told him that they didn't believe he would be fit again that season, that they'd select someone else.

There was now no way that Chris could avoid the scalpel. In February 2001, Paul Armour, Chris' orthopaedic surgeon, cut into the flesh around Chris' knee and began the intricate repair work.

Chris had a focus — he would make the end-of-year tour to Australia. While Australia were storming through another Ashes series in June, and journalists started to use superlatives to describe them, Chris travelled to South Africa to continue his rehabilitation. There were two main reasons for going there. First the weather was warm. Chris hated the cold, particularly when injured, as his body seemed to creak and groan in the wintry weather.

The second reason was more cardiac — Carin and he had decided to take their friendship to another level. They found a place in Jo'burg together and while Carin studied, Chris worked furiously in gyms to prime his body for November.

It wasn't all hard work though. The couple went on safari with Wayne Allport, and his wife, Carlene, and down to Cape Town to watch the All Blacks play the Springboks in the Tri-nations. Gilbert Enoka invited him to have dinner with some of the South Island ABs, including Jeff Wilson, Andrew Mehrtens and Anton Oliver, and he experienced the sheer amount of meat the rugby players ate. Taine Randell was the most carnivorous. His affection for T-bone steaks would have impressed Fred Flintstone.

Chris, meanwhile, was dieting. On his return to New Zealand he got himself into the best shape of his life. He spent two months working with Billie Kaine, a champion body-builder at the Pro-Fitness Gym in Christchurch, to build up his upper body, and was a regular at Lincoln, honing his bowling technique.

After the September 11 attacks, New Zealand had cancelled their cricket tour to Pakistan, anticipating the conflagration in Afghanistan. Instead they elongated the tour to Australia. It was this extra time that Chris credits their subsequent success to. The team had time to prepare thoroughly, to sit down and draw up a plan of attack.

When he joined the Black Caps in Australia, Chris felt underdone. Maybe he was unconsciously favouring his knee, but in the lead-up matches he didn't bowl well. He just didn't have the requisite number of overs behind him. His batting was another story. He scored 119 off 81 balls against an Academy XI with such regal batting that

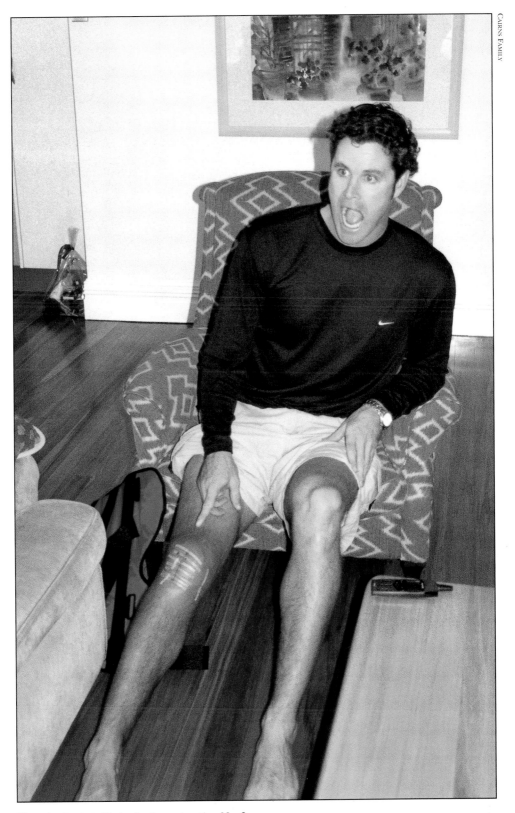

X marks the spot. Chris after knee operation No. 2.

CAIRNS FAMILY

Chris (centre) and the Black Caps make their way onto the Gabba for the first test against Australia in 2001. It was Chris' 50th test.

he should have been wearing imperial purple rather than white.

The next tour match was not a memorable one for Chris. External events would make cricket seem a distant irrelevancy. In South Africa Carin went to visit a doctor. In Australia Chris was dining with his good friend, Tim Barry and several others all the while nursing a mobile phone anxiously. The phone rang, Chris answered to hear Carin's brogue via satellite, 'We are having a baby.'

He returned to the table and saw Tim looking a little puzzled. All evening Chris hadn't uttered a word. Now he had a Cheshire grin! His mum, Sue, was ecstatic at the idea of her first grandchild. To Chris' amusement, Lance replied, 'I never thought you had it in ya.'

Normally when sides tour Australia, they get pummelled by the state sides, because the gap between the full federal side and the Sheffield Shield sides is not that great, but against Queensland, Nathan Astle scored a double-century and then the Kiwis bowled well to take a small lead into the second innings. It was a draw but in the Kiwis' favour. It signalled that they were ready.

It was Mark Richardson who was a major catalyst for the side. During a meeting about tactics for the forthcoming tests, Richie said, 'We know what we have to do, we know our plan A, but what do we *really* have to do, what's our plan B, plan C? Rather than just looking at the best-case scenario, what if that doesn't work . . .' To win a test series against Australia they had to go deeper than normal, investigate, probe, research.

Stephen Fleming allotted each player an Australian to prepare a dossier about. It had to be thorough. They went to the Internet and found stats, run charts. They found how bowlers took their wickets, where batsmen were most vulnerable. They investigated weaknesses and strengths and developed stratagems for each. They noted

PHOTOSPORT

Chris celebrates Matthew Hayden's run out in the second innings of the first test against the Australians in 2001.

that Glenn McGrath rarely hit the stumps — perhaps he could be left more often. Damien Martyn scored freely through point, but the shots were often aerial. Some were poor starters. Going into the test series the Kiwis had the gen.

They also had the inspiration. The night before the test, Jeff Crowe arranged a private presentation of the black caps to the team. As the team sat in a semi-circle, the manager introduced his cousin — Russell.

Russell Crowe pulled out his New Zealand passport and said simply, 'This is who I am.' The Hollywood star spoke quietly about achievement, his love of cricket, about winning. 'I've followed my dream. It's about belief and giving things your best shot. If you go hard here, you can achieve something that can never be taken away from you. Ultimately it's about winning and for me winning is about this.'

Crowe then pulled out of his worn satchel a little gold statuette, his Academy Award. As Chris was passed the Oscar he was amazed at how heavy it was. It read: Best Actor Russell Crowe — Gladiator.

It had been a great lead-in to the first test at the Gabba. Chris was hyped for the match — he hadn't played test cricket for a year. Fifth ball of the test Chris struck Justin Langer on the pads, dead in front. He screamed for Darrell Harper to raise his finger, but the umpire's hands remained at his side.

New Zealand having won the toss, to get a wicket in his first over back would have started some momentum for Chris, given him some sense of reward for the efforts over the months before. But it wasn't to be and Langer went on to make a hundred, and another in the next test as well. Chris, meanwhile, dwelled on that delivery, how unlucky he had been. His head was cluttered and he took the next half hour to get over it.

The Aussie openers put together a double-century partnership but then the Black

Caps came back taking some middle-order wickets in the last session. However, the Kiwi bowling attack suddenly started to fall apart — Nash tore a stomach muscle, O'Connor's knee blew and Chris was suffering from a bout of food-poisoning.

Chris kept bowling through the nausea. He had three wickets and he was determined to get 'five for'. Eventually Chris snaffled the last wicket, Adam Gilchrist — 5 for 146 wasn't pretty but he'd done it.

The game had been badly affected by huge rainstorms brewing over the Pacific Ocean. Chris got to bat only on the fourth day with New Zealand struggling to save the follow-on. Chris considers the bowling of Jason Gillespie that day, on a pitch that had freshened up, some of the finest he has ever seen. Chris was out for 61 the final morning, his 24th score of 50 or more in test cricket. As Parore and Nash pushed towards the follow-on target, Chris and Stephen Fleming were in the viewing room. Chris suddenly turned to his skipper and suggested that they declare as soon as the follow-on target was secured. Flem nodded. He'd been thinking about it already.

'But should we bat on for a bit or what?' he asked.

'We're here to play positive cricket,' Chris replied.

As soon as New Zealand were less than 200 behind, Fleming called his batsmen in. It was game on.

Nobody had thought any result other than a draw was possible but suddenly the ball was in Steve Waugh's court. One good declaration deserves another, and after run rates and overs remaining were carefully considered, Waugh left the New Zealanders 284 to score in 57 overs. Chris thought it was a very generous target, but the Aussie skipper was backing his bowlers.

The Black Caps batted positively but Warne took three wickets and Chris arrived at the wicket with the match in the balance at 190 for 4. Chris and Fleming started to find gaps in the field and suddenly Chris heard Steve Waugh yell, 'Can anyone show me some body language out here!' For the first time Chris felt they were on top.

Then Waugh himself produced a moment of brilliance — a side-on run out of his opposing number. Craig McMillan joined Chris. Seventy-odd was needed with less than 10 overs on offer. Suddenly these two muscular hitters struck — 31 runs came off two overs, one each from McGrath and Warne. Macca hit two sixes, Chris likewise, and the Black Caps were down to a run a ball to win.

There was a cyclone of protest about what happened next. McGrath changed his line, bowling yorker-length balls, three feet outside off stump. They couldn't be hit. That over conceded just one run against batsmen bristling with aggression. Critics claimed that this was somehow not in the spirit of the game. Chris disagrees. It was a masterpiece of control at a vital time. There is no place in the last overs of a tight test match for outmoded etiquette.

Chris lined up Brett Lee in the penultimate over but as he swung he felt his bat turn in his hands. He hadn't quite connected, and Ricky Ponting took the catch on the boundary ropes. Steve Waugh then put most of his fielders on the boundary and the test was drawn. Chris had almost taken them to a miraculous victory but in the end the Kiwis weren't disappointed. It had been a great game of cricket, and the chance of winning had only been created because of Steve Waugh's declaration, which has to be remembered. On reflection, a draw was the fair result.

What the match did show was that the Black Caps were not the canny nondescript journeymen that New Zealand had often sent across the Tasman.

Chris has always believed in playing aggressive cricket. Here he cuts Jason Gillespie for four in the Gabba test against Australia in 2001.

They demanded a measure of respect and attention.

Leanne noticed this one night at a Brisbane restaurant while dining with Chris. A steady stream of people came up to the table to wish Chris well for the series, to congratulate the all-rounder. All of them were Australian. Ockers know and love their cricket and it was a great compliment to the Kiwi.

Before the second test in Hobart Dion Nash was replaced on tour by rookie Shane Bond. The Australians began the contest with intent, scoring 400 on the first day, but then rain came and hour after hour dripped by with no play. On the last morning the Kiwis were 156 for 4 in their first innings, but they arrived at the ground at 9 a.m., for a 10.30 start, to find the covers still on the pitch. The tarpaulins should have been removed a couple of hours earlier but had been left to sweat and enliven the pitch. When Stephen Fleming pointed this out to the curator he agreed in a very non-plussed manner and unhurriedly removed the tarps.

Fleming was out first ball of the morning and Chris came in to face McGrath and Gillespie. It was the most challenging forty minutes of fast bowling he ever experienced. The ball was moving great distances laterally. Gillespie was jagging the ball back a long way and for the first time in his career Chris was worried that he couldn't avoid being hit. He was caught behind for a brave 20 and drizzle arrived to cease the Kiwis' torments.

The series was still 0–0 and suddenly the Kiwis had a gilt-edged chance to take the series in Perth if they could play to their potential at the WACA. The hype before the match was about the pitch — it was going to be the fastest and bounciest wicket for years and the Kiwis would be blown away by the troika of Aussie speedsters. But when Fleming won the toss, he surprised everybody by choosing to bat.

Chris was one of the three tour selectors and the day before the test Fleming had been adamant that he wanted to give Matthew Bell a rest. Bell's footwork was all over the place. He had altered his technique and had numerous movements in his stance that the Australians were exploiting. It was sad to see, as he was a very good batsman but Chris thought they should stick with Bell — they wanted their most experienced side for this crucial match.

The skipper made a big call — he wanted Lou Vincent to open, on his debut, at the WACA. Chris thought it was a huge gamble but Flem went through the positives — Lou was infectious, he wanted to play, he was a great fieldsman. The plusses of Vincent playing far outweighed the minuses.

It turned out to be a stunning decision by Stephen Fleming. Vincent scored a century in his first knock in test cricket, and Fleming watched delighted at the other end as he progressed to three figures himself.

Steve Waugh took the second new ball late in the day and four quick wickets fell — including Chris, who first astonished Gillespie with two boundaries off his first two balls before clipping a 100-mph Lee away-swinger to the keeper. Occasionally a ball is simply too good.

In spite of the ferocity of the bowling, the pitch wasn't all it was cracked up to be and on the second day Astle and Parore became the third and fourth centurions of the innings. The Kiwis were well on top.

The next day Vettori bowled superbly, and Australia might have been in real trouble had Astle taken a catch off Warne. In the end, the great spinner scored 99 and New Zealand had a lead of 183 runs.

All thoughts went to an appropriate target to set Australia for the last innings. Stephen Fleming wanted more time to bowl them out — but Chris and the senior players implored the captain to set a target over four runs per over. After all, the Australians had been scoring at four an over throughout the series.

New Zealand set Australia 440. Most teams would have done the bulwark thing, sought to defend for a draw, but this was no ordinary team. No matter what total was set, the wizards of Oz would have a tilt at it.

Before the team went out to field, Stephen Fleming announced that Chris Martin and Shane Bond would share the new ball. Chris accepted the decision but was gutted. He was the most experienced bowler and usually expected the shiny red sphere with the gold embossing by right. But he knew he hadn't been bowling well the whole tour.

Early on, Bond beat Langer for pace, then Chris was brought back for the last few overs of the fourth day. His second ball was short and wide and Ponting rocked back and smacked it through the off side. Chris groaned with frustration. He was the match-winner, the player to lead from the front. He should be taking wickets. Then Ponting slashed at another short ball. It took the inside edge and shattered the collection of wood behind him. Chris had bowled him. The Kiwis needed just eight more wickets.

On such a pitch, wicket-taking was like working in the salt mines. Wickets came, but only after toil. Only three wickets fell in the first two sessions, although it might have been different had Ian Robinson spotted a clear caught behind off Vettori. Australia slipped behind the run rate — it inflated to over a run-a-ball — and a draw seemed inevitable at tea with Waugh S. and Martyn batting soundly.

But Vettori yorked Martyn and Adam Gilchrist came out to bat. They weathered the new ball and the Australians kept accumulating but the run rate required was soon 10 an over. Then Gilchrist switched it on. This magnificent timer of the ball attacked Vettori (18 off an over) then Cairns (14) in consecutive overs. Thirty-two runs in 10 balls. The Kiwis were suddenly confronted with two batsmen well set, coming for them.

Just as things seemed to be getting beyond their control, a slice of luck — Vettori got half a hand to a Gilchrist drive and Steve Waugh was run out at the non-striker's end. Warne joined Gilchrist and the Aussies kept hunting runs. Warne, trying to give his partner the strike, pushed the ball to short cover and set off for a quick single. Chris, the bowler, was at the ball in moments with his long strides. In bare fractions of time he weighed up his options. He could throw at the stumps, but just in his peripheral vision he saw Matthew Sinclair sprinting to the stumps. Chris turned and lobbed the ball to the fielder, who removed the bails — and Warne was run out by an inch.

Gillespie was next in and the batsmen had a mid-pitch conversation. Gilchrist blocked the next ball and left the one after that. The chase was over. It was now the Kiwis' turn for an onslaught. With a full five overs to be completed, Chris bowled a short ball to Gillespie, who attempted to flick it to leg. The keeper and slips went up. Chris screamed. They'd all seen the batsman blatantly glove the ball but Ian Robinson was the umpire and the Zimbabwean official remained unmoved.

The tail-end would have been exposed, but it was not to be. The great joust was over. The match and the series were drawn. The Kiwis had competed — in fact, in the last match they had made all the play.

Like 1980, New Zealand had played the best team in the world and matched them. And just like 1980, they were the topic of conversation everywhere. Housewives had begun watching cricket again. Lou Vincent had a chat group on the Internet. The *Press* called the Black Caps 'The Magnificent Eleven'. It was the start of a great summer.

One talking point, though, was Chris' bowling. He had averaged over 45 with the ball. Chris' rhythm was all wrong. Maybe he had tried too hard to make an impact by bowling wicket balls, rather than that old mantra 'line and length'. He went back home and had huge debates about technique with his father. He watched videos. He trained hard. However it was all too easy to forget that he was returning from major surgery.

New Zealand had an inaugural series against Bangladesh next. Bangladesh was not a top-drawer opponent and Chris saw the two tests as chances to get back to his best with ball in hand. Before the Hamilton match, he went to his captain and asked for the new ball. It was important to him. His captain assented. Fleming had faith in him.

Bangladesh lived down to expectations. They were young and inexperienced. Masrafe bin Mortaza was 18, Mohammad Ashraful 17 and Mohammad Sharif, who bowled Chris in the first innings, was 16 years old. Chris initially struggled to dismiss the schoolboy batting line-up. Then on the last morning, six wickets were required for the win. Within an hour, Chris had five of them. People were still walking into the ground carrying their picnic baskets when Chris took the last wicket to confirm an innings victory. Twice he had been on a hat-trick. With one spell (9.2-2-20-5) he quelled any speculation, confirmed his fitness and found his rhythm. It had been a great work-out.

Christmas was again in Wellington, with all the team and their families celebrating together. The Boxing Day test that followed was as one-sided and finished in less than three days. Chris took five more wickets. He was closing in on 200 test wickets.

After New Year, the coloured clothing was shaken out again as the VB series began across the Tasman. It was the familiar Tri-nations teams. New Zealand went into the series having failed to beat South Africa in 12 matches in a row. Australia meanwhile, home nation and World Cup holders, had won 18 of 21 ODIs.

The news seemed to get worse when the Black Caps played Australia A in a warm-up game. It proved to be that in every sense of the word. In the hottest conditions Chris had played in, Shane Bond 'blew a gasket'. He overheated and had to be assisted from the field. The Kiwis' fitness and form wasn't looking so good. But as a journalist wrote: 'If this New Zealand team were a racehorse, it would probably need to be swabbed.'

The first match was at the colossal MCG. The Australians were hyper-confident, having just whacked the South Africans three-nil in the test series. On a lively pitch, the New Zealand top order fell to the pace merchants — Chris was out early, fending away a vicious short ball from Brett Lee. Chris Harris and Daniel Vettori rescued the effort and saw the team through to 199, but it didn't seem enough against the cocky Australians.

Chris considers Mark Waugh to be the best one-day player in the world since the latter half of the '90s. With him as a batsman, Australia always seem to progress to victory. He has been the linchpin of the Australian one-day team. But if that pin can be drawn, Australia seem vulnerable. The chance of winning rises dramatically. On that Melbourne night, Shane Bond took the wicket of Mark Waugh in the first over.

The rest of the top order seemed seduced by the allure of a bonus point, awarded if the New Zealand total was passed quickly. Chris did Gilchrist with a slower ball but Australia were 95 for 2 after 15 overs. Then continuing to push for the extra point, Martyn and Bevan both fell to Bond. The Kiwis bowled to their extensive plans of attack, and on a wicket that was helpful they picked up regular wickets. McGrath might have complained about his decision but when he was last out his team were still 22 runs shy. It was a great victory, a great start to the campaign.

That night virtually the entire squad went out and had a tremendous night of team bonding — there were the old hands, Cairns, Nash, Fleming — mixing with the young'uns, Franklin, Vincent, Adams and Shane Bond. Harry was Man of the Match, but it had been Bond who had picked up vital wickets. Shane Bond advanced the game.

Chris had played alongside Bond for Canterbury in the late '90s and Bondie had been a good provincial medium-pacer. Then Chris had been injured and Bond had spent a year away at the Police Academy. When Chris next met Constable Bond, at the Performance Centre at Lincoln, he was bowling very quickly indeed. Whether his police training had bulked him up or whether it was simply that he had reached the prime fast-bowling age (26–31 years old), he had become a much faster bowler.

Often in the '90s Chris would play a team with a very fast bowler and lament the fact that New Zealand didn't have an out-and-out greyhound. Now one had developed right under his nose. Shane Bond is in the same league as Younis and Donald at their peak, and is very nearly as fast as Brett Lee. The New Zealand effort that month was driven by Shane Bond.

The next match was against South Africa in Hobart and the hoodoo continued. South Africa set a challenging target, and a good captain's innings dragged the Kiwis close. But 'close' doesn't shoot the rabbit. In fact it should have been a lot closer.

Chris was bowling to Mark Boucher, when the African hit a ball back to him. It looked like a bump ball, but when Chris caught it it felt all wrong. Bump balls have some weight behind them. This seemed too soft, too loopy. So Chris turned to umpire Harper and appealed. He was the only one in the entire stadium who thought it was out and his 'Howzat' could be heard around the ground. Not out. TV replays showed clearly that it was a catch. Boucher went on to slog a quick 30. South Africa won by 26.

There was drama before the next match. In the nets at the SCG, Dion Nash pitched a ball short that hit Stephen Fleming on the elbow. Dayle Shackel, the physio, ordered an immediate X-ray. Flem asked Chris if he wanted to lead the side if he couldn't play. Chris thought about it for half a second and said it would be an honour. Chris hung on to Jeff Crowe's mobile phone during warm-ups as the captain went off to hospital. Then with less than an hour to go before kick-off, the phone rang. Fleming wouldn't be back in time. Chris was to make his debut as an international captain in front of a packed SCG.

Captain Cairns salutes the fans after leading New Zealand — in the absence of Stephen Fleming — to victory over Australia at the Sydney Cricket Ground in the 2002 VB series. Other Black Caps pictured are Brendon McCullum (left), Chris Harris and Craig McMillan. PHOTOSPORT

The captain has a lot to do before a contest. There are the team lists, the media contacts, the toss. Chris met Steve Waugh as he was walking out to toss. Waugh enquired about Flem's absence.

'Flem won't be with us today,' said Chris.

'Is this your first time captaining?' asked Waugh. Chris nodded.

'Good luck. Enjoy it. All the best,' were Waugh's sentiments.

The coin spun, Chris called 'heads', and the Queen's profile landed up. Chris had won the toss. Then he got stage fright. His mind went blank for what seemed to be five or 10 seconds with Waugh and the TV crew waiting. He couldn't think whether they had intended to bat or bowl. He looked at the coin, then the pitch. It was brown, it looked a good batting surface. 'We'll have a bat.'

In fact it wasn't. The ball seamed and jagged. McGrath, with his control, was next to impossible to play. Chris thought for a while that they'd be all out for under a hundred, and that he'd be the captain with the worst-ever record. But the Kiwis weathered the storm. They were 25 for 1 after 15 overs, but they could have been five down. Chris was missed first ball but contributed a knock of 31 (29 balls!) Thanks to that, and good efforts by Harris and McMillan, Chris' team managed to set a very reasonable target of 235. It could have been much worse.

Mark Waugh was run out early but Chris dropped Ryan Campbell. As captain, though, he was conscious of keeping in control. He couldn't show his disappointment. The wicket was still helpful, a couple more wickets fell. Then Chris received a message from Fleming. They were behind the required over rate. With all the thoughts of keeping the game tight, he had clean forgotten about the pace of the game.

Chris brought himself on for his last bowling spell and ambitiously kept a slip in. Bevan edged a ball directly to the slip. Another ambitious decision followed. The ball was swinging and they needed wickets. Although James Franklin had been expensive in previous games, he swung the ball substantially. Chris believed in the young Wellingtonian, who proceeded to swing the ball into Lee and get an LBW. Suddenly the Kiwis had done it. A victory by 22 runs.

One can think of his test debut, or the triumph at the Oval, or Kenya, or the century at Lord's, but captaining his country to a victory over that great Australian side at the SCG is the highlight of Chris' career. His mum and Wayne were there, as was his manager, Leanne. And to top it all off, Chris is the only New Zealand captain to have a hundred per cent record!

Chris loves the Gabba. The pitch always does a bit to start off, then it flattens out, but doesn't lose its pace and bounce. The ball comes on to the bat allowing stroke-makers to flow through their shots. Chris has played many of his greatest innings at the Gabba.

While New Zealand had done their homework on Australia, their prep for South Africa was not as thorough. The Africans always seemed to get away from the Kiwis. The Africans were on target for a big score that Saturday, but Bond again got wickets, and Chris picked up the dangerous Jonty Rhodes, a player who is fiendishly difficult to bowl to once he's set. Still, 241 seemed a long way off when the top order collapsed to 73-4 in the 19th over. Chris joined Craig McMillan but Macca was soon out. Three figures were not even on the board and half the wickets were down. And the required run rate was over six an over.

Chris was joined by Chris Harris. One thing these two veterans knew was that there was more time than they might think. They could gather runs, and target a couple of bowlers and the short boundaries at one end. They had the experience, the precedent of Kenya to call upon. There was no need to panic, patience would win out.

A crucial moment occurred when Ntini came back onto the field after a break. He warmed up then handed his hat to the umpire. But Chris was alert. The bowler had been off the field for longer than 15 minutes. He wasn't permitted to bowl immediately. This threw the South African bowling scheme. The pattern was broken and Pollock had to shuffle his bowlers differently.

Chris hit the spinner Justin Ontong back over his head for four then six — momentum had shifted to New Zealand. When Harris was out, Chris was joined by Parore. After Adam had settled, the pair started to look for boundaries. One an over was all that was needed. Chris pulled Kallis for six, then drove Ntini for four and sent Elworthy to the third-man boundary. Suddenly, the Kiwis were on the verge.

Chris had a plan for Jacques Kallis in the 49th over. Kallis is a good bowler at the death with a good yorker, but Chris knew that he'd miss, just once, and Chris would swing through the ball. It was the fifth ball. Chris drove the half-volley, high over long off. A single and Chris was on 98 with two needed to win. He lofted the first ball of the last over to the cover boundary. He had won the match and scored a century with the same shot.

The record Brizzie crowd rose to salute a great victory and Bill Lawry in the commentary box screamed in near-falsetto, 'That was one of the best innings we've seen in 25 years of televised one-day international cricket.'

He had wanted a century in Australia and achieved it. It was his fourth one-day century. To run off having carried 10 men, and another four million people, to victory, was the greatest feeling he'd experienced. It was emotion enhanced by the hugs and cheers in the dressing room. Then later to share the moment with friends Smithy and Emma and his family, who were all there to witness it. At these points of adrenalin and joy the only practical thing to do is to soak it up.

Nathan Astle returned for the next match, at the Adelaide Oval, and promptly scored yet another 90. Chris helped the score along with 39 not out from just 23 balls, including three straight-driven sixes over Adelaide's enormous boundaries. Then Shane Bond tore the Australian batting apart with 'five for'. It was Australia Day.

That win put New Zealand on the brink of finals cricket. Just one more victory was needed to assure them a place. In fact the Black Caps didn't win again in the competition. The day after having destroyed Australia, they were in turn destroyed by South Africa. The folly of playing a double-header against two different teams was displayed. The Proteas were fresh and never allowed the exhausted Kiwis near the match.

Chris' back was playing up. A slight twinge had been magnified when he had dived into the crease to earn a single during the Brisbane innings. He was sent for scans and X-rays and a cortisone injection.

Carin, who had come to Australia to join Chris, could see the damage for herself. Every morning, Chris would virtually fall out of bed, then spend 10 minutes getting his body moving freely. She was upset when Chris decided to play in the next match against Australia at the MCG, but for Chris the decision was easy. This could be his last match against Australia in Australia. He wasn't going to miss it.

Playing only as a batsman, Chris scored a half-century. The Kiwi total seemed well

Turning to his team-mates, Chris signals his triumph after the Black Caps' remarkable come-from-behind win against South Africa at the Gabba, 2002. Chris' final shot went for four to secure the victory and take him to his hundred.

beyond Australia when they slumped to 6 for 82, but Michael Bevan had begun to play another great one-day innings.

It is ironic that two of the best innings ever played, not a fortnight apart, finished on the same score — 102 not out. But while Chris' was full of bellicose drives and cuts, Bevan's was almost surgical in the way he would push the ball into the wide open spaces of the MCG and steal two. While Chris takes great gouges out of the opposition, Bevan uses a thousand little cuts to inflict the same amount of pain. New Zealand had their chances to dispose of the Australians — Brendon McCullum and Daniel Vettori both dropped catches, Vettori banging his head so badly in the attempt that he can't remember bowling the last couple of overs. Australia won and the chances of their making the final at New Zealand's expense increased.

Chris sat out the next match at Perth which South Africa won. It was in this match that the New Zealanders staged a go-slow, to gift South Africa a bonus point. This would increase the chance of the Black Caps progressing. The bonus point had been introduced, to much praise, to replace run rate as a tie-breaker (ironically run rate would have produced the same two finalists). Like the Super Six system in the World Cup it was open to abuse. The points system is also slated for use in the 2003 World Cup, but Chris fears that that will create a farce or even collusion that will damage cricket.

Cricket is a funny game and even the most surreal events have a habit of occurring within the boundary. Chris believes the full consequences of the bonus points system have not been contemplated and that it should be scrapped. If it is implemented in the future, Chris fears a nasty incident, perhaps between players, or even nations. When two of the test fraternity are India and Pakistan, the full volatile consequences could be huge.

As it was, in Perth, New Zealand doctored the result too overtly for Chris' liking. Censure was inevitable, but Australia failed to make the finals in the next match and the tactic achieved its ultimate objective. It was within the rules, for sure, but it was against the ethics of the game of cricket.

Nevertheless, for the first time in 11 years, New Zealand were playing finals cricket, and while they would have preferred to play Australia for sentimental reasons South Africa promised to be challenging. Unfortunately the Kiwis didn't play well in either match. A middle order collapse in the first meant a tally that should have been in excess of 240 was 50 less and South Africa hardly broke sweat in meeting it.

During that match, Chris caught the edge of Boeta Dippenaar's bat, but umpire Harper, for the third time that summer, didn't give Chris the wicket. Chris said a few things to the batsmen, all of which were well within the code of conduct. He didn't swear, or abuse. But at the end of the match 'Chopper' Crowe came to Chris and told him he'd been cited by the match referee, Hanumant Singh. Stephen Fleming, in the invidious position of having to control his players, was also cited.

The hearing was so petty it was ridiculous. Dippenaar stated that nothing he heard was offensive, as did the umpires. The referee stated that no matter what the content, the style was aggressive. He couldn't find the relevant footage and eventually dismissed the charge after several uncomfortable minutes and full-term pauses. After the Mike Denness affair, this seemed to be another situation where the structure of the disciplinary arm of ICC was too much like a kangaroo court. A full system of right of reply and appeal needs to be set up.

It was all forgotten when the pair returned to the dressing room. There was silence until first Flem, then Chris, announced their innocence. As soon as the verdicts were revealed there were cheers or groans and money changed hands — the squad had taken bets on the outcome!

The second final at Sydney was affected by rain. Chris scored 57 in 73 balls. New Zealand's 170 was never enough and South Africa had clean-swept the finals.

Nasser Hussain's England arrived in New Zealand trailed by a flotilla of press and a pod of supporters. They met a spirited New Zealand side at Jade Stadium only four days after their return from Australia. However, they were determined to put the disappointment of the finals behind them. England collapsed, assisted by two wickets and a great diving catch at fine leg by Chris Cairns. Eight wickets fell for 40 runs and New Zealand was back winning.

The support around the country, after the exploits in Australia, was huge and Chris received a great ovation at the WestpacTrust Stadium in Wellington. The atmosphere was supercharged but while he hit one ball into the crowd, it was not a hitter's pitch. Only 74 of New Zealand's runs came in fours or sixes, which meant the Black Caps ran almost 7 km worth of ones and twos. England was routed for 89, their worst-ever performance against New Zealand.

At Napier, the roles were reversed as New Zealand collapsed chasing a big score. Chris scored a good half-century at Eden Park but the match was blighted by those banes of fair cricket, rain and a calculator. Suddenly the series was 2–2, with the decider to be played in Dunedin. The New Zealand team just seemed exhausted. The one-day game was taking its toll on everybody.

The night before the match they had a team meeting. After the functional stuff was worked through most of the players remained sitting around talking, laughing. They had congregated because all of them felt the lack of atmosphere in the side. The next day, walking out to bowl first, Chris was still feeling flat. He needed an artificial stimulant so he went and fielded in front of the terraces. Hundreds of students, primed on Speight's, roared with approval as he approached the boundary. It was the boost he needed. Chris bowled a superb spell in the middle of the innings and each time he returned to the crowd the reception lifted him again.

New Zealand fired with the bat and when Chris came to the wicket Carisbrook gave him the greatest reception he could remember. Unfortunately he tried too hard to reward their faith in him that night. He chipped to mid-off third ball, but there would be other times. It was Nathan Astle's night. He hit his fifth six to win the match. It had been an extraordinary innings — yet it wasn't to be the most extraordinary innings he was to play that summer.

Sometimes a series win is pure joy, but at the end of this match there was simply a sense of relief. It had been hard work. The team sat drinking wine for a couple of hours as Carisbrook emptied.

Chris was disappointed to miss Canterbury's 125th anniversary match against the tourists but his back was badly affecting him. He needed rest. He did attend the jubilee dinner and was honoured to be selected in the all-time Canterbury team alongside Richard Hadlee — one hell of an all-rounder combination!

Before the test, Jade Stadium CEO Bryn McGoldrick took Chris out to see the drop-in wicket that was going to be used for the first test. Chris liked the look of the wicket. He was on 194 test wickets. He would love to get 200 on his home ground.

It seemed like Chris would get those wickets in the first morning. His first over was one of the finest he has bowled. The first two balls beat Marcus Trescothick, the third was edged to Parore, the fourth was a short ball fended away by Butcher and the fifth was another wicket. Two wickets down for no runs. Later he got Michael Vaughan as well to have the first three wickets.

The attack was a little inexperienced to fully exploit the helpful conditions. On another day, England could have been all out for 120, but the wickets just didn't come. Then just before tea on the first day Chris bent to try and stop a full-blooded drive from James Foster, and something went in his knee. He couldn't bowl.

The knee dominated his thoughts. He got a duck in the first innings but he was in a bad headspace. Chris was told not to bowl the next morning by the medical panel, but after listening to their advice and their detailing of the ramifications if he did, Chris still chose to bowl. He wanted to contribute.

Chris sat in the viewing room and watched Graham Thorpe rattle up a tremendous double-century. New Zealand required 550 to win. It was a ridiculous target, impossible. Chris talked to his captain and said he would only bat if he needed to, if one of the top order was still batting.

When Ian Butler was dismissed the score was 333 for 9. If anyone else had been at the other end Chris may not have batted on. The target was impossible, the run rate had air-bagged, he needed a runner. But Nathan Astle was not only his friend, he was also the cleanest hitter of the ball Chris has played alongside.

Having just recorded his century Astle had started to launch into some expansive drives. Maybe Chris would help Nathan get 150. Astle hit a six off Hoggard and so did Chris, reminding everybody that he too could swing a bat. A short ball from Flintoff made Chris sway and his knee almost gave way. His glass joint was obvious to everybody. But then Nathan Astle started hitting. There were drives through cover for four, then crisp pulls for six. There were outrageous hooks and swats to cow corner. He was middling the ball every time.

Chris had the best seat in the house — he was standing at square leg — and watched as the most extraordinary innings test cricket has seen unfolded. Caddick was smote for six after six, and suddenly Astle was on 199 and Chris had three balls to negotiate before Nathan could face again.

Chris was really nervous so defended the first, then drove the next for a boundary. He was determined not to let his mate down. He planned to bat on off stump and just step into the ball, letting it hit his body but in the end he didn't have to avoid the delivery so radically. Next ball, Astle pushed a single. He had scored the fastest double-century of all-time.

And he didn't stop. Chris and Nathan had a conference. Incredibly just 110 was needed to win so they agreed to keep teeing off until the target was less than 80.

With 98 to win, on 222, Nathan Astle charged down the pitch but only managed to nick the ball to the wicketkeeper. The fantasy was over — an hour's fantasy that was like a highlights package, and a tribute to a great batsman.

With 15 overs to go, Chris had contemplated winning a test by running down a target of 550. As he hobbled off, he was disappointed — with his own efforts, with the loss — but he was also proud. He was proud of his friend, and proud to have been involved in such a sensational test. He was also proud to have been a test cricketer, of having chosen this profession, of having lived his dream. Because he wondered as the spikes rattled on the concrete of the dressing room, whether he had played his last test.

Epilogue

The story of Chris Cairns is not a cricketing story. It is the story of the evolution of a human being. It is how a young boy with attitude and dreams evolved into a champion.

While it is easy to talk of the last stanza of his career, of retirement and last orders, it is easy to forget that Chris Cairns is only 32 years old. He has whole parts of his life ahead of him that are unimagined. He is currently a sportsman but if the slings and arrows have taught him anything it is that there is a life beyond the pickets. He knows this because he has lost a sister and a half-brother. He knows this because his parents lost love and found it again.

It is his body that will ultimately decide how long he plays. The surgery on yet another tear to his patellar tendon, that took place in April 2002, may sustain his career three or four years if successful. If it is unsuccessful, it may allow him to play only one season. He has played through pain for the last three years. He is sick of the pain, but would play through it to achieve one thing. The day he went into hospital he joined 29 other players at Orana Park for a vision statement for the World Cup 2003. It would be Chris' fourth World Cup. With players like Shane Bond, Chris Harris, Craig McMillan, Nathan Astle and captained by Stephen Fleming, he believes New Zealand can win the trophy in South Africa next year.

Paul Armour, his surgeon, cannot believe he is still capable of playing with so damaging an injury, yet Chris is fuelled by determination. He loves cricket. He has things he wants to achieve. He needs just three wickets to become only the second New Zealander to take 200 wickets. He needs just 147 runs to score 3000 test runs. To do both would be to join a list of just four people — Imran Khan, Kapil Dev, Ian Botham, Gary Sobers.

He is second on the list of six scorers in test cricket. Thirteen more sixes and he will be above Viv Richards, his idol. He would love to play test cricket against South Africa, against his three rivals for the best all-rounder crown — Kallis, Klusener and Pollock. He would also dearly love to beat Australia in a test series. He would also love to play another season for Nottinghamshire, where it all started.

He is also aware that he is only renting space for the next generation. He has enjoyed being an icon and mentor for the young crop of bowlers that have arrived in the New Zealand team over the last few years — talents like Shane Bond, Ian Butler, Daryl Tuffey, James Franklin, Chris Martin. He would love to play alongside them as they develop but he is all too aware that time marches. In the last few months, two of his friends — Dion Nash and Adam Parore — have retired. They are both younger than him. He thinks back to the sad and bitter end to the cricketing careers of people he respects — Jeremy Coney, Danny Morrison, Lance Cairns — and he wants to make his own destiny.

And once he has closed the lid on his cricket coffin for the last time, where will the future lead him? He has enjoyed planning and strategising with Stephen Fleming,

The two most important people in Chris' life – Carin and Thomas.

An extended family who enjoy each others' company. From left, Sue, Carin, Carol, Wayne, Chris and Lance.

CAIRNS FAMILY

Chris and Lance in the family business, Cairns Fudge.

David Trist and Steve Rixon. Perhaps he will enter the world of coaching. There are few people with such a treasury of cricketing knowledge, and the ability to express that knowledge. Yet maybe the game of his life will be left behind altogether. He has for some years owned a company that makes confectionery, with his father and Lance's wife Carol — Cairns Fudge. (On the recent Australian tour, he was called Willy Wonka by his opponents.) Lance is the chef, but Chris loves the marketing side of things, the negotiations, the ideas and strategies. It is a different kind of cut and thrust than he is used to. Perhaps the world of commerce will snare him.

In Carin he has a special partner, someone he respects and loves immensely. She has a passion for the earth. Carin's dream has always been to farm the land. Perhaps her vision of following in her father's footsteps will be realised.

And where? South Africa, the Netherlands, England, America or New Zealand. Chris and Carin are young. It is a portable world for those with certain skills.

The future is uncertain but the past is black and white. Chris has done it. He has climbed the pinnacle. On the way he slipped sometimes, the path was rarely easy. He has performed remarkable feats that are burned deep in the collective memory. His straight drives, his slower balls, his throws from the deep that defy Newton will exist for as long as cricket exists. The stats are there forever.

But there is one other statistic that he now considers his greatest achievement. Seven pounds, three ounces. On 5 June 2002, Carin gave birth to a boy, Thomas Robin Cairns. Chris has another life now. He is a father.

Statistics

TO 31 AUGUST, 2002

FIRST-CLASS
Debut for Nottinghamshire v Kent at Dartford, 1988

Highest Score
126 New Zealand v India at Hamilton, 1998/99

Best Bowling (Innings)
8-47 Nottinghamshire v Sussex at Arundel, 1995

Best Bowling (Match)
15-83 Nottinghamshire v Sussex at Arundel, 1995

TESTS
Debut v Australia at Perth, 1989/90

Centuries
120 v Zimbabwe at Auckland, 1995/96
126 v India at Hamilton, 1998/99
109 v Australia at Wellington, 1999/00
124 v Zimbabwe at Harare, 2000/01

Five Wickets in an Innings
5-75 v Sri Lanka at Auckland, 1990/91
6-52 v England at Auckland, 1991/92
5-137 v Pakistan at Rawalpindi, 1996/97
5-50 v Zimbabwe at Harare, 1997/98
5-62 v Sri Lanka at Colombo, 1997/98
6-77 v England at Lord's, 1999
5-31 v England at The Oval, 1999
7-27 v West Indies at Hamilton, 1999/00
5-44 v West Indies at Wellington, 1999/00
5-31 v Zimbabwe at Bulawayo, 2000/01
5-146 v Australia at Brisbane, 2001/02
7-53 v Bangladesh at Hamilton, 2001/02

Ten Wickets in a Match
10-100 v West Indies at Hamilton, 1999/00

ONE-DAY INTERNATIONALS
Debut v England at Wellington, 1990/91

Centuries
103 v India at Pune, 1995/96
115 v India at Christchurch, 1998/99
102* v India at Nairobi, 2000/01
102* v South Africa at Brisbane, 2001/02

Five Wickets in an Innings
5-42 v Australia at Napier, 1997/98

DOMESTIC ONE-DAY
Debut for Northern Districts v Central Districts at Levin, 1988/89

Centuries
115 Canterbury v Wellington at Christchurch, 1992/93
143 Canterbury v Auckland at Christchurch, 1994/95
113 Canterbury v Otago at Christchurch, 1996/97

Five Wickets in an Innings
5-23 Canterbury v Central Districts at Timaru, 1995/96
6-37 Canterbury v Wellington at Christchurch, 1996/97

MOST SIXES IN A TEST CAREER

6s	Runs		
84	8540	IVA Richards	West Indies
72	2853	CL Cairns New Zealand	
71	7515	CH Lloyd West Indies	
67	5200	IT BothamEngland	
67	7558	CG Greenidge	West Indies
61	5638	CL Hooper	West Indies
60	5248	N Kapil Dev	India
57	2898	Wasim Akram	Pakistan

2000 RUNS AND 200 WICKETS IN TEST CRICKET

Name	Mat	Runs	HS	Ave	Wkts	Ave	BB	Team
R Benaud	63	2201	122	24.45	248	27.03	7-72	AUS
IT Botham	102	5200	208	33.54	383	28.40	8-34	ENG
RJ Hadlee	86	3124	151*	27.16	431	22.30	9-52	NZ
Imran Khan	88	3807	136	37.69	362	22.81	8-58	PAK
N Kapil Dev	131	5248	163	31.05	434	29.64	9-83	IND
SM Pollock	63	2242	111	31.57	261	20.72	7-87	RSA
GS Sobers	93	8032	365*	57.78	235	34.03	6-73	WI
SK Warne	101	2091	99	16.59	450	26.52	8-71	AUS
Wasim Akram	104	2898	257*	22.64	414	23.62	7-11	PAK
also								
CL Cairns	55	2853	126	32.79	197	28.80	7-27	NZ

TEST RECORD AGAINST EACH COUNTRY

Opponent	M	I	NO	Runs	HS	Ave	100	50	ct	O	M	R	W	Ave	Best	5W	10W
Australia	14	26	1	863	109	34.52	1	6	2	437.1	88	1636	39	41.94	5–146	1	–
England	11	19	1	533	80	29.61	–	5	2	327	69	1045	35	29.85	6–52	3	–
India	8	12	1	377	126	34.27	1	3	–	216	47	698	19	36.73	4–44	–	–
Zimbabwe	8	13	2	480	124	43.63	2	2	–	356.5	98	944	39	24.20	5–31	2	–
Sri Lanka	6	10	0	175	70	17.50	–	1	5	132.4	18	491	19	25.84	5–62	2	–
Pakistan	4	8	0	238	93	29.75	–	2	4	135.5	23	533	16	33.31	5–137	1	–
West Indies	2	2	0	103	72	51.50	–	1	1	85	30	169	17	9.94	7–27	2	1
Bangladesh	2	2	0	84	48	42.00	–	–	–	50.2	10	159	13	12.23	7–53	1	–
TOTAL	**55**	**92**	**5**	**2853**	**126**	**32.79**	**4**	**20**	**14**	**1740.5**	**383**	**5675**	**197**	**28.80**	**7–27**	**12**	**1**

ONE-DAY RECORD AGAINST EACH COUNTRY

Opponent	M	I	NO	Runs	HS	Ave	100	50	ct	O	M	R	W	Ave	Best	RPO
Australia	29	26	2	584	67	24.33	–	4	11	207.2	11	1021	29	35.20	5–42	4.92
South Africa	24	22	3	720	102*	37.89	1	5	7	190.5	10	956	26	36.76	2–26	5.00
India	23	21	3	720	115	40.00	3	1	1	173.1	14	781	24	32.54	3–26	4.51
Pakistan	20	19	2	384	54	22.58	–	1	5	161.2	9	708	22	32.18	3–18	4.38
England	17	16	0	290	79	18.12	–	2	9	88.1	4	447	20	22.35	4–55	5.06
Zimbabwe	13	10	1	199	71	22.11	–	1	3	70.3	8	316	9	35.11	3–24	4.48
West Indies	11	10	1	297	75	33.00	–	1	3	72	5	320	11	29.09	3–25	4.44
Sri Lanka	10	10	0	335	72	33.50	–	3	6	51	1	265	8	33.12	2–39	5.19
Bangladesh	1	1	1	7	7*	–	–	–	–	7	1	19	3	6.33	3–19	2.71
UAE	1	1	0	6	6	6.00	–	–	3	10	2	31	1	31.00	1–31	3.10
Holland	1	1	0	52	52	52.00	–	1	–	7	1	24	0	–	–	3.42
Scotland	1	1	1	20	20*	–	–	–	1	8	0	26	1	26.00	1–26	3.25
TOTAL	**151**	**138**	**14**	**3614**	**115**	**29.14**	**4**	**19**	**49**	**1046.2**	**66**	**4914**	**154**	**31.90**	**5–42**	**4.69**

CAREER SUMMARY

	M	I	NO	Runs	HS	Ave	100	50	ct	Wkts	Runs	Ave	Best	5W	10W
First-class	190	297	35	9254	126	35.32	11	61	70	597	16415	27.49	8-47	29	6
Test	55	92	5	2853	126	32.79	4	20	14	197	5675	28.80	7-27	12	1

	M	I	NO	Runs	HS	Ave	SR	100	50	ct	Wkts	Runs	Ave	Best	RPO
One-day International	151	138	14	3614	115	29.14	81	4	19	49	154	4914	31.90	5-42	4.69
Domestic One-day	67	60	8	1763	143	33.90	88	3	8	15	82	1835	22.37	6-37	3.90

Note: * denotes not out